SELFLESS BEYOND SERVICE

A Story about the Husband, Son and Father Behind the Lion of Fallujah

DENVER, COLORADO

Outskirts Press, Inc.
http://www.outskirtspress.com

ISBN: 978-1-4787-2935-8

Outskirts Press and the "OP" logo are trademarks belonging to Outskirts Press, Inc.

PRINTED IN THE UNITED STATES OF AMERICA

TABLE OF CONTENTS

INTRODUCTION

On May 11, 2007, a part of me died when my husband was killed in action doing what he loved most: leading men in battle. Several stories have been written about this man, Major Douglas Zembiec. He was known by most as "The Lion of Fallujah," which namesake was given to him in 2004 when he encountered several battles against insurgents after the brutal Blackwater murders. Others knew him as Major Zembiec. Some knew him as Zemmie, and still others simply knew him as Douglas. I, being his wife, knew him in a different way. We were friends, lovers, and soul mates. This story celebrates Doug's life as the husband, father, and son: the sides of a warrior that get lost inside the battles and the eventual tragic death. Every warrior struggles with balancing his family and his country, and Doug wasn't an exception.

I initially began this quest as a means to work through my grief by writing about the struggles of my loss and to also give my daughter an idea of what her father was like as a boyfriend, as a husband and as a father. I gathered all his letters from Iraq, many personal quotes and his words of wisdom in my quest to accurately depict his unique and somewhat "eccentric" qualities. A short time before Doug's death, we had a discussion about what he would do after he retired from the Marine Corps. "Babe, the first thing I'm going to do is write a book. A book about the bravery of my men, and you will help me by saving all those letters I wrote you from Iraq."

This book is dedicated to my daughter, Fallyn Justice Zembiec, so you will one day understand why you never knew your father in the flesh, but will always know him in spirit.

I love you, Mommy

CHAPTER 1

ANNAPOLIS MD, FRIDAY, MAY 11, 2007

*"May you never take one single breath for granted. God forbid
love ever leave you empty-handed."*
Lee Ann Womack

Where was I on this night? It didn't feel like my guest room, the one I slept in next to my daughter when my husband was deployed. I felt like I was lying next to Doug, in my own bedroom where I slept like a rock, so soundly, my subconscious was incapable of dreams. When I first heard the barking, I tried to ignore it. I was too comfortable and didn't want this to end. Doug left over six weeks ago, and my body was desperate for a solid 8 hours. Unfortunately, the barking grew louder along with the doorbell ringing, and then knocking fists on hard steel. I jumped up from the guest room bed more concerned with the noise waking up my baby then anything else. When I noticed it was still dark outside, my mind started racing with anxious thoughts. *Who is at my door this time of night? Is one of my neighbors in trouble?*

I quickly ran up the stairs and peered through the glass pane door only to see four men standing on the carport next to the entrance of my home. Immediately, I was able to notice one familiar face out of the four men; it was Colonel Ripley. His face was drawn and gray in color. He stood in front of the door pacing with his hands pressed so firmly inside the pockets of his beige zippered jacket, I could see the outline of his fists. Something was terribly wrong. I met the colonel over five years ago and never saw him look this way. Doug and I visited Colonel Ripley on many occasions, and he was always calm and unswerving. He had gone through many struggles in life and always recovered. The man was an

1

icon. He was a highly decorated war hero and had survived several obstacles; the Vietnam War and two liver transplants, just to name a few. The colonel was the ultimate war hero and a true Southern gentleman. Doug's dad was the only man whom Doug respected more in his life.

Why was the colonel at my door during this hour? *Oh my God!* I thought to myself. *One of Doug's friends is in trouble.* I quickly opened the door and let the colonel in the house. The three other men followed slowly behind him with faces full of doom. They proceeded through the doorway without making a single sound and after a second look, I was able to recognize another one of the three men. It was Doug's boss, John. I remembered the last time I saw John. He came to visit us in Annapolis to watch a Navy wrestling meet. He brought his two children with him to enjoy the experience. I was five months pregnant with Fallyn and was too tired to join them. Doug came home embarrassed because he mixed up the match days and there wasn't a meet after all. John understood and was happy just to show the kids the wondrous Naval Academy. I liked him and his children instantly. I anxiously asked him, "What's going on? Has one of Doug's friends been killed?"

The colonel and John looked at me with sad eyes. They didn't have to say a word. My entire being knew what was coming next. I screamed, "No, no. Not Doug. I just talked to him. It's impossible!"

My mind hurriedly regressed back to our morning conversation . . . "Babe, did I wake you up. I'm sorry, but I couldn't help myself. I had a moment to call, and I had to hear your voice, but I can let you go if you're busy," Doug said.

"No, no, honey. I'm up, and I want to talk to you. I would never miss an opportunity to talk to you," I responded in a whisper because Fallyn was still asleep.

"I'm so excited about life. I have everything planned for us. When I get back, we're going to Idaho for our second honeymoon, and I'm going to get you pregnant again. What do you think about that?" he excitedly asked.

"I'm ready, honey, and just in time. All my baby weight is gone. I can't wait, but I hope it's a boy this time because I want the Zembiec name to be passed on for generations," I said.

Doug replied, "No worries, baby. I read that you can get some type of medical procedure to pick the type of sperm. If it's a girl the second time, maybe we can get that medical thing done the third time." Doug always had a solution to every problem.

I laughed when I answered, "Sure, honey, but we should just want healthy kids."

Doug answered in an excited tone, "Babe, with your genetic masterpiece of a body and immune system, and of course, my genetics, we have nothing to worry about."

Fallyn started to cry so I walked into her bedroom. Doug heard her and said, "Babe, put the phone up to her." I placed the phone on speaker, and he began to talk. "FJ, or should I say Fallyn Justice Zembiec, you are a rock star! Be good for your mother and I will be home soon," he said.

Fallyn curiously looked into the mysterious receiver and babbled, "Dada."

"Babe, did she just say dada?" he asked.

"Yes, honey. She is smiling ear to ear. She knows her daddy's voice," I answered.

"That made my day. I love you, Fallyn J, and I miss you. I love and miss you too, baby," he said.

"I love you too, honey," I replied.

I was getting ready to hang up the phone when I heard him yell, "Babe, wait a minute! I have to tell you something before I go! We're doing great work over here! The Iraqi people are awesome, and things are getting better. You should see what we're doing!" he said excitedly.

"That's great. I'm happy all your hard work is paying off," I answered.

"I know, it really is, but I really gotta go now. We're getting ready to go out. I love you," he said.

I answered, "I love you too."

The colonel tried to talk to me and get my attention, but his words weren't registering. "Pam, I am so sorry, but Doug was killed tonight during a night mission."

"What?" I asked.

His voice grew louder. "Pam, Doug is gone. He was killed in an ambush."

A big rush swept me from my feet as reality set in. I couldn't breathe; it felt like someone had kicked me in the stomach with enough force to fall into the kitchen table. My body was lifeless, and I felt nothing until the tears and sobs began to take control of my body. I was in another world, so far away from my happy life. The colonel grabbed me by the arm and carefully placed me on the sofa in the living room.

I sobbed uncontrollably while all the men respectfully bowed their heads and waited for me to say something . . . anything. When I realized this was really happening, I began to rationalize. "Are you sure it was him?"

"Yes, Pam. Definitely," John answered.

I couldn't hold back my anger. "Did they get the monsters who killed my husband?"

"Yes. All of the insurgents were killed. We are 100 percent positive they got the ones who killed Doug," John answered.

I looked at one of the men I didn't recognize and asked, "Why can't we just bomb that country?"

He methodically replied, "Sometimes we ask ourselves the same thing."

My emotions were wavering from anger to sorrow, and it was once again sorrow's turn. I paced around the room, not knowing what to do next. "Pam, is there anyone you want us to call and come stay with you?" the colonel asked.

"Call my parents," I quickly answered. My heart dropped when I thought of my other family, so far away. I cried out, "And we have to call Doug's mom and dad. I want them here right now. I need them with us."

"Pam, we have a Marine Corps representative who will be paying Doug's parents a visit in the morning. We wanted to come see you now before the news got wind of this," John said.

"No, call them right now! They need to know right now! I want them with me and Fallyn as soon as possible!" I screamed.

The colonel came over and told me my mom and sisters were on their way. "Do you want me to call Kap?" the colonel asked.

"Yes, call Kap. He will know what to do. He's been through this before," I answered. Kap lost a few of his marines in a helicopter accident, and I knew he was a huge support system for the families. He would be able to help us, especially since we were the family of his best friend.

My head was spinning and for a split second I thought maybe I was in a dream. Doug wasn't supposed to die. He was invincible with muscles like steel. How the hell could a bullet penetrate steel? I looked at John and asked, "How did they get him?"

He answered slowly. "We don't know all the details. Once I find out I will tell you everything. The report stated a gunshot wound to the head."

I spoke aloud, "That would be the only way to kill him. He was larger than life." I saw the colonel from the corner of my eye.

"Pam, I have the Zembiecs on the phone." I hurriedly grabbed the receiver, and I could hear Jo Ann screaming in the background. I said hello as I sobbed.

Don spoke, "Pam, we are booking our flights right now. I don't know what to say. *He was the son of our universe.*"

I sat silent for a few moments thinking about his words and answered, "I know. What are we going to do without him? How am **I going to live** without him?"

My mom and sisters suddenly appeared next to me and surrounded me with a temporary protection barrier. The phone rang again, and I frantically grabbed at it, knowing it was Kap. I desperately wanted someone—anyone—to tell me what to do. I cried to him, "Kap, he wasn't supposed to die. What the hell is going on? What are we going to do?"

He answered calmly, "Pam, I will be there first thing in the morning. The colonel and I are going to take care of everything." I couldn't say another word. My world was gone. The only thing I had left was sleep as my sister Tammy forced me to go downstairs and get into bed. The sun was still going to rise.

CHAPTER 2
VIRGINIA BEACH, VA, 2001

"Happiness itself is sufficient excuse. Beautiful things are right and true; so beautiful actions are those pleasing to the gods. Wise men have an inward sense of what is beautiful, and the highest wisdom is to trust this intuition and be guided by it. The answer to the last appeal of what is right lies within a man's own breast. Trust thyself."
Aristotle

It was the spring of 2001, and my lease on life was renewed. My move back to the East Coast was about to take me on a journey full of fresh faces with high hopes for countless, exciting adventures. I was in Virginia Beach, and the locals promised the spring winds would bring the beginnings of summer fun. Virginia Beach was a small town filled with beach lovers, strong families and the military: Navy SEALs, the Coast Guard, the Marine Corps and the Army were stationed in this little beach town nestled on the edge of the Southern Virginia Atlantic coastline. The town was filled with a sense of country I never felt in my life. My father was retired Air Force and patriotism was instilled in my brain at a very young age. As a family, we never lived in an actual military town, but I do remember watching my dad shine his black patent leather shoes in preparation for guard weekend. My sisters and I were amazed at how dashing he looked when he left for those weekends and how proud we were to have our father serve his country.

When I first arrived in Virginia Beach, my civilian friends warned me about the military men, especially the Navy SEALs. They had their own personal experiences, which made the idea of dating a Navy SEAL seem like a nightmare. I guess the words "love them and leave them fast" would describe how the SEALs treated the majority of women. I respected my friends' experiences, and I decided to stay as far away from them as possible. Besides, my life was interesting enough and leaving military men out of the equation was easy. The respect was there, but I wasn't about to be another female casualty. I was too good and was at a place in my life where I wanted someone who's influence made me a better person—not an insecure one. I knew from my past men loved women with self-respect and confidence and losing mine wasn't an option, but being alone was.

The first time I met him was during the middle of April. The weather was beautiful, sunny and warm, but breezy. It was a Saturday night and an off night for the Hot Tuna which was the place to be in Virginia Beach; a seedy, dark, smoky bar located within a strip mall. There was a small stage for live bands and the music was respectable, especially after a couple drinks. The bar was located in the center of the room with small tables surrounding the edges of the bar's boundaries. Bartenders and waitresses were always at your service, and the drinks were poured heavily. The Tuna attracted beautiful men and women on the usual nights, and if you showed up on Wednesdays or Fridays, familiar faces were always there to greet you.

One thing I noticed about living in a beach town was the women all looked the same; athletic and somewhat skinny bodies with a youthful glowing tan. Most had an unhealthy, needy attitude that emulated through a superficial-looking exterior. The men were similar in appearance, but with arrogance seeping from their pores. I guessed both sexes in the Hot Tuna deserved each other, and when my girlfriends and I decided to visit on a Saturday night, we were happy to bring in a different crowd. We simply ignored the patrons and enjoyed each other's company. Our group danced as the band played our favorites, but I had a sinking feeling someone was watching me. I finally glanced over my shoulder only to notice a man standing along the windows, tall and masculine, with a commanding presence. His hair was short, and I suspected the cut was service related, especially when I noticed his broad shoulders and squared jaw. This man had a confident, but friendly stance, and his stares penetrated my body like x-ray vision. I silently waved off his presence and thought, *Not now. I'm not ready for this one.* Besides, I decided to move to the area after my fiancé and I broke off our engagement and I didn't want a boyfriend right now. I could tell from looking at this guy there was something about him that made him definite boyfriend material, but he was too persistent, and I couldn't escape his presence, even on the other side of the room. After 2 hours of feeling his presence and trying to ignore it, he finally approached me with hesitation in his movements. He carefully stood next to me and said, "Hi, I think you're beautiful and an extremely confident woman. My name is Doug. What's your name?" The voice was deep and commanding. I thought to myself. *He's certainly different. Who has ever used that type of pickup line before?*

"My name's Pam," I answered as I observed his face. Up close, his eyes were dark and intense, and his lashes were excessively long for a man.

Before I could say another word, he introduced me to his friend Ken. "This is my friend Ken. Isn't he a movie star?" I didn't answer because I thought Ken was handsome, but thought Doug was the movie star of the two. Ken was different from Doug. He had perfect, straight white teeth that were bright enough to light up a room, especially against his tanned face. He was tall and muscular like Doug, and his hair was thick and dark. He was a looker indeed and reminded me of the warrior from the movie *Black Hawk Down*. I wasn't sure why Doug took me over to meet his friend when we immediately dismissed ourselves to a small table away from him, never seeing him again. I thought maybe it was a way to shield his nervousness. Whatever the reason, it didn't matter when our talk smoothly flowed into a very deep conversation.

As Doug and I discussed our families, he pulled all of the good moves by showing me a picture of his friends' little girls. I was touched because of my close relationship with my nieces and nephews. He asked about my career, family, friends and life. I had never been this closely examined in the middle of a seedy, dark bar before. What was this guy doing? I could tell he was interested, but I wasn't. I had to get away from him because I knew instinctively he was the type who would be in my life for a very long time, and I wasn't ready. I was able to turn the interrogation around and asked about his profession. He was reluctant when he answered, but finally said, "I'm a Force Reconnaissance Marine." His answer merely verified what I already knew. I was trying to stay away from the military, but here I was, talking to someone who was part of the most powerful military group in our nation.

Run, I thought to myself.

After 2 hours but what only seemed like 10 minutes, the lights came on and the night was over. "Can I get your phone number?" Doug asked. I already knew my answer before he asked the question.

"No, I don't give my phone number out to men in bars, but I can take your number and give you a call."

The look on his face was one of extreme shock and disbelief. He hesitated for a moment, but eventually wrote his number on a small piece of white cardboard in red pen. When I got home, I placed the piece of paper on my computer desk, knowing I would never call. As the months rolled by, I glanced at the white piece of paper on numerous occasions. I knew when I was ready it would happen with someone, but my meeting with Doug made me wonder if life events were a person's fate or free will. There was something about that piece of paper with red ink that made me wonder if my fate was already planned.

CHAPTER 3

VIRGINIA BEACH, VA, 2001

"Adapt yourself to the life you have been given; and truly love the people with whom destiny has surrounded you."
Marcus Aurelius

Summers in Virginia Beach were supposed to be the best time of the year. It was my first summer as a resident, and being single brought a high level of excitement. My friend Christine and I went to all the summer events that exposed us to many new and interesting people. A mutual work partner thought the two of us would get along because of our similar backgrounds. She was right; we were very similar in behaviors and looks and by both being single new residents, we formed an immediate bond. Christine was blond, and her body was athletic and toned, just like a gymnast. She would joke at times about me being "Barbie" and her being "Skipper." It was a funny, but true comparison considering our height differences. Both of us had careers as successful pharmaceutical sales reps, which gave way to many afforded opportunities. We, therefore, enjoyed our first summer in style, and the Duck Inn was one of our favorite spots to be during hazy Friday afternoon sunsets in Virginia Beach. The Duck Inn sat at the beginning of the Lesner Bridge and was nestled along a beach on the Chesapeake Bay. Anyone who experienced it would immediately notice the small tiki bar situated on the shoreline as they crossed over the bridge. There was also a small restaurant on the property, but the bar was certainly remembered for the sunset beach parties outside, not the food inside.

On this particular Friday evening, the weather was beautiful. It was sunny and warm with low humidity. As always, the entrance to the Duck Inn was filled with numerous Harley-Davidson motorcycles, and as I glanced their way, I wondered what it would be like to ride on the back of one of them. Each Harley belonged to a military man, and I figured riding on a Harley might fill some type of need for men who wanted to blow off high levels of testosterone when they were on shore duty.

As I entered the Duck Inn, I was thrilled with the wonder of what the night would bring. The beach party was always fun, especially when the weather was perfect. And it was one of those perfect nights where Christine, Pete and I were ready for some fun after a long workweek. I grew up with three sisters and never had the pleasure of knowing a brother. Pete was the brother I never had. He was blond and muscular with a caring personality. We knew each other for around six years and formed a close friendship from the beginning. Pete was an avid boater and moved to Virginia Beach for his job, but I was sure the boating on the Chesapeake Bay played a huge part in the final decision. The three of us gathered outside on the deck and discussed our crazy work industry while we enjoyed fruity cocktails.

Our conversation came to a screeching halt when I looked over my right shoulder and noticed Doug standing by the railing in the sand, but he looked different this time. He was dressed in a green tee shirt and beige shorts; Teva sandals were on his feet. His hair was cut close to his head, and I noticed he was going bald. He was even more handsome than I remembered.

What were you thinking? I thought to myself. I immediately realized I made a terrible mistake by not calling him and was embarrassed to have run into him again at a completely different setting. *It has to be fate,* I thought to myself. I hoped he wouldn't completely ignore me for being so rude, but my thoughts eluded me when his look came my way. He wasn't hesitating this time and walked over to greet me with complete confidence.

"Hi, Pam, do you remember me? My name is Doug."

"Of course I remember you," I said.

Doug motioned his friends over to us and introduced them by name. "Pam, this is Joe and Kap. Kap and I just completed the Armed Forces Echo Challenge. Kap is an avid biker, and I thought you would be interested in talking with him because I remembered you like biking." I became immediately alarmed when I got the impression Doug might be trying to fix me up with one of his friends. I guess he figured I wasn't interested in him because I never called.

What am I going to do? I thought to myself.

I decided to briefly speak to Kap and Joe, and then turn all of my interest back to Doug. "What is the Armed Forces Echo Challenge?" I asked.

"The military has the race every year and teams from each branch compete against one another. This year it was held in Alaska. There are four members to each team. Each team member is responsible for completing each section of the race. There is mountain biking, hiking and canoeing for 24 hours straight. If you take too many breaks you're doomed," Kap answered.

"Wow, pretty intense. I can mountain bike, but I'm not sure about the rest of it," I stated.

Doug quickly intervened. "You'd be surprised at what your body can do. It's mind over matter. Most people never push their body to the limits."

That was all it took to separate us from the rest of the crowd; everyone around us seemed to disappear into the loud music and fun fare as our conversation went on and on. I guessed his friends were sick of being ignored when they came over and motioned to Doug that the sun was setting and it was time to head to the Hot Tuna. Doug looked at me and asked, "Would you like to go with us and ride over on the back of my Harley?"

My immediate thought was yes, but I still needed reassurance from my friend Pete and motioned for him to come over and meet Doug. Even though their conversation was brief, Pete decided I was safer with a Recon Marine than with any other person in the world. His response was all I needed to feel comfortable. I was filled not only with the thrill of being on the back of a Harley, but also holding on to an extremely handsome man. Doug escorted me over to the hundreds of Harleys lined up next to the entrance. We stopped in front of a black Harley and Doug turned to me and explained, "This is my friend's bike. I loaned mine to Kap. The next time I take you for a ride, it will be on my bike." He motioned to our right, and I saw his bike. Wow! It was beautiful. The bike was a 1996 Fat Boy Harley-Davidson. The tank was bright yellow with black and red stripes going around the perimeter. I could tell Doug was proud of his toy, but his friends seemed to come before any type of material object, considering he loaned his bike to Kap and rode the lesser of the two. I liked that about him; he was handsome and confident, but already I could tell he put his friend's needs before his own.

We stood next to the Harley, and he carefully placed a borrowed helmet on my head. As we drove away from the Duck Inn, Doug instructed me on how to stay on the bike. "Hold me around my waist and stay away from the pipes." I grabbed him around the waist and was pleasantly surprised as I felt muscles rippling from his back and abdomen. I quickly withdrew my arms and inconspicuously brushed over his shoulders, and then placed them back around his waist. I admired people who took care of their bodies, and his body was a physical masterpiece. Doug must have thought I wanted him to return the favor when he moved his arm and gently caressed my lower leg. I guessed my extra touch might have provoked him, but I couldn't help my curiosity and allowed him to continue, knowing the caressing would go no further. I especially knew this when I looked up and noticed a sticker with the words "Orgasm donor" plastered on the back of his helmet.

As the men entered the Tuna, it seemed like the entire standing room crowd stopped in midsentence to view the group of strapping lads who just walked in. I noticed Doug and his friends all ordered Jack and Cokes, which was odd to me, but I heard this was the drink choice for military men. I stayed at the Tuna a bit longer to talk with Doug, but as soon as I saw shots being ordered and cigars lighting up, I knew it was time for me to go and let the men have their time. I walked over to Doug and said, "Thanks for the Harley ride. I had fun, and it was also nice running into you again."

He looked at me with a puzzled look and asked, "Can I call you this time?" I didn't hesitate to answer while I handed him an invite to my party for the following weekend.

"Here is an invitation with my number."

Doug looked at it with questioning eyes and asked, "Are you sure this is the right number?" I looked at him and with a half laugh, said, "Yes, I promise." He smiled, but I knew he was still unsure about me. Who would blame him?

I left the Tuna that night looking back at Doug and his friends engrossed in conversation while they drank Jack and Cokes and smoked cigars. I could see their bond was immeasurable. I decided on my cab ride home. I was ready for him and hoped I hadn't already ruined what could be a wondrous adventure.

Because I wanted him to call this time, Saturday came and went without one. I woke up Sunday morning shocked I hadn't heard from him. He seemed so eager to see me. Normally, men would call within a few days, but Doug was different. I thought he would call immediately because of his confidence. He didn't seem like the type of man who played games. I, on the other hand, knew that in order to keep his interest, I would have to play some type of cat and mouse game. Men wanted women with self-respect, confidence and beauty. Doug was different, but he was still a man. I secretly yearned for the phone to ring with his number, but tried to pretend like I didn't.

Finally on Sunday morning he called. "My friends and I are going to Chicks for lunch; do you want to come with us?"

Was he serious? I probably would have said yes a long time ago when I was young and stupid, but now there wasn't a chance in hell I was going to accept a lunch date *one hour* before the occasion. Besides, I already had plans with my girlfriends and told him this when I rejected his invitation. He promised he would call later and make plans for another time. I was completely disappointed with our conversation, but knew I made the correct decision. He kept his promise by calling a few days later, and when he tried to pull a similar stunt, I, once again, rejected him. The game continued for two more phone calls, and finally he scheduled a Sunday date well in advance for lunch at a popular oceanfront restaurant called Mahi Ma's.

Dining at Mahi Ma's was a treat with its elegant beach atmosphere inside for climate comfort and outside for ocean views. Fresh locally caught fish were always on the menu, and Sundays were particularly fun at Mahi's during the summer with the afternoon beach parties and live bands. I knew Doug was coming home from a weekend with friends in Annapolis and after he showed up late for our first date, I decided to pretend I wasn't ready and made him wait for his tardiness. I guessed he was accustomed to dating women who didn't care about lateness and last-minute dates. Not me, I was different.

I went downstairs to greet him, and before I could say anything, he showed me a picture. It was a photo of his face completely battered with scratches, bruises and edema. "What happened?" I asked. He looked at me with serious black eyes and said, "I crashed on my motorcycle a few months back, and this is what I looked like. I could have been killed." I looked out the front door and noticed he kept his promise; we were going to ride on his Harley to Mahi Ma's. Doug's Harley sat in my driveway and seemed to stare at me, daring me to come over. Why did he show me that photo?

I swallowed tightly, then said, "Are we going to be safe on that thing?"

"Of course," he said. "I will be carrying precious cargo." And with his comment, for some reason, I trusted him with my life. There was something about being in his company that made me feel safe. My fears melted away, and I felt free with him as we cruised on the Harley in the summer breeze. Once again, I held him around his thin, muscular waist, loving the feel of his body close to mine.

Lunch was satisfying, the food was incredible and the conversation even better. I was comfortable and excited all at the same time. We ate, walked on the beach and talked about the future. Our conversation took a twisted and highly personal turn into exploring our past relationships. I spoke about my prior relationship that led me to Virginia Beach. Doug also shared a story about a past relationship, which ended badly. He said, "She was the first woman who I thought I loved. I got deployed for six months, and when I came home, she confessed to cheating on me. We tried to work it out, but my trust for her was broken. I haven't been in a serious relationship since."

I sympathized with him by sharing my thoughts and said, "Doug, I have found in my life that it's much more difficult for a man to recover when a woman breaks the trust. Women get their hearts broken all the time and bounce back remarkably well. I think it's human nature because the woman is always in search of true love and the 'happily ever after' ending. Men, on the other hand, are in search of fulfilling their 'manly' needs, and falling in love takes a long, long time. When the trust is violated by a woman in a committed relationship, the man is in a state of sheer turmoil because it took him forever to 'fall in love' in the first place."

Doug agreed and told me he was over what happened. Even though I just met him, I didn't believe him. I felt honored he shared his story with me and wondered why he chose to do so on our "official" first date. Was he already thinking of a future with me? I wasn't sure, but knew I had to see him again. He dropped me off with a small hug and left, knowing that behaving like a perfect gentleman would draw me to him all the more.

CHAPTER 4

VIRGINIA BEACH, VA, 2001

"You've gotta dance like there's nobody watching, love like you'll never be hurt, sing like there's nobody listening, and live like it's heaven on earth."
William W. Purkey

The next week brought an air of excitement with my friend Patty from Michigan coming for a much-needed visit. Patty and I met during pharmaceutical sales training. We spent countless hours together studying and training to become representatives, which created a strong bond between us. To make things exciting, I planned the weekend around the Dave Matthews concert and my Ravens party. When I picked her up from the airport, the music of Dave Matthews filled the air . . . *"Crazy how it feels tonight . . . crazy how you make it all all right . . . love . . . crush me with the things you do and I'll do for you anything . . . Lovely lady, I'm at your feet . . . God, I want you so badly . . . Is this real or am I dreaming."*

Patty and I planned our days well before Doug was ever in the equation. So, when he asked if he could make dinner for both of us on Thursday evening, I made sure I discussed it with my friend before I agreed to change our plans. Because she was looking out for my best interests, she agreed, and we simply moved a couple of things around to fit in his generous invitation. When we arrived at Doug's place on Ocean View Drive, he was already preparing a chicken dish with artichokes and sun-dried tomatoes. He was trying to cook us a healthy meal because he knew about our obsession with health and fitness.

Doug welcomed us in his home and quickly asked, "What can I get you ladies to drink? A glass of wine? I have both white and red."

We both answered together, "Red." The three of us discussed many different topics, and I was pleasantly surprised by Doug's knowledge of things that didn't involve the military. Doug and Patty enjoyed talking about her bodybuilding competitions and Doug's wrestling meets. I was overjoyed in knowing Patty already approved of Doug, which was a good sign.

Our dinner went so smoothly, we both wanted Doug to join us on our next stop at Crocs. He thanked us, but said he had an early morning. I knew what he meant by "early" morning for the simple fact that Thursday nights at Crocs were crazy, and I took off work in order to avoid that. Croc's was a little corner bar on the ocean side of Virginia Beach. It was another local hangout, and I took Patty there because it was the place to be in Virginia Beach on Thursday night.

Because of the incredible dinner, we weren't up for much after we left Doug's. When we arrived at 10 o'clock, the bar was already packed inside; thank goodness for the outside area where the air was cool and the crowds were scattered.

As we stood by the railing, Patty shared her opinion about Doug. "Pam, I like him. He's fantastic and hot! But he's also nice and considerate. Do you like him?"

I didn't hesitate when I answered, "Yes, I do like him, and I feel a connection, but I haven't kissed him yet. You know you can't measure passion and friendship until the initial kiss. If a guy can't kiss, forget about it!"

We both laughed until I noticed the expression on Patty's face. She had a look of surprise when she said, "Don't look now, but here comes your 'maybe' new boyfriend." I turned around, and there he was. It was difficult not to notice his large stature as he came barreling over to us both. Before I could say hi, he picked me up high in the air and tossed me around like a rag doll. When Doug carefully placed me on the ground, he decided it was time to dance as he spun me around and around. This guy was something else. Our conversation was kept to a minimal because of the loud music, so we ended our evening a lot earlier than expected. Doug, once again, being the perfect gentleman, walked us to my car. Patty took her seat while Doug and I stood along the driver's side.

"Thank you for a wonderful evening," Doug said.

"No, thank you," I answered.

He reached over and wrapped his body around mine. The embrace was so tight I could hardly breathe. I moved my head to face him because I wanted to kiss him and he knew it, but he looked me in the eyes and turned away. The passion between us was completely intoxicating. Even a stranger walking past my car would've felt it. All I wanted was a kiss. What was his problem? Two can play this game, so I quickly said good night, got into my car and drove away. I was thankful for his gentle character, but I wondered about the kiss. I needed it to confirm what I already knew; we were connected and being together was just a matter of time.

Friday brought beautiful weather, and Patty and I worked out hard during the day to feel good about lounging by the pool in the afternoon. The concert started at seven, and we could hardly wait to dance on the lawn to the meaningful songs of the Dave Matthews Band. Sometime in the afternoon, I noticed a teal green Ford 150 truck pull into my driveway. Behind the driver's seat was a man in a military uniform. He wore a beige shirt and a beige cover on his head, and when he opened the driver door and stood up, I recognized him immediately. It was Doug. What was he doing in my neighborhood? He looked statuesque in his military uniform; tall and lean with many ribbons of valor and service planted upon his well-developed chest. Seeing him in full uniform made my stomach fill with butterflies.

As he approached my front door, I begged Patty to stall him so I could run upstairs and throw myself together. Surprise again. Was he testing me in some way? I could hear their conversation as I quickly applied a small amount of mascara and changed into a cute beach cover-up. He was talking about his court appearance for a speeding ticket and was at the courthouse, which was around the corner from my house. He thought he would stop by and say hi. As I walked down the stairs, I looked at him and waved hello.

"Hi, Pam, I wanted to stop by and let you know I will be coming to your party tomorrow night, but I wanted to make sure if it was okay to bring by two friends, Chris and Doug."

"Of course," I replied. "Your friends I've met so far seem to be great, so I'm confident all of your friends are cut from the same cloth."

Doug smiled and said, "Okay, then, I'll see you tomorrow." He walked out the front door, got into his car and sped off around the corner. I could see why he was in court for a speeding ticket. The Harley-Davidson accident, the speeding tickets and the Armed Forces Echo Challenge were elements to his personality outside of fighting for our nation. I wondered for just a second if I could be with this type of man and knew immediately the answer was yes.

That evening, being at the concert was incredible. The air was cool for a summer night in July, and we danced under the stars to songs that would inspire a snail to jump out of its shell. "*. . . I'm coming slow, but speeding . . . I will go in this way and find my way out . . . it's coming to much more . . . I'm coming . . . YEAH . . . I wanted to say, wanted to play . . . wanted to stay.*" Dave Matthews's words were singing in my soul. Life was good, and it was about to get better.

I woke up the next morning excited about my Ravens party, but even more excited about who would be coming. The party originated as a fun gesture to celebrate the Ravens' Super Bowl win just one more time. The house was filled with purple, black and gold. Stars and balloons painted every corner of the house. Outside, there was a football toss and random trivia. We had purple shooters, purple martinis and purple slushies. The theme party was working out well. People wore football gear for their favorite team. We had Ravens, Steelers, Packers and Redskins. Doug and his friends showed up casually late and, of course, without football gear. I wasn't surprised as Doug already mentioned he wasn't a big pro football fan. He felt the players didn't play for meaning or purpose, just for money. I did see some truth in his reasoning, but I liked professional football all the same due to the entertainment factor.

I could tell immediately Doug's friends were great. Chris and Doug were both Marine Corps officers and served with Doug during some point in his career. They were men of character with a very dry sense of humor; never laughing too loud at any remark. Chris was an avid Steelers fan and made snide remarks about the Ravens such as "a bunch of criminals" and "the old Browns." Chris was tall with blond hair and blue eyes. His physique was lean, and he had a pale complexion. I wasn't surprised when I found out his Irish nationality. The conversation between the three men was fun, but I was getting impatient to get Doug alone. When he arrived, I was on my second martini and felt a little daring. I said to Doug, "Hey, let's walk over to this side of house. I want to show you something." He nodded his head and I quickly grabbed his hand while we strolled to the side of the house where no one could see or hear us.

As soon as we reached the fence, I pushed Doug against it and tried to kiss him. He quickly grabbed me by the hands, turned me around and pushed me against the fence. He stared long and hard into my eyes and said, "You will never initiate our first kiss." Then he immediately lifted up my face and starting passionately kissing my wanting lips. A bolt of lightning ran through my entire body as the fire ignited tenfold between the two of us. Kissing him was like every girl's dream a first kiss should be; it was the best kiss of my life. We walked back to the party, hand in hand, without saying a word. The connection was made. Our kiss remained a secret when we returned to the party while making sure we had plans to see each other again as soon as possible.

The next morning, as I drove Patty to the airport, we couldn't help but talk about Doug and the connection she saw between the two of us. We said our sad good-byes, and I went home to prepare for the evening. I already planned to be in control of this date by meeting him at his house to see *The Planet of the Apes,* letting him pick because he was definitely more passionate about movies than I was. Doug seemed to love movies, books and music, and he appealed to me in so many ways . . . but not with this movie pick.

When Doug invited his roommate Joe to the movies with us, I thought that maybe he might be getting some additional feedback about me from another friend. Joe was Doug's good friend and an infamous "Navy SEAL." I met Joe originally the night at the Duck Inn. He looked familiar with his fire engine red hair and a body stacked with muscle inside his 5 foot 8 frame. Doug referred to him as "Mighty Joe," and I could definitely see why. He was Irish in descent with a witty sense of humor, which I liked in a person. Joe chose to sit in another row and gave us some privacy, but being in the movie was awkward because I wanted to talk to Doug about everything, especially the kiss. We held hands during the movie and laughed at the ridiculous scenes. I think Doug was embarrassed about picking such a horrible movie and tried to apologize.

"I'm sorry. I promise you can pick the next time." I simply nodded my head and was certain my choice would be a sappy love story just to be funny.

We wanted more time together and after the movie, the three of us went to one of their favorite Thai restaurants. Thai wasn't my favorite, but I could see that Joe and Doug were foaming at the mouth for a taste of Thai. I learned about levels of heat in Thai cooking and how Thai iced teas were made. Doug loved Thai iced teas and was open by saying, "I love them; they are full of fat, sugar and calories." I certainly wasn't going for any additional calories besides what was in the food, so when they both ordered their "high caloric drinks," I opted for a water with lemon.

The three of us shared great stories about everything. We talked about the navy and Marine Corps. We talked about sports and women. Joe was still single, and I was trying to figure out his type of woman. I was hoping maybe I could find him a friend. The conversation led to my family, and I spoke of my father being in the air force for twenty-five years. I was overwhelmed with curiosity about the differences in military forces, which led me to ask the guys a question, "Who is tougher, the Navy SEALs or the Recon Marines?"

Both Joe and Doug looked up at each other, smiled, but didn't say I word. I broke the silence by responding for them, "I was only asking because, according to my father, the marines are the toughest. He told me that if you need something done, they go in and get the job done, no matter what the consequences." Still neither answered, and I guessed I touched on a soft spot for both of them; neither wanted to take credit for their great service to the United States. Once again, I was in complete admiration of Doug and the company he kept.

We returned to Ocean Drive after dinner, and I ended up giving up control by eagerly retreating to his small downstairs apartment. I was nervous about being alone with Doug after experiencing the passion of our first kiss. I was afraid of giving into my physical needs, but I knew I could be strong by looking at the big picture: I wanted this relationship to go slowly and mature into a meaningful bond.

Doug turned on the CD player and chose a beautiful, romantic song. He lit a couple of candles and seemed to be getting a little too comfortable, so I decided to be up front with him to avoid any romantic, preconceived notions. I shyly said, "Doug, I hope you know I just wanted to talk with you a little longer in private. I have no intention of sleeping with you."

He looked at me with a smile and said, "I know." We sat on his bed and talked. He leaned over and kissed me, and it was what I remembered from the previous night; his kisses were like kissing no other. We both controlled our desire by deciding to lie down and rest for a little while.

As soon as our heads hit the pillow, we heard a soft knock on his door. The knock was gentle, like that of a woman, and the look on Doug's face confirmed my answer. I could tell he was very nervous and tried to ignore the knocks, hoping they would go away. Whoever it was, she was persistent, and I started laughing to calm his mood while saying, "Maybe you should answer the door."

He looked at me with honest eyes and said, "I swear I'm not playing two women against each other. I know who it is, and as soon as I met you again, I broke it off with her."

I laughed again and said, "Douglas, I completely understand. Just answer the door and tell her to go home."

He immediately got up and went outside. I could hear soft whispers, and then a car start. She was leaving. I didn't feel threatened by her at all because I was confident Doug and I were going to be together. We both knew our connection was strong. When he returned to me, he tried to explain himself, but I stopped him and said, "Douglas, I just entered your life. Who am I to judge you when we just started dating a month ago?" He looked relieved and knew I meant every word I said to him.

CHAPTER 5

VIRGINIA BEACH, VA, 2001

"There is never a time or place for true love. It happens accidentally, in a heartbeat, in a single flashing, throbbing moment."
Sarah Dessen

Romance was in the air. I thought about him throughout the day and had dreams about him at night. Just thinking about his touch made me tremble, and the sight of him made my stomach jump. It was a good idea, for now, to never let him know how I was feeling. He was a man who was accustomed to getting what he wanted, and I knew it was mandatory for me to be a wise woman with someone like this. After the experience with the other girl at his door, I knew he was someone who could date whoever he wanted, and my last wish was to scare him off by sharing too much. I even read books like *The Rules* to help me maintain my cool.

With all that being said, Doug and I were similar in many ways. We were both extremely independent and wanted to be with each other at the same level, but I let him take the lead and never, ever called him unless he called me first. I also never answered the phone when he called and tried to instill a sense of mystery in order to keep his curiosity in check. Maybe that was why he didn't back away. He was a man full of testosterone and wanted the chase, so I gave it to him. Even with all the cat and mouse games, it was impossible to deny the fact that we were getting closer and closer as the days passed. I wanted him to be mine, and I didn't want another woman knocking on his door ever again. *How could I tame a wild animal?* I thought to myself. Time was moving quickly, and I knew I was going to be with him completely, but I would never unless I knew he was mine exclusively.

I kept the mystery going by planning a girls' weekend away from him. It was the first time we would be away from each other since we started dating, and I thought it would be good for our relationship. Besides, I enjoyed being with my friends, but knew I would still miss him. The girls' weekend was filled with shopping, dancing and sunning, but Sunday ended up being too much fun when brunch turned into another party, and I ended up getting stuck at the beach because of my lack of discipline from drinking too many mimosas. There was no way I could drive back in my condition, but I knew someone who would come save me.

I dialed Doug's number and was elated when he answered. I desperately told him my story. "Doug, I'm stuck at the beach. I drank too much and can't drive back. Can you come get me? Everyone else has to leave, and I'm by myself." He didn't hesitate.

"I'll be there in 3 hours."

"Okay," I answered. "We can stay the night here and leave first thing in the morning."

As I waited patiently in front of a Mexican restaurant, I couldn't stand the butterflies swimming in my stomach. He arrived shockingly in only 3 hours, riding the entire way on his Harley through a series of terrible thunderstorms. I felt horrible when he showed up covered in a black trash bag, which didn't give him much protection from the rain; he was soaked to the bone. Seeing him in this condition and knowing how he saved me from my own mistake touched my heart.

By the time we checked into the Hampton Inn, I knew we wouldn't be getting separate rooms. He kissed me in the entranceway of our king bedroom suite, picked me up and walked over to the bed. Before this went any further I had to be sure of one thing and whispered in his ear, "If we are going to be together, then you need to promise me you won't be with anyone else."

I thought maybe the question wasn't asked at the best time, but he immediately replied, "You are the first woman who has ever said that to me." He didn't even think for a second and said, "I promise."

Our lovemaking was everything I imagined it would be. He was all I could ever want in life from a lover. Doug filled all my needs and was as passionate about sex as he was about being a marine. Selfless, undying and eternal were the only words to describe our special first time together. I knew I would never want for anyone else again.

We returned to Virginia Beach the next morning with Doug driving in front of me on his Harley as I carefully followed behind. Driving home alone in my car, I dreamt of going back to his place and staying with him the entire day. We had crossed the line last night, and it both scared and excited me. I didn't want to lose control by falling deeply in love with him too soon. My barriers had to stay up until I knew for sure he was in forever. He already committed to a monogamous relationship, which was the first step. The second would be meeting more of his friends, and then his family. He already invited me to meet Andre and Steph for the 8th and I parade so I felt sure about our relationship moving forward in a positive direction.

After crossing the Chesapeake Bay and entering Virginia Beach, we parted to our separate homes. The ball was in his court now, and I was curious to see if he was, indeed, a man of his word, but it was extremely difficult to keep my head on straight when all I could think about was him. I kept to myself and waited for his call in the evening. He didn't tell me he was going to call, and I didn't ask. I only prayed and by five P.M. my phone was ringing. I picked up the phone.

"How is the most beautiful woman in the world doing?" he asked. Doug passed the test.

CHAPTER 6

WASHINGTON, D.C., 2001

"If I had a flower for every time I thought of you . . . I could walk through my garden forever."
Alfred Tennyson

It was finally our time to attend the Marine Corps 8th and I parade in Washington, D.C., where I would meet two more of his best friends: Jon, Doug's spiritual Jedi master, and Andre, Doug's big brother. Doug and I decided to drive separately, since I was in Richmond calling on physicians, and would continue to make my way north after work. As usual, I was early and Douglas was late. He told me to go in and introduce myself to Andre, but having never met him, I felt awkward and was still unsure about my relationship with Doug. Was I his girlfriend or friend? I wasn't sure, so I left it open.

I hesitantly knocked on Andre's door, only to be greeted with a huge smile from a very large man. We chatted briefly, and I immediately knew he was like all the rest of Doug's friends who were all great people. His house was neatly kept with two sofas in the living room, a large television set and a small kitchen with matching table and chairs. I noticed he had a dozen red roses on the table, and I guessed they were for his girlfriend, Stephanie. Doug bought me many different types of flowers, but never red roses. It was probably due to the meaning behind them. The red rose symbolized everlasting love. We never discussed why he didn't bring me red roses, but I already knew. This man wasn't one to throw those words around or give symbols of love unless he was 100 percent sure. Our relationship was still new, and I was positive it was going to take much longer for me to earn a red rose. I was happy when Doug finally arrived, all smiles, while straddling his Harley.

I certainly liked the way he looked on his bike, but the picture he showed me when he crashed flashed in my head. All my worries faded as Doug walked into the room and the entire house lit up with his energy. His smile was from ear to ear as he grabbed Andre and hugged him hard; he seemed to take the breath out of him. That wasn't an easy task with Andre being a heavyweight wrestler in a frame around 6 foot 2 and 225 pounds of muscle.

Doug greeted Andre with excitement. "Hi, Dre, it's so great to see you. I've missed you, my friend." I noticed he wasn't afraid to show his emotions with his friends and family. He used the word "I love you" freely with all of them and never left his friends or ended phone conversations without saying "I love you."

I excused myself to freshen up and let Doug privately catch up with Andre. It was difficult finding the right thing to wear because I wanted to look sexy for Douglas, but classy in front of his friends and the Marine Corps. The best choice for me was to be myself, so I decided to go with a nice pair of maroon slacks and a black sleeveless shirt. It didn't matter anyway because Doug didn't care about outside appearances. He spent his entire life surrounding himself with people who were beautiful on the inside. When he told me he was borrowing an outfit from his roommate for the parade I laughed, knowing I didn't choose him for his fashion sense. He wore a white button-down shirt, yellow tie and beige slacks. He looked handsome, but I knew in time, I would help transform his civilian wardrobe . . . or at least get rid of his Lee jeans.

As we finished dressing, I could hear a female voice upstairs and guessed it was Stephanie. I couldn't wait to meet the woman behind the voice, especially since Doug told me all about Andre's plan to make her his wife. From the moment I met Steph, I could tell why Andre wanted to marry her. Beautiful in appearance, she had long blond hair and cute tiny freckles that danced when she laughed. They would make a handsome married couple one day. The four of us shared some champagne and waited for the third couple, Jon and Anya Sanchez.

Jon and Anya were married when Doug was fighting in Kosovo, which made it impossible for him to be in the wedding. Jon was so disappointed he didn't fill Doug's spot and carried on the wedding with one less groomsman. I was beginning to realize, I wasn't the only one who knew Doug was irreplaceable! When Jon and Anya entered the house, Doug's emotions were in full force. Once again, he grabbed both Jon and Anya and hugged the breath out of them.

Jon and Anya were the ultimate married couple. They just looked like they belonged together; the way they looked into each others' eyes and their close body language made me feel the love they shared for each other. At first glance, both were beautiful in outward appearance. Jon was handsome with dark hair, hazel eyes and a gleaming smile. His smile lit up the room and, along with Doug's gleaming face, made lighting completely unnecessary.

Doug described Anya as "the most beautiful wife out of all of my friends." Anya was definitely a looker with her blond hair, piercing blue eyes and the most incredible white teeth I had ever seen. I was able to have a brief talk with them and instantly realized, like with Doug's other friends, their outward beauty was only hitting the surface.

Excitement filled the air as the marines took center stage on the lawn of the 8th and I Barracks. All were handsome and dressed in their finest, the Marine Corps Blues uniform. I looked at Doug and asked, "Why didn't you wear your Blues?"

He answered, "Babe, they may look nice, but they're hot as hell. If I don't have to wear them in the scorching heat of August, then I won't. Besides, you will see me in them when I take you to a ball one day." I was determined for him to keep his promise.

The 8th and I parade was everything Doug promised. The rifle patrol and the band were unbelievable. It was like Broadway in Washington, D.C. At the end of the parade, Jon whispered in my ear, "If you stick with Doug, that's where you'll be living one day." I looked over to where Jon was pointing and saw the most magnificent white house. I could tell it was a historic house and was most likely built with the barracks. All of the windows had small lights glittering in the night sky; it was the home of the commandant of the entire Marine Corps. I thought about Jon's statement and decided then I would gladly accept the invitation.

After the parade, we were invited to the Center House within the 8th and I Marine Corps Barracks. Doug explained the tradition of the Center House. "Back in the day, marines would invite their girls back to the Center House. The marines would have a couple of drinks, and then lift the women up so they could kiss the ceiling and leave their lipstick marks." When Doug finished his story I looked over at him and noticed an air of mystery in his smile. Before I could blink, he swiftly picked me up to kiss the ceiling. I ducked my head and yelled for him to stop. With my fighting, and along with the looks of several other guests, he finally stopped his pursuit. Of course, our group loved it by the sound of their boisterous laughs filling the room.

We began to lose some of our friends as the night progressed to Georgetown. Jon and Anya decided to head home, and we promised to get together sometime soon in the future. Georgetown was another place Doug wanted to take me, and I was excited about the adventure. Andre was the "mayor" of Georgetown, as Doug would say, and we were well received into a club called Modern.

Modern was a small nightclub with blue fluorescent lighting. The club was packed, and we could barely move to the bar to get a drink. Doug grabbed my hand and quickly maneuvered us around the crowd. He ordered drinks, and we settled in the corner by the swing for some elbow room. This place was definitely filled with lots of singles on the prow, and I was a little worried by what I would find when Steph and I left for the ladies' room.

Sure enough, when we came back, there were women surrounding our men. Doug and Andre looked innocent and immediately returned their attention to us. However, the woman interested in Doug wasn't going to stop; she was all over him. When he tried to get away, she bumped into me and spilled my entire apple martini all over Doug's shirt. *How dare that woman?* I thought it was apparent by the way we looked at each other and by our body language we were together. The martini incident spoiled our mood, so we escaped the bar scene to share the rest of our evening among good friends.

While we cabbed home, laughter about the stupid girl filled the air along with, more important, the incredible parade. Being with Doug and his friends made me realize just how special this man was. It was another sign of why I wanted him by my side and the thought of living in the big white house on the 8th and I Marine Corps Barracks was suddenly my dream too.

After returning from D.C., Doug and I became inseparable. I still enjoyed my alone time, but wanted to be with him more. Dates turned into sleepovers, and nights turned into weekends. My roommate and I moved into a new house in September, but I was never there; Doug and I liked the seclusion of his basement apartment. We discovered many things about each other and grew to like each other enough to fall in love. During our discovery process, I uncovered Doug's love for music. I think he had at least three hundred CDs. He would play songs like "You're Simply the Best" by Tina Turner and "Breathe" by Faith Hill. His romanticism was intense, which was empowered by the songs he played for me while we were together.

He would surprise me with flowers, song choices and photos. On one special day, he came over my house holding a picture of him while he was deployed. In the picture, he was posed holding three cute little kids. I discovered on the back of the photo some beautiful writing. The writing was a poem he composed for me.

> *You are an eagle's cry, high above the mountain peaks, full of strength and purpose. You are a deep blue wave, crashing into a jagged lava cliff, as a couple, embraced, watches in awe.*
>
> *You are a sunset, brilliant, lighting up the desert sky after an evening thunderstorm, the air cool and invigorating.*
>
> *Thank you for your friendship and positive attitude.*
>
> *Respectfully, D. A. Zembiec*

Doug had a way of surprising me when I least expected it. We were falling in love, but we both never said it. We kept our feelings about each other to ourselves, but we both knew what was happening.

CHAPTER 7

ANNAPOLIS, MD, FRIDAY, MAY 11, 2007

"I trust you to do the right thing and I believe in you."
D. A. Zembiec

I stayed in the guest room to see if there was a chance for my body and mind to rest. The task was daunting as I tossed and turned in bed for hours. I tried desperately to find sleep, with the hope of waking from a horrible dream. Sleep never came, and I finally gave in to the day. What was I going to do next? I was broken. For the first time in my life I thought of the possibility of not making it. I couldn't stop the negative thoughts from running rampant in my mind. Doug and I were supposed to grow old together. How would I ever move forward?

All I could think about was my life being over, and then suddenly, I saw her; she was sitting in her high chair eating breakfast with her sparkling brown eyes smiling at me. "Mama," she said. Looking into Fallyn's eyes was like looking into Doug's. She had identical dark brown piercing eyes in comparison to her father's. When I looked into her eyes, I saw my husband. She was the answer and would give me the power to move forward.

"Hi, baby. Good morning. Mommy loves you," I said as I kissed her forehead. For a few moments, I was able to concentrate on my daughter, which gave me much-needed hope.

I guessed people from the outside had heard the news when my phone began to ring off the hook, flowers started arriving in the hundreds and my front door had to be guarded. Kap and Tom Ripley, Colonel Ripley's son, arrived at the house and took the necessary guard duty to keep the news reporters and friends from flooding my doorstep. I was barely coherent when my sister Denise arrived with a prescription for Valium. She said it would help me sleep. At first, I refused to take it, and then after several failed attempts at rest, I decided there wasn't another option when I went to bed that night. I hated sleeping because waking up to reality was so difficult, but I knew I had to sleep or I would never make it through the viewing, the funeral and burial. I told my sister I would take a Valium for sleep and sleep alone because I wasn't going to drug myself into not feeling. Feeling in life wasn't always good, but I needed to feel the loss of my husband or I would never come to terms with his death. My life was over, as I knew it, and I couldn't believe how foolish I was in thinking my husband was invincible. We weren't prepared for this to happen because Doug wasn't supposed to die.

Don, Jo Ann and John arrived later in the day, and we were at a loss for words. The four of us sat on the back deck and just listened as friends and family arrived to console us. Nothing was working. I was empty. The heart, which housed the passionate love for my husband, was replaced with an enormous void that could never be filled. My chest was aching, my head was aching and I couldn't eat. The very thought of food made my stomach curl, and food was in every corner of the kitchen. My generous neighbors sent tons of food. I wanted only wine, but even wine wasn't affecting me in any way, shape or form. The alcohol couldn't numb the pain of my loss; this loss was too great and much too difficult to bear.

All day Friday, I sat and listened. I could barely speak, and when I did, I could only make out a whisper or whimper from the pain of my heartbreak. No one knew what to say or how to say it, but what could be said except Doug was dead and my wonderful life was gone.

When Doug's friend Chris arrived, I felt a small amount of comfort. He was wearing a crisp white linen shirt and jeans. He was completely relaxed on the outside, but I knew he was hurting. Chris was a marine and highly trained on the consequences of war. We both walked Vahli while Chris shared his last conversation with Doug during their visit in March.

Doug was at Camp Lejeune for training with the marines and stopped by Chris's house to see him and his family. I remembered telling Douglas to stay the night and spend time with his good friend. Doug was disciplined about coming home when he wasn't deployed because he wanted to be as close to Fallyn and I as much as possible. His voice was filled with relief and joy when I suggested he stay. Chris and Doug were able to share stories, drink scotch and smoke cigars. Chris said to me, "Pam, I remember talking with Doug about his future in the Marine Corps. He told me he was tired of the job he was doing and was ready to stop traveling and spend more time with his family. Pam, I never heard Doug talk like that. He was always the one to stay and continue the fight. Finally, after all his tours, he was getting tired. He couldn't wait to go to Major school in Quantico with me. If it's any consolation, Pam, Doug was ready to settle down and just spend time with you and Fallyn."

"Thanks for telling me that, Chris. It means so much to me to hear he was beginning to unwind and become more settled down with his family, but what the hell, Chris? One tour too late, I guess," I cried.

"Pam, I know. The more you go over there, the higher your risk. Doug thought he had nine lives. He thought he was going to live forever. Nobody does, and it's the chance you take every time you go back." I thought about Chris's statement, "he thought he had nine lives." Yes, he did think he had nine lives, but they were all gone.

My conversation with Chris echoed back and forth in my head. If only we could have one more chance. I wished and prayed I could go back in a time machine and warn Doug of his impending doom. Life wasn't fair, and my situation was grim. I kept asking myself over and over again, "How am I going to make it?" The day worsened when I found out the official Caco officer assigned to me was coming over to give me my options. He was going to discuss our benefits and what was entitled to our family, but I didn't care about that stuff and certainly didn't want him at my house. Seeing him would make it so "final," and I wasn't ready to actually believe it.

Colonel Ripley was so kind to come over to my house the moment he received word, but hearing it from a marine in uniform was the dreaded moment. He was coming over, and I wasn't able to prevent it. As the doorbell rang, my body began to collapse. I screamed, "No, I don't want to see him, tell him to go away. I'm not ready!" I quickly ran outside to the deck. The deck was my refuge. It was outside and surrounded with trees and the view of the tranquil creek. Doug and I loved our evenings on the deck in the spring. I felt his presence with me when I sat out there.

Doug's parents, Colonel Ripley and Kap quickly followed behind me. Kap said, "Pam, I know it's hard, but you have to see him. Major Hart and the chaplain are the official representatives of the Marine Corps, and it's a must."

33

"Why can't Chris be my Caco officer? He's a major," I cried.

"It doesn't work that way. Major Hart is a great guy. Give him a chance," Kap said.

"I don't want to see them, Kap. It's too final for me right now and makes everything real," I cried.

"Pam, we held it off for as long as we could. They must come and talk to you."

I finally gave in to my first of many life-changing responsibilities and knew there would be many more to come. "Okay, I will deal with it."

Major Hart and the chaplain came outside to the deck and gave me the official Marine Corps notification of Douglas's death. He carried a large binder, which contained all of the pertinent information I would need in the upcoming months. They spoke, but I couldn't hear them. Everything was cloudy, and I sat still and sullen without a word leaving my mouth.

When they left me on the deck, I sobbed. I sobbed for the sheer sanctity of sobbing. It was all I could do; it was all I knew how to do. That evening, I welcomed the Valium because my lack of sleep for over 48 hours was inhibiting any ounce of sanity I had left.

CHAPTER 8

VIRGINIA BEACH, VA, 2001–2002

"Tolerance does not mean acceptance of people who try to destroy the principles which made our nation free and strong."
D. A. Zembiec

September 11, 2001, changed everything. I was up for work early that morning to get over the Hampton Roads Bridge Tunnel and see physicians in West Point, Virginia, before traffic hit. During my drive, I noticed bright blue skies and cooler temperatures. The weather was spectacular along the entire Eastern seaboard without one cloud in the sky.

I showed up at my first doctor's office at 9:00 A.M. sharp, hoping to be the first representative for the day. I entered the office, went to the sample closet, and waited to speak with one of the physicians. In the middle of my conversation with Dr. Cooper, one of his nurses was screaming as she ran down the hallway. She was out of breath and yelled, "One of the Twin Towers had a plane accidently crash into the top of the building!" Dr. Cooper and I looked at each other in horror and quickly went up front to see the television. We both could only stare and realized, yes, a plane had crashed into one of the Towers.

A few moments later, another plane crashed into the second Tower. At that point, we were speechless and knew this wasn't an accident. Who hated Americans enough to do something like this? From my conversations with Doug, he warned me this could happen. He said our country was too comfortable and our guard was down; terrorism finally got us. There was no other explanation. We all held hands in the office and listened as Katie Couric and Matt Lauer talked about the "accident." I knew we were under attack and the news was in denial. There was no way our nation wasn't going to retaliate. The United States of America was about to go to war, and I was petrified. I left the office shaking, and as I entered my car, I noticed Doug calling on my cell phone. There was an urgency but calmness to his voice. "Babe, get back over the bridge as quickly as you can. We're under attack, and Virginia Beach is a prime spot to bomb. I want you back here with me so you're safe." As I hung up the phone, I listened to the radio and heard the Pentagon was being attacked. I drove as quickly as I could back over the bridge for safety.

When I arrived in one piece to Doug's house, I planted myself right next to him because he made me feel safe and secure. Each time the sliding glass door opened, another marine or navy SEAL would enter. The room was filled with our finest warriors who were all very pissed off and couldn't wait to get the Taliban. Those mindless criminals were celebrating as the Towers crumbled to the ground with thousands of innocent victims. I hated them and wanted them to pay for this horrific act. Everyone gathered by the television and waited to see how our nation would retaliate. Breaking bread together and waiting for President Bush to address the nation passed the time. We talked about the future of our country and how each military branch would do their part to seek justice against this extreme act of terrorism.

After we finished dinner, the president of our country began his address. Everyone gathered in front of the big-screen television and listened carefully to President Bush's words. The silence in the room was frightening as the words resonated throughout every room in the house. The warriors respectfully listened, but I could tell no one was satisfied. We all wanted justice now. Doug being Doug said, "We need to be patient and not worry. Justice will be served in good time."

The next few months turned into the land of many changes. The entire country was in turmoil, and we struggled to make our way out of the terror that killed over 3,000 innocent men and women in New York, Pennsylvania and Washington, D.C. The land of the free and the home of brave would never be the same. When President Bush declared war on terrorism, Doug and his friends couldn't have been more ecstatic. They wanted to go the war, seek justice and restore safety to the American people. Most of Doug's friends knew they wanted to serve in the military from childhood and had prepared their entire lives for this.

Doug wasn't different from his friends. He knew by the age of eleven he was going to be a Marine Corps officer. He spent numerous hours with his father's friends who, like his dad, were retired military. He listened to the acts of heroism each shared about one another. Of course, no one spoke of himself or herself; they were humble men and women, like Doug's father, and Doug grew up surrounded by greatness. He chose the sport of wrestling to instill himself with self-discipline and determination. Wrestling also helped prepare him in achieving the warrior mentality. He ensured his success by applying to every military academy in the United States. Doug thought he would get accepted into at least one of them, but in the end, every military academy wanted him. Doug's dream of becoming a Marine Corps officer was turned into reality when he accepted his position into the Naval Academy. The academy was the best at preparing men for the Marine Corps, and Doug knew it. Most of Doug's great friends were from the Naval Academy, and all of them were warriors; most remained in the military even after their required service was completed.

The SEALs were the first to leave, and Joe was soon on his way to the Middle East. When Joe told Doug he was leaving for battle, Doug was very proud, but there was no denying the envy in his eyes. He wanted to be there, but it wasn't his time. His job as an instructor for 2nd Force kept him on shore duty, and I was relieved he wouldn't be going, but also felt compassion for his need to fulfill his dream. As I tried to understand how Doug felt, I looked at my own stance in life. It was like the need I felt to become a mother. As a woman, you prepare yourself for motherhood your entire life. How would I feel if God decided not to grant me a child? I would be devastated; therefore, my compassion for Doug was immense. We watched several of our friends leave, which turned Virginia Beach into a ghost town. The Hampton Roads area wasn't the same with everyone gone. Even Doug commented on how "dead" the town seemed. We were relieved to occasionally hear from Joe and knew he was doing everything to keep terrorism out of our country.

Doug did his best to ignore his wants about being in the Middle East and served his country by leading his training class to a scheduled trip in Key West. To make it fun, we decided to vacation there for Thanksgiving and my birthday. I planned the trip around his schedule and would fly into Ft. Lauderdale, rent a car and drive to Key West. Once there, I would stay with him at the military hotel, and we would have some fun in the sun. I also planned on spending Thanksgiving dinner with my friend Kim and her family in Ft. Lauderdale, and

Doug agreed to come along. It was our first trip together as a couple, and he was going to meet one of my best friends. Kim and I met in high school and knew we would be friends for life. By knowing her for over fifteen years, her approval was something I needed.

The month of November crept by like a tortoise moving up a hill. Doug's training group left a week before our planned trip, and the week without him seemed like an eternity. My nights were sleepless without him beside me. My dreams were also strange. One night I tossed and turned and dreamt I was lying in my bed and could see that my stomach was swollen. I took a second glance and noticed it was not just bloated. It was immense.

Oh my God, I thought. *I think I'm pregnant.* I turned to the left of my bed, and he was standing at my bedside. He was in full dress Blues with medals hanging off on his muscular chest. There was a white cover on his head. He placed his hand on my swollen belly and smiled at me. It was Douglas, and it was his baby. When I woke up from that dream, I was smiling. For now, I knew I wasn't pregnant, but I would be someday, and the child would be Doug's.

CHAPTER 9

FLORIDA, 2001

"Two people in love, alone, isolated from the world,
that's beautiful."
Milan Kundera

I arrived in Ft. Lauderdale three days before Thanksgiving and traveled along Route 1 to Key West, filled with excitement, because I would be with him in one of the most beautiful tropical areas in the United States. When I arrived in Key West, the Naval Hotel couldn't be missed with its large, multilevel structure and the words "Fly Navy" in immense, bright colored letters painted on the front side. I noticed Doug immediately when I pulled up to the entrance, and we embraced like we hadn't seen each other in years. He told me he planned a nice trip that evening, cruising on a historic clipper ship along the bay stocked with plenty of rum runners, wine and beer. I was sure he did this because I shared a great time in my life with my girlfriends when we went on a similar ship in Baltimore called the *Clipper City*. I loved the way he always listened to everything I said.

We could hear Reggae music as soon as we boarded the boat and decided to retreat to the front mast with our drinks while the cool breeze surrounded our bodies and the sun disappeared into the crystal blue waters. We didn't talk much while we enjoyed the rhythm of the music and nestled into each other. Romanticism filled the air, along with the gentle motion of sails moving in the wind.

The next morning I went for a run around the island while Doug finished up with his training group. As I ran through the charming town, I noticed all the palm trees, historic inns and quaint bars. I ran down the main strip to the dock where all the boats chartered for daily snorkeling trips. The sun was warm on my face and body, and I started to feel the sweat trickle down my neck. I looked down and noticed my stomach; it was normal in size although I couldn't help but think about the dream I had before leaving for the trip. I knew I would never tell Douglas about the dream. We were going on our fifth month of dating, and it was too soon to even speak of the possibility of marriage and kids. I didn't want him to think I would, in any way, shape or form, "trap" him into marrying me because I wanted the dream, and I knew in time I would get it. The question was . . . how long?

Time was ticking so I headed back to the room to get ready for our evening together. I wanted to look extra special for my birthday dinner in the Keys. The weather was extremely warm so my options were limited. *Definitely a skirt,* I thought to myself. He loved my legs and preferred me in skirts. I chose a rayon skirt with bright pink and yellow flowers on a white background. The colors were more than appropriate for Key West. I matched a white button-down tie shirt with the skirt. When Doug saw what I had on, he too wanted to be tropical, so he pulled out a beautiful red Hawaiian shirt and explained the history behind it.

"My grandma gave me this shirt before she died. She was born and raised in Hawaii, along with my mom and the rest of her family. I was born in Kona as well, and one day I'll take you there and show you the little hospital. We're all Portuguese." I knew Doug was a "passionate" nationality, but I wasn't sure which one. It was nice to hear about his family heritage. He promised to share more about his Portuguese ancestors during our dinner, which included the legend of his great-great-grandfather who traveled to Kona from Portugal. His boat capsized shortly before arriving on the shores of Kona, and he was forced to swim his way in the cold Pacific.

I didn't have a clue where we were going when Doug put me in the back of the cab. As usual, he jumped in the front seat of the cab in order to question the driver. "It's for our protection," he would always say. During our few cab rides, he seemed to ask the cabdriver the same question every time. "Where are you from?" Some cabdrivers took offense to him being up front, while others liked it. On this evening, the cabdriver loved it. He was from Key Largo and decided to move to Key West for a change.

Doug said, "Can you take us to Louie's Backyard? I made reservations there for my lady's birthday dinner." The cabdriver immediately looked at Doug and said, "Nice place. You'll have a fabulous meal."

The cabby pulled up to the front door of the restaurant and gave us a warm good-bye. "You two have a great meal and call me if you need a ride home."

Louie's Backyard looked like something in a movie. It was a small, restored mansion and the house was painted a soft pink, which I could barely see in the setting sunlight. The staircase leading to the entrance was very wide with embossed green carpeting. Looking into the front glass doors, I could see only a few tables. Louie's Backyard was extremely quaint and deliciously romantic. All the tablecloths were white, and each large window was opened wide to allow the evening breeze to pass through the entire dining area.

As the hostess led us to our table, I noticed many young and old couples engaged in conversation over candlelight. She sat us at a table situated in the front room next to a large window, which was open to the evening air. I was completely impressed by Doug's choice and could tell he did his research when he picked this place. Doug always chose the seat where he was facing the doorway. He explained to me once, "A man should never have his back to a doorway. You never know who may enter—good or bad." I, of course, had no objections because it was nice being taking care of by a real man. Doug also sat next to me; never across the table, to be as close to me as he could, every time.

It was difficult letting him take the lead when it came to choosing a wine. I developed quite an interest in wines and usually chose. I gave in this night because it was his time to completely take the lead on all things. He already knew my favorite, some type of red wine. The wine Doug chose was a 1995 bottle of Bordeaux from a region in France called Pauillac.

"I'm choosing a 1995 bottle because that's the year I graduated from the Naval Academy and became a marine." Every choice with Douglas was always symbolic, and I loved him for it. His actions were always thought through and important choices always had a specific meaning behind them.

At dinner we talked about life. *What is the meaning of life? Are our actions determined by fate or free will? What is the meaning of integrity? Is self-esteem more important than self-respect? Who would you die for? What is more important, inner beauty or outward appearance?* The questions we pondered on went on and on and each answer we shared showed the similarity between our values and goals. However, I noticed Doug was extremely black and white with his answers, and

I believed in some circumstances there was room for a shade or two of gray. I guess that is where we complemented each other. He gave me the strength to believe, and I toned down his judgmental attitude and I knew we fit . . . but did he? All of his actions led me to believe in yes, but one should never make assumptions. I barely ate my dinner because of the excitement, but we did enjoy the lobster and crab soufflé as well as the fresh caprese salad.

The Oceanside bar, waiting for us after dinner, was made of dark wood with a small awning wide enough to barely cover the seats aligned along the length of the bar which seemed to span over the ocean. It was getting late, and the bar was deserted, leaving the place to us. While enjoying the calmness of the moment, our focus quickly turned to the soft sounds in the background. We both looked at each other with identical expressions. I already knew what he was thinking, and before I could comment, Doug said, "What kind of music is this? It's romantic and sensual, yet angelic. I have never heard music like this before." I agreed with him, and we asked the bartender if he knew who was playing, but he didn't recognize the musician. It was difficult to comprehend the tone, and the lyrics were nonexistent. We started to move to the sounds of music as he gently touched my face and kissed me softly. I looked at him in the moonlight and knew I would love this man forever.

You would think our amazing dinner was enough, but we didn't want the night to end and Doug guided me to Sloppy Joes where we both knew there was a band or a DJ. Doug and I both enjoyed dancing and he told me we would feel right at home with Sloppy Joes being frequented by the military, especially navy pilots. On this evening, the bar wasn't crowded, but navy pilots were the first people we spotted sitting on stools near the entrance. Doug knew these pilots and introduced me. I didn't pay attention to their names because I knew they were only acquaintances, and I could tell by Doug's behavior he didn't particularly care for these men. He told me they were helping out in the training classes.

Doug excused himself to use the men's room, and I was left standing there next to these two men. I tried to pretend like I was reading something, but one of the pilots tapped me on the shoulder and asked, "So, you like the big and stupid guys?" I was flabbergasted and wanted to punch him in the face knowing full well his comments were made out of jealousy. This guy knew he could never be anything like Doug and maybe he was joking, but my devoted nature wanted to scratch his eyes out. I tried to ignore his comment and move away, but he proceeded to continue with his ridiculous "pickup" lines. "You have the most beautiful white teeth I have ever seen." I looked at him and rolled my eyes while saying, "It's called bleach."

Before my anger took hold of me any further, I decided to walk away forcing Doug to search for me in the large crowd. When he finally made his way back to me, he knew something happened and I decided it was best not to tell him what the pilot said, but I did ask if we could dance and stay away from them. Doug questioned, "Did they try to pick you up?"

"Yes," I said.

He started laughing. "Typical navy pilots. I don't blame them."

Doug and I danced the night away and returned to our room ready for peace and quiet. We both wanted to spend alone time together on my birthday, away from all others. In our world, on that night, no one existed but the two of us.

On Thanksgiving Day, we traveled north to Ft. Lauderdale for dinner with Kim, Paul and Josh. We all appreciated a comfortable setting while stuffing our bellies with Kim's cooking. Kim couldn't wait to pull me aside after dinner.

"Pam, I've met all your boyfriends, and I want you to know he's the one. Mark my words. You will marry Doug." I agreed with her, but I knew it was going to take time. We watched Thanksgiving football, and I tried to help Doug understand the game a little more. I definitely enjoyed the game much more than he. It was refreshing to be with a man who wanted me more than a football game. The next morning, Doug returned to Key West, and I was on my way back to Virginia Beach. Doug left me with a good-bye kiss and a postcard that read,

Dearest Pamela, Brutal winds lash my face, sweat grows into daggers.
Fingers grow numb on unforgiving metal.
Relentless weight cuts deep into my shoulders.
Shadows surround me. I am with many, but I am alone.
Painful isolation descends in cold darkness, but I remember and I take refuge.
I see the beautiful strength of your character. I hear your encouragement.
I taste your soft lips. I smell the sweet scent of your warm body.
I feel the electricity of your passion. Icy winds cut like a steel knife.
Ominous storm clouds advance like armies, but I am warm.
A fire blazes in my soul. You are in my heart.

Happy Birthday!

I wrote this poem for you, Pam. Your friendship shines like a jewel in the crown of life. You are the most positive, confident, energetic, self-assured, driven woman I have ever met. You will go farther than you already have, and I admire and respect you more than you will ever know. My soul smiles every time I think of you. Thank you. Semper Fi, D. A. Zembiec.

When Doug came back to Virginia Beach, the first stop we made was to find the angelic music we heard in Louie's Backyard. Unfortunately, we left every store empty-handed.

CHAPTER 10
THE HOLIDAYS, 2001-2002

"All the happiness you ever find lies in you."
D. A. Zembiec

The holiday season for the year 2001 was here. I couldn't believe it was already Christmastime and this year, I was happy about the holidays. They usually brought a sense of renewal for many lives, and I was truly in love with someone for the first time in my life.

Doug and I were both scheduled to go back to our hometowns and see our families. He would travel west to Albuquerque, and I would head north to Baltimore. We decided to exchange gifts after we returned, but I couldn't wait. I left the Christmas present on his bed to surprise him and asked him to take it with him to New Mexico. He could open it on Christmas Day. It was difficult not being with him on Christmas, but necessary. Both of our families missed us, and we weren't ready to exclude either family from their deserved visits. Besides, meeting the parents was a big deal. It would happen when we were both ready.

Doug and I spoke on the phone every day while he was away visiting his parents. He opened up his present on Christmas Day and was overjoyed to receive a new Casio watch to replace the old one, which puttered out while we were in Key West.

After visiting with my family, I went to Las Vegas to ring in the New Year with my friend Stevie. I lived in Las Vegas for over two years and met Stevie one day while I was calling on a physician. We were both waiting for our time to speak with the doctor. The conversation between Stevie and I was so comfortable, and

I felt as though I had been friends with her for a long time. We decided to go to lunch after the call and remained friends since that time. She was gracious enough to take me to the airport when I left for Virginia Beach, and I promised her that I would visit the next year for New Year's. I am one to never break a promise . . . even for a man's company.

We rang in 2002 at an exclusive spot in the Mandalay Bay called the Foundation Room. It was a good time, but I couldn't wait to get Doug's Happy New Year's call. Of course, I called him one hour earlier in New Mexico, and he returned the call 2 hours later. Our plans were to meet in the Baltimore airport where he would pick me up when my flight returned. I loved visiting Stevie, but couldn't wait to get back to Doug.

I was early for my flight home in anticipation of seeing Doug. While waiting for my plane to take off at McCarran National Airport, I noticed two Baltimore Ravens players sitting close to my seat. It was Jonathan Ogden and Michael McCrary, and I desperately wanted to ask for their autographs. However, I didn't want to look like some female "groupie" because I was a true football supporter. During the entire flight, I contemplated how I would get their autographs. Doug would be my savior; no one would say no to him, and the players would definitely not think much of a guy asking for an autograph.

The plane landed as scheduled, and my anticipation for seeing my man was overwhelming. I saw him standing at the beginning of the baggage claim, carrying two red roses. *At last,* I thought. He was sending a sign this might be love. We embraced each other and once again, I received a welcoming embrace that took my breath away. However, instead of telling him how much I missed him, I said, "Michael McCrary and Jonathan Ogden were on the plane with me from Las Vegas. Can you get their autograph for me?"

Doug looked at me with complete disappointment in his eyes, and I knew I made a terrible mistake. He finally showered me with red roses, and to him, all my attention seemed to be on getting a stupid autograph. Doug gladly went over to the players and both signed without hesitation. He came back with the autographs in hand and looked at me with defeat and disappointment. He said with a heartbroken voice, "I think you're more excited about getting the autographs then you are about seeing me." I simply stared at him and knew he was right. I made a dreadful mistake, but I wasn't more excited to get the signatures. He was most important.

"Doug, of course I'm more excited to see you. I'm sorry. I was just amazed to see some players from my football team. You know how I am about the Ravens." Unfortunately, it was too late. The damage was already done. We drove home to Virginia Beach, me trying to make my mistake go away. My only hope was to take away the hurt of my thoughtless actions. Although Doug was a tough marine, he was also extremely sensitive when it came to me. I was the stoic German girl, and Doug was the passionate Portuguese. When we arrived at his apartment, I hugged him tightly, and we made up in the only way we knew how.

I'm sure he was better the next day when he brought me a Christmas gift, which was a beautiful framed portrait of "The Kiss." Doug signed every card, book and gift. On the back of the portrait he signed, *"Dearest Pamela, Kissing you is like kissing rose petals from a banquet off God's dinner plate. Love, Z."* He explained the portrait to me. "This picture reminds me of you and me, entwined together. You can't see a division between the two bodies. It's how I feel when I'm with you." I didn't know what to say. His romanticism was leaps and bounds over anyone I ever met. I knew he would remain this way because it was part of his being. He would always be the strong marine and the true romantic combined together into one amazing Doug.

CHAPTER 11

VIRGINIA BEACH, VA, 2002

"Take into account that great love and great achievements involve great risk."
Unknown

The holidays brought joy and a sense of renewal; the year 2001 was over, and it was the time to rebuild our nation. 9/11 took a huge toll on everyone, especially the military. Doug was still anxious to play his part in the redemption; however, he was to remain in Virginia Beach until the end of the summer. At that point, he was scheduled to move to Quantico and be part of Captain school for one year. I was thrilled he wouldn't be going away for another year and a half. He would move to Northern Virginia, but that was an easy drive from Virginia Beach. Doug said, "Shore duty isn't the real Marine Corps. Wait until I'm sent away for seven months."

I could definitely wait for that, but knew I could handle it. Doug, however, wasn't as sure.

The winter of 2001 proved to be much colder than other years, and we tried to keep ourselves occupied with movies, reading and dinners. During one cold January night, Doug invited me over his place for dinner. I knew he had something up his sleeve when he asked, "Babe, can you please come over tonight. I have a big surprise for you, and I have to give it to you at my place." I wondered what type of surprise this was going to be. Once again, he had me guessing, and I couldn't help but feel as though he was going to propose. Why did I feel this way? It had to be that dream. The dream was so real, and I told

Doug everything about my life, but not about that dream. He had to figure it out on his own.

I showed up at his place just after 6 P.M., and he said, "Put on your coat, we're going to the beach." Doug lived on Oceanside Drive, and the beach was one hundred meters from his yard. We walked out in the freezing night air with the wind blowing profusely when we got to the beach. Doug looked at me with deep brown eyes and said, "We're going to do something that will invigorate your body, mind and soul."

"Oh boy," I said to myself. I was secretly scared to death. This was a man who didn't show fear, and if he felt it, he certainly didn't let anyone know, not even me. I tried to stay calm, but knew it was probably something I would never do. I was sure it was another test to see if I was strong enough to be his woman.

Doug's eyes were as dark as night, and I could hear the excitement in his breath as he whispered, "The bay water temperature is around 32 degrees. It's just about freezing. We're going to take off all of our clothes, jump in the bay, wrap a towel around us, run home, and then shower our bodies in hot water."

"You are a crazy man!" I said.

"Are you scared?" Doug questioned.

I would never back down from a challenge. I could do this. "No," I said. I immediately stripped down with Doug. He grabbed my hand, and we both ran into the water. The water was bitter cold, and when we ran out of the bay and into the wind chill, my body was covered with tiny ice crystals.

We quickly gathered our things and ran back home to a hot shower. Our bodies were pink from the ice-cold air and water. The shower brought our body temperatures back to normal and he was right. I was completely invigorated. This man brought every aspect of life into my world. Love, tenderness, romance, challenge, intellect, but most of all, the greatest excitement I had ever known.

Valentine's Day approached with the man of my dreams; I could only imagine what Doug had up his sleeve. The relationship was moving forward, and I wanted to talk to him about the future. How could I bring up the subject? I knew I loved him, and I knew he loved me, but we both never said it to each other. I, being the stubborn female, refused to say it first. I would patiently wait for him to make the first move. I thought to myself, *Maybe on Valentine's Day I would get the "I love you" statement.*

On February 14th, Doug came to my house and asked me to leave so he could set up his surprise for me. I returned to a house filled with the scent of vanilla and rose petals showered on the floor, down the hall and into the bedroom. On the bed, he placed an exquisite card. Inside, the card read *"Princess Pamela, thank you for spending time with me. You are the most positive, energetic woman I have ever known. The thought of you makes me smile. Love Z."*

I appreciated the romantic gesture, but where was my "I love you" and why was he signing all his cards Z? I didn't think it was a good sign. I had to talk with him about our future because I was ready to settle down and have children. I wanted it to be with Doug, but if he didn't want the same things, then I would have no choice but to move on. I knew the talk was a must, but I wanted to enjoy the rest of our Valentine's Day together, so I put my thoughts to rest . . . temporarily.

CHAPTER 12

ANNAPOLIS, MD, SATURDAY, MAY 12, 2007

"Always maintain your levelheadedness, especially under pressure, especially in life-or-death situations."
D. A. Zembiec

I awoke to the sounds of my baby laughing in the kitchen. She drew me out of my darkness, but my body was still aching from the inside out. The loss was real, and it wasn't a nightmare I would be able to shake off. This was my new reality. I walked into the kitchen and noticed everyone sitting in the dining room so I decided to sit and listen while Colonel Ripley and Kap made the arrangements. The two of them would travel to Dover where Doug's lifeless body would be welcomed home. I was honored that the colonel was bringing my husband home. Both Kap and the colonel would be at Dover when the body arrived. I knew I wasn't physically or mentally capable for the trip, and neither were Doug's parents.

I pictured the arrival of the plane, the opening of the cargo area and the casket draped with the American flag. Doug's Michelangelo's David body would be lifeless, and I couldn't and wouldn't picture it. Kap and Colonel Ripley would determine whether the viewing would be an open casket. I was petrified of the thought and didn't want to see my husband like that, without life.

The trip was planned for Monday morning, the viewings would take place on Tuesday and the funeral would be on Wednesday. I listened to their plans for as long as I could, and then walked away to my couch. Kap, Colonel Ripley, Tom Ripley and Chris sat together and made the plans on yellow legal paper;

the same paper where Doug and I would write our family goals. When they all agreed on something, they walked over to get my approval. I wasn't in the state of mind to make the tiniest of decisions, but I tried to listen and make choices, which seemed right.

It was going to be another extremely difficult day. Doug's teammate in Iraq was coming over to tell me what happened. He was there when Doug was killed, and I wanted to know every last detail. I needed to know because the situation was completely unreal and I still didn't believe, or simply didn't want to believe, it. How could a man made of steel, guts and glory get killed? He promised me he wasn't going to die in Iraq. He gave me his word, and I believed it, hook, line and sinker.

I was unresponsive to almost everything and everyone around me. Thank God I had the help of my mother, sisters, and Fiorella. They were there for Fallyn because I wasn't. Christine was there with me. The two of us sat together all day long and were in disbelief as we drank wine amidst the air of Chase Creek. It was the best time of the year in Annapolis. May was filled with sunny days and low humidity.

Christine and I sat alone until we were joined with two more of Doug's friends, Captain Ed Solis and Captain Ben Wagner, and I was happy to see them both. They were two marines who fought side by side with Douglas during the battles in Fallujah. Doug had the utmost respect for both of them, and so did I. Ben and Ed also made me feel closer to Doug. They were both dressed in their Alphas, and it made me think about the time when Douglas showed up unexpectedly at my door in Virginia Beach while we were dating. He looked amazing in his Alphas. I would never see them on him again. I said to them, "Guys, I wish Doug would have been in Iraq with you two. He would have never been killed." Ben and Ed didn't know what to say. They looked at me, and Ben responded, "Pam, who knows what would have happened. Iraq is a dangerous place, and you are never safe."

"No, Ben. I know that if Doug were with his marines from Fallujah he would be alive. I'm sorry. I can't understand why he died now. I never worried about him. I worried like hell when he fought in Fallujah. If he was going to die, it should have been there; not this way." I cried.

Ed tried to change the mood by chiming in, "Pam, I think you need to run the Marine Corps Marathon with us. We are running this year, and you should do it." I didn't have to think at all; I wanted to run the marathon again.

"Yes, I'm in. I will run it in honor of Douglas, but trained and with a better time."

Kap walked out on the deck and joined in. "Okay, I'm running it too. I bet we can get a lot of people to run it this year. We'll start training when everything settles down. It will keep you focused." I was running the marathon again. However, it was different this time because I would train to keep my mind off my misery.

The clock ticked away, and I knew with dread Doug's coworker would be arriving any minute. Another step into entering reality was about to happen. The entire story was going to help me believe, or would it? He arrived on schedule with his wife; both were filled with looks of nervousness and dread. Doug's parents, his brother John, Kap, Colonel Ripley and I headed to the deck. We all took our seats, and he asked, "How much do you want to know?"

"Everything," I answered. I looked over at the Zembiecs, and they nodded in agreement. He sighed and sat down with his wife to my left. The air was thick and dead silent; I couldn't hear anything but my heart pounding out of my chest.

He began. "OK. Our mission that evening was to secure an area in the city of Baghdad that was harboring terrorists. The way we work things is to divide the men into three teams. The first team enters into the area first to secure the site and access the situation. The second team follows to complete the search, and the third group stays behind for backup. Each team leader would take a turn.

"On this night, it was Doug's turn to lead the first group. He led his men down an alleyway in the city. It was very early in the morning, around 4:00 A.M. Baghdad time. Doug had a sixth sense when it came to spotting the enemy, and on this night he noticed impending danger. He saw an oncoming ambush and warned his men to get down. It was too late for Doug as he was shot in the process. I wasn't with Doug's group, but I noticed one of our guys dragging a man out of the area. I saw the long legs, and I knew it then. It was Doug. I was pissed. One man was down, and it was him. He was one of our guys. We did everything we could to try to revive him, but it was too late. He was killed instantly."

He stopped for a long pause. It was difficult for him to tell the story. His wife was holding his hand in support, and I wished I were she. I wished I were holding Doug's hand. I didn't say a word. I sat there motionless with anger brewing in my stomach, and then decided to speak out. "What the hell went wrong?"

He answered, "We didn't see it coming. That's all I can say. I have to tell you, Doug was never left alone at any time during the process. I sat with him and stared into his right eye and talked with him for a very long time. Pam, he was a hell of a warrior, and I can't begin to express my deepest sympathy. I was pissed that he put himself out there and ended up getting killed, but I know he wouldn't have had it any other way. That was the type of guy he was . . . a true hero and warrior. What a shame to lose a man of such high caliber! He was a hero. He saved the rest of the group because he warned everyone else of what was coming."

The conversation was too much for me to handle. I controlled myself long enough to thank him for coming and then quickly retreated to my room. I stayed there for the rest of the evening, but was never left alone. Christine kept me company through each passing night because I was too scared to sleep alone; too afraid to wake up alone in my living nightmare.

CHAPTER 13

VIRGINIA BEACH, VA, 2002

"Love knows nothing of order."
Saint Jerome

It was difficult having the talk with Doug, so I bravely approached the subject and never looked back. I gently said, "Doug, you know I enjoy being with you; we just get along. You also know I care about you and don't want to lose you, but I need to know if you see us together in the future. I'm not wasting any more time because I want to get married and have children, and if you don't think you want to do those things with me, then we have to break up."

He looked at me puzzled. I could tell he didn't know what to say. He stumbled on his words. "I feel the same way, but what's your time line?"

Time line? I pondered the thought for a second because I already knew the answer to his question. My life was moving forward with him, and I didn't want to wait around. I looked him in the eye and said, "I want to be married by the time I am thirty-four, and I want to start having kids at thirty-five." I could see his mind racing and knew he was adding up the years in his mind.

He answered, "So, in two years, you want to be married or engaged?"

My eyes diverted over to him, and I said, "I want to be married. That means we should get engaged in one year."

I was surprised when it took him a matter of seconds to answer. "Okay then, I can do that." Relief and happiness flooded me. It was great knowing we were moving in the same direction, but something didn't seem right about the way he answered.

It was March and time for my company's National Sales Meeting in Tucson, Arizona. By being a salesperson, I prepared myself all year for the meetings. The entire company would attend, and each rep would have the opportunity to meet all the higher management. I was well on my way in my territory. The territory I started was progressing nicely, and I was in the top three in our region. The top three reps all had high hopes of coming home with the coveted President's Club win. The President's Club winner and a guest of their choice would receive an all-expenses-paid trip to Maui for five days. Doug was confident in my abilities and had strong feelings I was going to win. However, my hopes were shattered when I didn't get the prize. I called Doug the evening of the awards crying, and he tried to console me. He always knew what to say and always made me feel better.

"Babe, you are the greatest salesperson in my book. We can go to Hawaii without your company." His words lifted my spirits, and I couldn't wait to get on the flight home.

When Doug arrived at the airport, he came to me holding a dozen long-stemmed red roses. I squeezed him tightly and thanked him for making my day.

As we climbed into his truck and made our way home, he said, "Those roses are just the beginning of my surprise. You have to wait in the car until I tell you to come out." When we arrived at his place, I waited patiently in the car for him to come and get me. He grabbed me out of the passenger side and said, "Close your eyes." Then he glided me around the side of the vehicle. "Now open them."

I opened my eyes to a candlelit walkway. There must have been twenty white candles paving the way into the front of his basement apartment. The doorway was open and candles continued around the corner, into the bedroom and covered each nook of his room. Candlelight illuminated the presence of roses all over the room. Pink, peach, yellow, white, yellow with red, purple and red roses were in every corner; there must have been at least ten dozen. In the center of his bed was a heart made of red rose petals, and in the middle of the heart sat a picture of us. My dreams were coming true.

The more time we spent together, the more we planned our future together. Trips to visit family and friends were another part of the equation, and our first stop was with Kap in Annapolis, Maryland. We also had a dinner planned with my family at the Charthouse. It was Doug's birthday on April 14th, and I wanted it to be special. He wanted my family at his birthday dinner. If they were going to be his family, he wanted to share a bond with them. My mom, my sisters, nieces and nephews all joined Doug and me at the Charthouse.

During dinner, my family immediately bonded with Doug. He brought out the funny side of my sisters, which only revealed it self under comfortable conditions. They were in awe of his humble nature and eccentric ideas. I was always the one who sought different things in life, and my family finally felt like Doug was "the one."

When we left dinner, it was my turn to spend some time with Doug's friends. Kap and Ray were meeting us at a local pub called Griffins. Ray was Doug's roommate for three out of the four years they spent at the Naval Academy. Ray was a quality guy and, just like the rest, was extremely handsome. He was tall and muscular with an excellent sense of style. I was beginning to wonder if having movie star looks was a requirement for friendship in this group. I also wondered why Ray, along with the majority of Doug's friends, wasn't taken. Doug told me Ray and the rest of the clan were extremely picky and someone would come along for all of them soon enough.

Doug and Ray shared some fun stories about their Academy days. Doug reflected on one story and told it like it had happened yesterday. "It was so hot in our room I decided that I would sleep naked. Bo, our other roommate, slowly decided to sleep naked as well, but Ray took a bit longer to adjust. One night, a female Mid performed room check. When she opened the door, she saw three naked midshipmen, screamed loudly and slammed the door. She never checked on us again." We all laughed.

Doug always talked about Bo who was a Marine Corps pilot. He said Bo was most like him out of all of his friends. Bo was married to Tandy and had the dream wedding immediately following graduation. Bo and Tandy were both from Texas, and the wedding was held on a huge ranch in their hometown. Doug described it as "the best wedding I had ever been to in my life." They decided to have kids right away and were blessed with two, a boy and a girl. I would have to wait to meet Bo because, like many of their Academy friends, he was fighting the war on terrorism. Talking about Bo made Doug slightly draw away from us, but I knew why; he wanted to be there, fighting alongside his friend. When he came back to us, he led a toast to Bo's safe return.

When we left Annapolis, shortly after breakfast, I could sense something was terribly wrong. What happened last night? Did I do or say something wrong? Doug was silent during our four-hour drive back to Virginia Beach. When he took me home that evening, he walked me to the door and kissed me good night.

"Douglas, is something wrong?"

He replied. "No, I just have an early day tomorrow. I'll call you later tonight."

I walked into my house and began to cry because I could sense Doug's animosity. He was emotionally running away from me, and I didn't know why. We just had an incredible weekend with his friends and my family, and now he was sending negative signals. I waited for his phone call, and it never came. Doug not calling was a horrific sign because he always called. I couldn't eat or sleep, and my stomach was in turmoil. I was connected to Doug in a supernatural sense, and I could feel when he was mad. I could feel when he was sad. I could feel when he was hurt or sick or tired. He could feel those things about me too.

I was ready for the worst when I received his phone call the next afternoon. He wanted to come by and talk to me. When he arrived only 5 minutes after his call, he knocked but stood outside on the front porch. I opened the door and tried to kiss him hello, but he turned his head. I heard his voice, but felt like I was in a dream when he said, "Pam, I'm breaking up with you."

"What?" I replied.

"Yes, I'm breaking up with you. I decided that I couldn't agree with your time line. I'm not ready, and I'm breaking up with you." He couldn't look me in the eye.

"You don't mean this," I said in tears.

He replied, "I do. Here are a couple of the things you left at my house. Don't call me because it will only make matters worse." With that, Doug turned from me, got in his car and drove away. I ran into my house heartbroken. What was he thinking? Couples break up when they are having problems, not when they are good together. I called Christine. She immediately came over to console me. I was in hell.

My roommate Pete tried to cheer me up. "I can't believe he just did that because I know he loves you by the things he does for you. Guys who decorate their girlfriend's rooms in roses are definitely in love. I don't understand his reasoning. I have never looked at a woman the way Doug looks at you. He'll be back. He doesn't mean it."

Time crept by ever so slowly. Each second seemed like a minute. Every minute seemed like an hour, and every hour seemed like a day. Days turned into weeks and still not a single word from Doug. I poured myself into work and working out. I went out with my friends and tried to meet other men. I couldn't do it because my heart belonged to Doug. We were broken up for three weeks, and it felt like three years. My friend Susan coaxed me into coming up for a girls' weekend. She didn't have to twist my arm. I needed a break from Virginia Beach, and she was just the friend to get me through this sad time.

Susan was from South Dakota. She was gorgeous, Norwegian in descent, with crisp blue eyes and long, natural blond hair. She lived in Canton. Canton was the "yuppie" area in Baltimore City and had all the fun and happening places for singles. I stayed in Baltimore until Sunday night, and we ended up having an incredibly fun weekend. I cried when I headed back to Virginia Beach on Sunday, but my life was there, and it was time to move forward.

I arrived home late on Sunday afternoon and as I unpacked my bags, my phone rang. I noticed his number immediately, even though I deleted it out of my phone. There was no way I was answering. He called again 2 minutes later, but I still refused. *He must sense I had a fun weekend,* I thought to myself. How dare he barge in on my life again after breaking my heart? I knew this would happen. I knew he would come back. His relentless phone calls were beginning to wear on me. After the eighth time, I finally picked up.

"What do you want?" I asked in an angry tone.

He carefully spoke, "Can I come by? I have something of yours I found in my room."

"No, just leave it in a bag on your door and I'll pick it up tomorrow before I go to work."

The other line was dead silent. He finally answered, "Well, I'm right down the street. I was rock climbing with some friends, and I thought I could just drop it by."

My voice was stone cold when I answered. "Then just drop the bag on my porch."

He was silent for a few moments. "Okay, I'll be there in 2 minutes."

I kept reminding myself to be strong and not let him in. He can leave the stuff on the porch. What article of mine was so important anyway? I didn't miss it, so it obviously wasn't important to me. In exactly 2 minutes he was at my entrance with only a glass door as the barrier between us. He motioned for me to let him in the house. Lord knows I tried with all my strength to say no, but I couldn't. His physical presence was too overpowering. I motioned him in and said, "Just for a minute."

He walked in, sat on the couch and when he spoke, he stumbled on his words. "I need to ask you a couple of questions."

"Go ahead," I said.

"Your time line, is it flexible?" he asked.

"What do you mean by flexible?" I retorted.

"Well, you told me you wanted to get married by thirty-four and have kids by thirty-five. Can you wait until you are thirty-five and start having kids at thirty-six? Babe, I do see a future with you, but your time line isn't my time line, and I want to know if you can work with me a little bit."

I stared at him for a long time without saying anything. I loved him deeply, but could I wait three more years until marriage? I finally answered, "Do you promise to never break up with me again?"

He replied, "I give you my word I will not break up with you." Doug's word was his soul, and I knew he meant what he said at that moment. I slightly paused, and then answered, "I can compromise with one year and one year only. We get engaged in two and get married in three."

Doug excitedly asked, "I know I hurt you, and I'm sorry, but can we get back together?"

My eyes looked into his. How could I resist when I loved him so much? "Yes."

He almost jumped off the couch and grabbed me into his arms. I snuggled into his chest and we just sat together embracing the moment. I wondered what article he used to get back into my life.

"What did I leave at your house that was so important?"

Doug pulled out a pair of panties decorated with gold bows. I simply smiled at him because we were back together, but I still sensed something was amiss. He was afraid, but I didn't ask the question. In time, he would have no choice and be forced to tell me the answer.

CHAPTER 14

NEW MEXICO, 2002

*"It's not only children who grow. Parents do too. As much as
we watch to see what our children do with their lives, they are
watching us to see what we do with ours. I can't tell my children
to reach for the sun. All I can do is reach for it myself."*
Joyce Maynard

Our lives were back to normal, and Doug thought it was time to take me
to his hometown in Albuquerque, New Mexico, where I would meet his
parents. I was full of anticipation and nervousness. Would his mom and dad
like me? Doug assured me his mom would love me. She just wanted him to
get married, but to the right person, and Doug said I was definitely the type of
woman she would choose for him. He was a little nervous about his dad and
explained why. "My dad is more apprehensive and will probably not get close
with you until he knows for sure we are going to get married. He is a retired
FBI agent so watch out. He might interrogate you." I looked at him puzzled,
and he said, "Just kidding. He is the greatest man I have ever known. He will
treat you well."

I enjoyed listening to Douglas talk with his parents on the phone. Each time
he called them, both parents would get on the phone, and they would always
have a three-way conversation. Doug would start the conversations by saying,
"Mama, how are you?" I could tell he loved his parents dearly, and they loved
him back in return.

The trip was planned for the middle of June, and Doug also planned trips to Santa Fe and Taos, where we would visit New Mexican wineries, mountain bike and relax. Our plane ride was uneventful. Doug fell asleep as soon as the plane took off, but I couldn't sleep. How could I when my stomach was full of butterflies? His parents were the most important people in his life, and I was on my way to finally meet them. This was a big deal knowing he hadn't brought another girl home since high school, and even then, it wasn't serious.

My first impression of the New Mexico airport was different from most of the usual airports I had been in. It was small and quaint without the usual airport crowds. The airport was decorated in cactus, Kokopelli and stucco, and as soon as we exited the plane, the dry New Mexican air was already soaking up the humidity we brought with us from Virginia Beach. Doug warned me his dad would be wearing a cowboy hat because he truly loved the western apparel and didn't wear it just because he lived in the West.

As we walked through the airport, almost immediately I noticed an extremely tall man wearing a beautiful cowboy hat. He was thin, but toned, wearing a western cowboy shirt and Wrangler jeans. Next to him stood a stunning lady; she was elegantly dressed and had the most thick, shiny dark hair I had ever seen. *They must be Doug's parents,* I thought to myself. Doug had his mom's dark eyes and gorgeous skin, but everything else was his father. Before I could say hi, Doug grabbed his mom and hugged the breath out of her. He hugged his dad with the same intensity while each patted the other hard on their solid backs; the sound was resonating. After Doug introduced me to his parents, we were off to their home in Sandia Heights. On the way, Don, Jo Ann and Doug explained the New Mexican history and pointed out many relevant landmarks.

Their home was at the base of the Sandia Mountains. It was picturesque; a ranch stucco home at the bottom of enormous mountains and blue sky. I walked inside and felt completely at ease. Doug's parents made me feel at home as Doug's mom showed me to my room. The house was built by Doug's family and was set up with an east and west wing. The west wing contained two guests room that used to house their sons. The hallway to the rooms had large windows with a sitting area to view Jo Ann's masterful garden. The middle of the house had a living area, office, dining area and kitchen with high ceilings that gave it an open and airy feeling. The east wing contained a television room and master suite. Doug's mom explained how the children were older when the house was built, and it provided privacy for both parties. I loved the idea and wished my parents had done the same thing. Doug's parents offered drinks and snacks, and

I became privy to the best guacamole I ever tasted.

Our first day in New Mexico took us to the highest point on the Sandia Mountain Range. A tram traveled from a visitor center where Doug and I purchased tickets, and then we rode the tram to the top of the mountain. What a beautiful place! New Mexico was one of the most beautiful states I had ever seen. As we traveled up the mountain, we could see cactus, rock and wildlife everywhere. At one point, we saw a bald eagle and watched him soar in the clear blue sky.

Doug was peering out the window of the tram when he shouted, "Look over to your left. See the dark spot moving on the side of the mountain?" I had to look closely, and then nodded my head yes. "That is a black bear," he said.

The man standing next to us decided to give his unsolicited opinion by saying, "That's not a black bear, that's an elk."

Doug looked at him and wasn't argumentative when he repeated out loud, "No, that is a black bear. Look at the way he is crouched over." The guy was a disbeliever, but we didn't care and ignored him. He whispered in my ear softly. "That is a black bear and seeing one is good luck according to New Mexican history."

"Good," I said.

When we reached the top of the mountain, we asked someone to take our picture overlooking the city of Albuquerque while the sun was setting for the evening. The sky was pink and purple as the sun disappeared to the west. Doug and I cuddled in the chilly night air, and he let me borrow his lumberjack shirt to void some of the westerly winds. I was thankful, but didn't need his shirt; his presence and the beauty of the moment warmed my soul. We left when the sky turned dark and was lit by twinkling stars.

We woke up bright and early the next morning to the smell of fresh omelets and ponduse bread warming on the stove. I walked past the greenhouse and couldn't help but notice the cactus and lemon trees in the yard. It must have been wonderful growing up in a house with such an extensive garden. Doug mentioned that his mom was a master gardener, and by looking at her garden, I was in complete agreement.

Our breakfast conversations revolved around Doug's plans in the Marine Corps to my family and career goals. Doug's parents were great listeners. I was curious about Don's FBI career, and he shared a couple reasons why he was an agent. Doug and his dad were two peas in a pod. They were tall and thin, but muscular, and walked with the same stance. Both behaved with the same mannerisms and were complete gentlemen. I studied how Doug's dad treated his wife, the way he looked at her with love in his eyes even after being married for over thirty years. They were still in love after all this time. I admired them and knew when I married their son, he would treat me the same way.

In the afternoon, we headed to Santa Fe and followed Doug's parents to spend the day there with them, and then we would go our separate ways. While in Santa Fe, we visited the oldest church in the United States, the Loretto Chapel, with the mysterious staircase, and the Georgia O'Keeffe Museum. The museum was my favorite. Doug and I viewed her artwork and bought numerous prints to bring home and frame for our future home together.

Doug looked at the flower artwork. "You see Georgia O'Keeffe was an extremely sensual woman and painted photos of flowers that resembled female sensuality. Look at the shape of this red one. What does it look like to you?" I just smiled at him and walked to the next canvas.

After lunch with Doug's parents, we made our way to Taos. While driving on Highway 40, we noticed several signs with wineglasses. We both looked at each other and without hesitation, headed toward the first landmark. We stopped at every winery on the way to Taos, tasting New Mexican wines while gaining knowledge of the types of grapes that thrive in the dry climate.

After visiting several wineries, we finally arrived at our beautiful bed and breakfast in Taos. The rooms were lined along a garden with chickens, roosters, cats and dogs. Our room had a picturesque canopy bed with a balcony that opened to breathtaking mountain views. The small town of Taos itself was artsy and quaint. Each shop was inimitable. It was extremely challenging trying to find a restaurant due to the vast array of choices, but when we noticed a small pub-style restaurant with a retro-style menu, we both knew it was the place.

Our first night in Taos was like living in a fantasy world. This place was spiritual, and I could feel positive Karma moving in the winds. For both of us, being relaxed was a chore, so we rose bright and early in the morning to ride mountain bikes on Angel Fire Mountain. The ride would certainly fill our need for adrenalin. As we drove up to the beginning of the slope, I noticed the ski lift with bikes on some seats and people on others. I asked Doug, "Why are people putting their bikes on the lift?"

He answered, "Because people want to ride down the mountain, not climb 2,000 feet to the top."

I was puzzled because I wondered what type of workout we would get from riding down a mountain. I lived out west and mountain biked on a frequent basis. I gained my strength from climbing up, not by flying down. I looked at Doug and said, "If you think we are riding the lift up, you're crazy. We're going to climb up and fly down. We don't need that lift."

He answered, "I'm game for whatever you are." I thought for one second that maybe I might be able to challenge Doug at one sport.

Mountain biking was my strength; running was his. As we started our ascent to the top, I was sadly mistaken from the very beginning. It nearly killed me trying to keep up with him, but he never once left me behind. He would come back just to make sure I was okay. Doug was a physical masterpiece. He had incredible athleticism and was an All-American wrestler while attending Navy. I admired so many things about him, but seeing his abilities in action gave me great pleasure and pride. I wanted a man who was physically stronger than I was, and he never left any doubt in my mind. Even though he outmatched my skills in all athletic activities, he encouraged me along the way and made me better. He was humble and gracious, both at the same time.

Once we reached the top, over 3 hours later, we had another couple take our picture as we rested on a huge rock. When Doug looked at his watch, he realized we were well over our time limit. "Oh shit, we have to go. Our massages are in 20 minutes and there is no way we can ride our bikes down."

We quickly loaded our bikes on the ski lift and enjoyed the record-breaking ride down the mountain. Thank goodness our massage therapist was waiting for us at our room. My body was in desperate need for a rubdown after the extreme workout on Angel Fire Mountain. The massage table was placed in front of the French doors, and the cool mountain air filtered in the room as the therapist kneaded the stress out of my muscles. I looked over at Douglas who was perched on the canopy bed. He had his journal in his lap and was writing something down.

"What are you writing?" I asked.

"Oh nothing, just my thoughts," he replied. I left him to his thoughts as I took great pleasure in the entire experience, our wonderful vacation and watching him in his thoughts.

The next morning we packed our bags to head back to Albuquerque for the evening. Our day was filled with exploring the city of Taos. Our first stop was a ski resort in Taos where Doug dragged me to the entrance of a food pavilion named "The Bavarian." He said, "I have to take your picture in front of this building because it bears your name. You are my Bavarian Princess." I, therefore, let him take endless photos before we set off to view a river gorge that was formed by the passage of the Rio Grande River. This area was full of tourists, and we had to park the truck and walk over a bridge, which contained a viewing area. The bridge extended over the gorge, which dropped to nearly 1,000 feet. Looking over the bridge offered spectacular views of the immense crack in the earth where the Rio Grande River was continually flowing. The height of the water was low due to a seasonal drought, and the people below looked liked tiny insects. Doug instinctively bent over the railing and looked at the bridge in an odd fashion. Before I could think about anything, he looked at me and said, "Take my picture quickly." At that point, he hoisted his body over the railing, grabbed on to the long rails and extended his entire body in midair. He screamed, "Take my picture!"

I snapped the photo as quickly as I could, and then burst into tears. He quickly pulled his body back onto the bridge and grabbed me. I was hysterical and crying uncontrollably. "Why did you do that? You could have been killed!" I screamed. He tried to console me, but couldn't. Just the thought of him dying made me ill from the inside out. My life would never be the same. "You could have been killed! I don't know what I would do without you in my life!" I screamed again.

He hugged me tight and apologized. "Babe, I'm sorry. I don't know why I did that. I knew I could do it and be safe. I'm not going to die. I'm like a cat with nine lives."

When we arrived home in Albuquerque, I told his parents about the stunt and his dad gave him an earful. I knew I didn't overreact. His life was too precious to be lost, and he had too many things to accomplish in his life. For me, it was he becoming my husband and the father of our children. For him, it was being the best marine the Corps ever made. We left for Virginia Beach the next morning, and I could not help but imagine Doug's parents as my in-laws. I enjoyed their company, and I knew that one day we could be family.

Chapter 15

Annapolis, MD, Sunday, May 13, 2007

"The city speculates and guesses as to why I elected those I did to the three hundred . . . I chose them not for their own valor, but for that of their women . . ."
King Leonidas

Sunday morning I rose out of bed. Was I dreaming? Yes, I just had a bad dream. I got up, walked into the kitchen and when the rancid smell of irises hit my nose as I turned down the hallway, I remembered where I was and realized this was my life now. I wanted to run back to my room, go back to sleep and wake up to my old life, not this one. But my stomach rumbled after days without food, and I was forced to eat something to rid me of the horrible noise. Things started to get worse when I was pressured to view the details for the funeral procession, the viewing and the burial. I didn't want any part of planning these things! Everything was becoming too final for me. This was my reality, and I didn't want to believe it. Some horrible person was playing a trick on me. The entire ordeal was a cover-up. Doug was really alive, and the Marine Corps was playing a game because it was safer for Doug to pretend like he was dead.

Maybe the country was protecting Doug's family from terrorists because Doug was such an individual threat to them they wanted to keep him undercover and one day he would come walking in my door. He would be Doug, but have hair and a mustache. I had to force myself to stop thinking in a fantasy world. DOUG WAS DEAD! The guy told you to your face. He was shot in the head and in the heart. He was killed instantly. *Instantly* . . . The word was resonating again and again. Doug never had a chance. He died a warrior's death, and I would be the stoic Marine Corps wife.

My mind took me back to our date when we saw *300*. Doug begged me to go see it with him. He told me it was the greatest movie ever made. I remembered the part of the movie when King Leonidas's queen said good-bye to her king right before he left to fight the Persians. She looked him in the eyes and said, "Husband, come home carrying your shield or on your shield." Doug turned, looked me straight in the eyes and said, "Babe, are you a Spartan wife?" I stared back at him and said, "I already am." Now, I wasn't so sure I was a Spartan wife.

When I married Doug, I always knew his death in war was a possibility, but I thought he was invincible. To me, Doug was the man of all men. He was my lover, my best friend, my life and my hero. God, how will I make it through? I was completely blindsided and never saw it coming. My life was wonderful, and now it was shattered into a million pieces. Thank God, Jon was coming today. He was full of life and would make me feel a little better.

When he arrived, we went to Doug's war room and began reading through his journals. Looking through the journals, Jon started reading some quotes out loud. *"Be positive, don't even think or speak negative thoughts." "Concentrate on your sphere of influence." "Be true to principle." "If something is worth doing in the first place, it is worth the sacrifice to finish."* The quotes went on and on. I grabbed another book and searched feverishly for a sign from Doug. I wanted to find a quote to help guide me during this time. What would guide me? All of his words were magnificent.

When I noticed Doug's photos scattered around the room, I instantly jumped up and starting tearing the pictures out of the frames. The photos were everywhere. I didn't know what I was going to do with them, but I knew they must be put someplace during the funeral.

My sisters came downstairs and volunteered to make a collage of his photos for the wake. They were also copying his wedding portrait. Jo Ann kept herself busy by going through all of Doug's important files and cancelling any appointments he wouldn't be able to keep. She discovered that Doug was planning a second honeymoon for us and graciously cancelled all the reservations for the bed and breakfasts and the other fun activities. Kap shared a conversation he had with Doug about the second honeymoon. "Doug told me he scheduled a hot air balloon ride for him and Pam and he thought it would be a great idea if he sky dived off the balloon once the balloon got to a safe height. The lady told him that wouldn't be a good idea since the balloons are weighted for both you and your wife. If you decided to jump off the balloon, then your wife would go flying high into outer space." I'm sure this was Kap's way of trying to cheer us up and it did, for just a moment, but then it got me thinking about our honeymoon and how I would never experience this or anything else with Doug ever again.

I was exhausted from those few moments of excitement and was forced to lie down. I couldn't sleep, as many questions were still unanswered. Who would give the eulogy? Who would carry the casket to the altar? Who would say the readings? Who? Who? The questions were endless. Who would give the eulogy? The colonel was my first choice.

I jumped up from my bed and joined the men at the dining table. "Colonel Ripley, I want you to give the eulogy," I stated.

"Darlin', I would love to, but I'm afraid that I wouldn't make it through."

"I understand," I said.

I looked over at the table. Doug had so many best friends. I was unsure of who to pick, but then it came to me like Doug was whispering in my ear, and then I spoke it out loud. "Kap, you do the eulogy. I think you are the only friend that could make it through."

Kap didn't hesitate when he answered, "Pam, I am honored."

One decision was down, but I wasn't able to make another. "Guys, you pick the rest. I have to take a break," I said as I walked back into my bedroom. I didn't want to face another thing. These decisions were difficult and hard to stand. The choices for my young husband's funeral were unbearable. It was against nature to become a widow at such a young age.

When I went back to my room, I tossed and turned in my bed. It was three o'clock in the afternoon. I was physically exhausted, but my mind was racing. "You need to get some sleep," I kept telling myself. I was also being ordered by everyone to stay in my bed. Everything was being taken care of for me, everything except bringing my husband home alive. How was I going to make it through the wake and the funeral like this? It was useless. I was trying so hard to stay in my bed, but there was no way I could sleep and decided to call my friend Andy. She would be able to tell me how Doug was doing. She was blessed with a gift. It was a gift for many, but Catholics looked upon it as sinning. Andy could feel things and sense things. She was able to meditate and see life in another dimension. I wasn't going to tell anyone I was calling my "gifted" friend, but I needed her, and she probably already knew I was going to call.

I dialed her number. "Hi, Pammy, I'm so sorry about Doug." She already knew.

"Andy, can you try to talk to him for me? I need to know that he is okay. I need to talk to him. Can you please, please, help me? I'm lost! I desperately need his guidance," I cried.

"Pammy, I'm coming to the funeral. I will meditate and see if I can reach him. I can't make any promises though," she said.

"Please try hard. I don't think I can make it without him," I cried.

"Oh yes, you can. Doug picked you for a reason. You have his daughter, and you will make it through. I will be there on Tuesday."

I hung up the phone and was out of my mind and helpless. I never felt this way before. My heart was broken many times in my life, but nothing like this. This was not a break. My heart belonged to two people: my daughter and my husband. By losing Doug, half of my heart was ripped out of my chest. How would I be able to replace half of my heart?

I was forced to eat something, but in the end, wine became the winner. I understood the depressant qualities of alcohol, but I didn't care. My feelings went beyond depression. Nothing was going to make me feel any worse.

CHAPTER 16

ALEXANDRIA, VA, AND VIRGINIA BEACH, VA, 2002

"So I can't live either without you or with you."
Ovid

Summer moved and passed us like a bolt of lightning, and along with its end came Doug's departure to Northern Virginia. He narrowed his search to Alexandria where he planned on purchasing a condominium for him and a roommate to share. After several trips, he found a great place to suit all his needs and asked me to accompany him for the final decision. The condo we both agreed upon was located in a subdivision called Manchester Lakes. It was on the third floor and had two bedrooms, two baths and a loft. All of the condos had an appointed garage where Doug could house his Harley. The area was great for him because he would be commuting against traffic to Quantico, and the Metro station was within walking distance for trips to Georgetown and D.C. I was excited knowing we would have weekends in Georgetown and also a change of scenery away from Virginia Beach. Doug couldn't wait to be back on a Marine Corps base surrounded by all his brothers in arms. Driving north on Highway 95, we would fantasize about the names of our kids and played around with naming our first dog "Quanti," which was short for Quantico.

When Doug finally closed on the condo, we celebrated with a nice dinner and planned our first event in D.C., where we would go to the Mall to watch the 4th of July fireworks. It would be a special 4th of July; our nation was recovering from 9/11. Doug and I both agreed we would spend the event underneath the Iwo Jima Memorial. There, we would celebrate the independence of our nation and toast to those who were in harm's way defending the very principles upon which our country was founded: life, freedom and the pursuit of happiness.

I felt honored going to D.C., even in the midst of lingering rumors of another terrorist attack. There were two others going with us, Ken and Kathy. Ken was a marine who served with Doug at 2nd Force and was with Doug the first night we met. Kathy was my friend from Virginia Beach who I met when she dated Doug's roommate Joe. She was a solid female, and we both shared similar ideas and beliefs on life. By being an aerobics instructor, she had a great body with gorgeous, long red hair and eyes the color of pool water. Even though Kathy and Joe didn't work out, she remained a good friend to us. For a moment, Doug and I thought of the possibility for romance between Ken and Kathy, but the idea was extremely short-lived.

Our night began with dinner and drinks at The Roadside Grill in Arlington, Virginia, and we rushed through the meal in order to get a memorable view of the fireworks. As we made our way to the Mall, the crowds were gathering at all the prime spots. The Lincoln Memorial, the Washington Memorial and Arlington National Cemetery were among the major crowd pleasers. Security was heavy, with the Capital being on Red Alert during our nation's birthday. We walked up the grass hills, through sidewalks, across intersections and up to the Marine Corps Memorial. Doug was mesmerized as we approached the memorial by the sight of the six men holding tight to the American flag. He gathered the group together and began to tell the story with fire in his eyes.

"On February 19th, 1945, the 4th and 5th Marine Divisions invaded Iwo Jima. The marines fought like lions, but were not victorious after 72 hours of hard fighting. The 28th Regiment went on to capture Mount Suribachi. They reached the base of the mountain on the afternoon of February 21, and by nightfall, had almost surrounded it. On the morning of February 23, marines of Company E, 2nd Battalion, started the crazy climb up the rough terrain to the top. Once at the top, a small American flag was placed on the mount. Marines were jumping up and down at the sight of the flag flying in the wind. They were so excited that they decided to put a huge flag in its place. Six men helped raised the flag that day, five marines and one navy corpsman. A photographer took the historic picture and the memorial was based upon that photo."

We were all amazed at the excitement in Doug's words and his precise historical recollection. I wondered how many Marine Corps battles he could recite in their entirety. Probably every single one. He finished his story just as the sunset filled the sky with purple, pink and orange hues. People were entering the memorial grounds on the left and right, filling every nook and cranny in view. When the sky was dark and clear with hints of stars flickering high above, we heard the first "boom" announcing the beginning of the show as the sky began to fill with reds, whites and blues. The only sound in the night was the bangs of exploding fireworks.

The entire crowd was silent under the booms of the fireworks, and then suddenly, from a distance, a small voice sounded, "Oh say can you see, by the dawn's early light . . ." Thousands began to chime in to the National Anthem. One by one, everyone joined in to sing the song. The sound grew louder and louder as everyone held hands. We were together as one nation under God at the Marine Corps War Memorial, standing together, united in this time of strife. Although war wasn't always the answer, it was in this case. Over three thousand innocent American citizens were killed for what? The answer was difficult to imagine, but as the marines fought at Iwo Jima defending our nation against the Japanese attack on Pearl Harbor, once again, marines would fight for that same reason. Innocent blood was shed on our soil, and marines would defend our nation, but in another time and another place. As the crowd finished the National Anthem, everyone clapped in unison. We just witnessed true patriotism in the highest form, and it was the most incredible 4th of July of my life.

We stayed in Alexandria for the remainder of the weekend and headed back to Virginia Beach where Doug would complete his transition from the Recon School, and I would go back to work. Doug's move was scheduled for the beginning of August. He planned on packing and moving his materials with the help of some friends; being a single man, he didn't have many large items. Doug's primary possessions were books and CDs. His library collection contained everything from Ernest Hemingway to Brian Tracy. He also read hundreds of books about military history and leadership. If a book was going to help him achieve his goals, he read it.

On our second date, Doug bought me a book by Brian Tracy called *Maximum Achievement.* He often bought books for his family and friends and always signed the cover. He wrote me a short note in *Maximum Achievement,* which stated, *"To Pam, a powerful book for a strong, beautiful woman."* We would often discuss this book when talking and planning our future because the focus of the book was on goal planning and positive affirmation.

We discussed topics on the importance of writing down goals because when goals were written down, they would rapidly materialize. His books were extremely important to him, and it took him days to organize the extensive library in boxes.

The rented U-Haul truck was packed and loaded in one day, and I helped Doug with as much of the move as I could. I stood by and watched as he hooked the U-Haul to the back of his Ford F-150 truck as I held back my tears. He would only be 3 hours away, but it wasn't going to be the same.

"I'll call you when I get there. It shouldn't take too long," Doug said as he backed out of the rocky driveway.

One hour passed and I was surprised when I received his frantic call. "Babe, the craziest thing just happened. I was driving through the Hampton Roads Bridge Tunnel, and all of sudden, the trailer started to sway. I didn't think much of it and kept going. I took a quick glance in my rearview mirror and saw that the trailer wasn't just swaying, it was moving all over the place. Cars were moving out of my way, and then the hitch came loose and the trailer came off of the truck. Thank goodness I attached a chain to the trailer because that was the only thing holding the trailer to the truck. The hitch was dragging on the ground, and sparks were flying everywhere! It was crazy. I finally slowed down, pulled on the side and reattached the trailer. I almost pissed my pants, but I was able to remain calm under pressure. You see, babe, that is the key, remaining calm under pressure."

After carefully listening to his story, I asked only one question. "How fast were you going?"

He replied, "Only around 80."

I retorted, "Only around 80! Are you crazy! You have a huge trailer attached to your car with only a chain and a hitch. You can't go 80 miles per hour with all that weight! Slow down!"

He giggled and said, "I promise I'll go slower. I learned my lesson on this one."

I hung up the phone and immediately starting worrying about his trip. I hoped he learned his lesson from getting three speeding tickets in one year. I didn't think Doug knew how to drive slowly. He performed every task at the highest level of intensity, which included driving. I, on the other hand, performed most tasks at the highest level, but knew when I needed to slow down because of safety precautions. He was excellent at judging most things, but driving was definitely not on the list. This was something I would help him with and make him understand the importance of driving carefully, especially after having a family.

Doug called me when he arrived, and we made plans for the following weekend for me to meet his close family friends, Jim and Shawna. Jim was Doug's surrogate "big" brother while he worked with Doug's dad in the Albuquerque FBI. Jim and Shawna were just newlyweds when they moved to New Mexico from California for Jim's career. Doug was a young teenager at the time, and he and Jim formed a tight brotherly connection by working out together on most days. The first night I met Douglas, he showed me a beautiful picture of their four girls. I was one of four girls and couldn't wait to share stories with the two. Once again, I was excited and nervous at the same time, being introduced to more of his family, but I tried not to worry too much, knowing this was a very good sign for our future.

The weekdays we spent apart went by so slowly as I moved through the daily grind of my life in Virginia Beach. My large territory ended up being a positive force in our long-distance relationship, which extended as far north as Richmond, Virginia. Alexandria was only another hour from this part of my territory, and I decided to plan my "Richmond Fridays" around my trips north to see Doug. On this "Richmond Friday," I arrived around 6 P.M. and quickly got ready for dinner with Jim and Shawna. We drove south to Quantico where we were scheduled to meet at a local Marine Corps hangout. During the drive, Doug gave me some much-needed information about Shawna, which he thought would prepare me for the interrogation, but it only made me more nervous.

"Babe, be prepared to go under the gun with Shawna. She is like my sister and is very protective. I can tell you she will be leery of you until you prove otherwise. However, once she gets to know you, she'll like you. Shawna didn't like my last serious girlfriend, and I eventually figured out why she wasn't supportive." I looked at him with worried eyes, and he protectively squeezed my leg while saying, "Babe, don't worry. Jim and Shawna are going to love you." He calmed my nervousness down slightly, but it was too late. I was already on alert. I was sure Shawna was a good judge of character because she didn't like the last girlfriend and, after all, the last girl's loss was my gain. I would simply be myself, and I knew deep down, if I did this, she would like me and be supportive of us.

The place where we decided to meet was the Globe and Laurel Restaurant in Quantico, Virginia. It was a classic place frequented by military patrons because a retired Marine Corps major owned it. The owners wanted to honor the men and women who "strapped on sidearms or wore a uniform or badge in service to this great country." The Globe and Laurel was dedicated to fine dining and the perpetuation of the proud history and traditions of the United States Marine Corps. It was a place where patriotism and Americanism were still regarded with dignity and respect.

As I walked into the Globe and Laurel, military memorabilia that dated back to the Civil War overwhelmed me. The setting was dark and masculine and overcrowded with dark oak wood tables and matching chairs that had black leather seats. Marine insignia displays were aligned all over the Pub Room which I tried to study while also watching Doug's facial expressions full of pride as he viewed the memorabilia which expanded over every inch of free space on the walls.

When I turned to my right, I saw a handsome couple smiling at us and knew they had to be Jim and Shawna. Jim was around 5 foot 10 with an athletic build and a high and tight haircut similar to the ones worn by most marines. Shawna was gorgeous with beautiful olive skin and big brown eyes; her figure was like a Barbie doll. I couldn't believe she gave birth to four girls! Looking at her gave me hope I would retain my figure after having kids. She was certainly an inspiration for any woman who ever worried about losing their bodies to childbirth. I knew Doug was right about Shawna because as soon as my bottom hit the chair, the inquisition began.

"Where are you from? What do you do? When did you and Douglas meet? What is your family like? What are your interests?" Shawna's questions were endless. Doug was engrossed in a conversation with Jim and didn't notice what was going on. I tried to join the guys and get relief, but was happily surprised when Shawna stopped on her own. I was finally able to ask her some questions, and we actually ended up having a fantastic conversation. Enough so that at the end of dinner, I knew I passed the test. Doug and I followed Jim and Shawna back to their place to see their four girls.

What a great family, I thought to myself. The girls were beautiful, especially when they all ran and jumped on Douglas, being overjoyed in seeing their big brother. We were able to stay for a while and enjoy time with the little girls. It was the first time I ever witnessed Doug interacting with kids, and I was confident he would make an incredible father.

I thought dinner with the McGees was a huge success, but when I got back to Virginia Beach, I discovered there were more important things I needed to put my attention on. I came home to a work e-mail explaining a company downsize, which meant over 65 percent of the sales force would lose their jobs. Of course, I turned to Doug for advice, and he was confident I would be part of the remaining 35 percent.

"Babe, you have nothing to worry about. You are in the top 10 percent of the company, and I promise you won't get the axe. Always remember this: In this country, the top 10 percent of people make it possible for the other 90 percent to live." I remembered Doug's words, but I still stayed up most of the night trying to be an optimist and not a realist. He believed in things like "if you think it, you will become it." But sometimes, even being a positive force couldn't control the outcome of falling pharmaceutical sales.

When I went to work on Monday morning, the entire sales force was told by voice mail to go home, get online and find out your fate. I never knew my company, the one I placed my heart and soul in, could be so disrespectful to their employees. I realized it was all about money, and I started to have my doubts about this career. After I got home and anxiously opened my e-mail, I found out, once again, Doug was right. I kept my job, but my partners, two friends I worked with closely for the past two years, had been let go, which meant I would be responsible for three territories now.

My life was changing both personally and professionally, and to make matters worse, even though Doug and I had an incredible weekend together, I started getting a sick feeling in my stomach. I was experiencing the same feeling like when he broke up with me the first time. Was I being paranoid because he was in a nice place with new people? I couldn't get the thoughts out of my head.

After I found out about my company changes, my manager scheduled a meeting in Baltimore, and I was planning on spending time with Doug before and after the meeting on Friday. My friend Kathy was also staying with us while she attended a wedding in Annapolis, Maryland. It was another opportunity to enjoy time with our friends from Virginia Beach. The weekend was planned, but for some reason, I was uneasy. I knew him too well; we just had a conversation with Jim and Shawna about having three not four kids. Things were getting serious between us, and I had a very bad feeling he was going to run again.

The stress of my company changing and Doug's cues must have lowered my immunity because when I left for my meeting I nursed the beginnings of a terrible cold. I knew this man too well so when I got his call halfway to

Alexandria, I didn't even say hello to his thoughtless and cruel words.

"Pam, I've decided I want a fresh start, and I'm breaking up with you. It's good we're in separate cities because it will make things easier; I can't marry you, I'm not ready. Don't come to the condo because I won't be here."

"You're kidding," I replied.

"No, I mean it. We're done," he said heartlessly.

I didn't know the person on the other line, and I couldn't believe this was happening again. He was a coward by breaking up with me over the phone, and I knew he had to do it this way because he couldn't look me in the eye. He knew he could easily run away from me if he wasn't looking directly in my face.

I slowly asked him, "Where am I supposed to stay tonight? My meeting isn't until tomorrow morning."

"Stay with your family or one of your friends. Don't come to my house," he retorted and hung up the phone.

Who the hell was this person? This wasn't the Doug I loved . . . or was it? I was boiling with anger inside and felt like a steam engine getting ready to explode. There was no way I was letting him get away this easily. What a coward! I felt completely disrespected by his actions, so I called him, and when he didn't answer, I left him a nasty message.

"You are a coward . . . Give me a C, give me an O, give me a W, give me an A, give me an R, and give me a D . . . What does that spell? COWARD! Your conduct is unbecoming of an officer, and I should report your actions to your commanding officer."

Who breaks up over the phone? His actions were like an adolescent boy entering puberty. My anger was out of control so I had to pull my car over and regain my sanity. I, luckily, was able to seek solace with a friend in Annapolis and got it together enough to make it through the sales meeting, surprising myself with my mental toughness. At least I still had my job, and knowing this, I would devote myself to work and be part of the President's Club.

As the meeting continued in Baltimore, my health deteriorated into an annoying cough with fever and chills. Kathy was still on her way North for the wedding, but both of us would stay at a hotel in Annapolis, closer to the Naval Academy Chapel, instead of in the comforts of Doug's condo. Of all places, the chapel. My wedding was going to be there, and now my world had come to a screeching halt. I got in my car and drove to Annapolis from downtown Baltimore, shaking from illness and heartache. I didn't know which hurt worse, my head or my heart.

On my way to Annapolis, I called Kathy to discuss the weekend, knowing I would probably sleep the entire time. "Kathy, I'm not going to be much company. I'm sick as a dog."

"No worries," she said. Kathy was my true friend. While she explained her plans, she caught me by surprise. "Holy shit, Pam. You are not going to believe who is next to me on the 95 freeway. It's Doug! I just passed the Quantico exit. Let me call you back. I'm going to catch his attention."

I waited impatiently by my phone and when she called, she explained what happened. "I started beeping my horn frantically, and Chris motioned to Doug that someone was trying to get his attention. Doug looked over at me with shock and with the face of a child who knew he was in trouble. He motioned for me to call him on his phone, so I called him and he gave me some shabby excuse why he broke up with you.

"'Kathy, I couldn't do it anymore. I'm not ready to get married, and she has this time line.' I told him if he truly didn't want to be with you, then he should have told you in person. I told him he was a coward and you, at the very least, deserved to have him tell you this in person and not over the phone. He agreed he should have told you in person, but he couldn't face you because he would have never been able to do it. That man is petrified of your relationship for some reason. I really don't think he wanted to break up with you, but he knows you aren't going to wait forever."

I cried. "Kathy, my heart is telling me he wants to be with me, but he has done it this time. I'm done. I never give third chances, and he was lucky as hell to get a second." I meant what I said at that moment, but would I be strong enough to resist him if he tried to return to me?

I returned home to Virginia Beach sick and heartbroken. Pete couldn't believe Doug broke up with me again and tried to console me. "I said it before, and I will say it again. I know that man loves you. He's just afraid of you. Who wouldn't be? You are one of the strongest, most independent women I have ever met."

"Thanks, Pete." But Pete's words weren't helping at all when I went to my room and cried myself to sleep.

The remainder of the summer I spent working and planning events with my friends. I ventured to Baltimore for a girls' weekend and once again tried to regain my composure. It never failed; I always met other eligible men when I visited my friends in Baltimore, but men were not the answer. I needed to at least get Doug out of my head on my own in order to move forward with my life.

I yearned for his daily phone calls and his words of encouragement. He wasn't just my lover, he was my mentor and friend. How could he break up such a bond? We were so good together. We had heated discussions about our disagreements, but never anything we couldn't work out. *People break up when things are bad, not when they're good.* I couldn't get this thought out of my head. I had to move forward because I knew if he did come back, my pride might not allow him to return.

Three weeks went by, and I started feeling better. I missed Doug terribly, but I didn't have a choice. I bought books on starting over, excessively worked out and tried to put my mind into my job. I went out some, but decided it was better just to stay away from the scene in order to regain my sense of self.

Labor Day weekend rolled in along with the Rock 'n' Roll Half Marathon and the American Music Festival. Virginia Beach's Rock 'n' Roll Half Marathon attracted runners from all over the country because of the fast course and great venue. I made a promise to myself I would run the Half one year, but first I had to get into running shape, considering my sport in the past had always been biking. Many of my friends at the gym ran the Half, which was a driving force for my desire to do it one year.

There was no way my friends were allowing me to stay in this weekend, so when Pete and his girlfriend, Lisa asked me to go out on Saturday night, I didn't dare say no. We planned on going to Shore Drive for some appetizers at Guadalajara's, and then head to the 501 Grill to see a band. For some reason, I felt good that day and was finally excited about having some fun; probably because it was the first day since my breakup where my mind wasn't totally consumed with Doug. And, of course, Doug probably sensed I was beginning to move forward when he called just as I was about to jump in the shower. I didn't dare answer and let it go to voice mail instead.

"Pam, I'm in town for the weekend to run the Half. I have one of your CDs, and I thought I could drop it by your place."

Once again, he had another excuse to see me and shake my world just when I was beginning to recover. How did he know I was moving on? He knew because we were connected at a higher level. I made sure Pete understood what he needed to do when Doug arrived. "GET THE CD FROM HIM, BUT

WHATEVER YOU DO, DO NOT LET HIM IN THE DOOR!" I quickly jumped in the shower in order to avoid him, but I could hear everything through the bathroom door.

When Doug knocked on the front door, Pete answered and immediately let him in. I should have known Pete would never be able to ignore Doug; they had a tremendous relationship.

I tried to wait in the bathroom until he left, but I could tell he wasn't going anywhere. Finally, Pete knocked on the door and said Doug refused to leave without seeing me first. My house was so small, there was no way of avoiding him, so I walked out of the bathroom in my robe and headed straight to my bedroom without acknowledging his presence. He took the liberty of following me in the room, which infuriated me even more, but I continued to ignore him. I felt him staring at me, and I finally looked up to his sad eyes, which seemed to beg for forgiveness. There was no mistake knowing how this man hurt me and my look back showed weeks of anger spilling out of every pore.

Doug finally spoke while standing on eggshells. "I had your *Shaggy* CD, and I thought you might want it back. How are you?"

I casually and coldly answered, "Fabulous."

"Good," he replied. "I'm running the Half with Ray and Karen Mendoza. Ray is a superstar, and Karen is his beautiful wife."

My words were few and emotionless because I was afraid if I said too much he could see how much I still loved him. He stood there for what seemed like an eternity and broke the silence between us.

"Well, I guess I'll see you around."

I didn't acknowledge his last statement and turned away from him as he left. When he closed the door, I stormed into the living room and yelled at Pete. "How could you betray me like that?"

Pete replied, "Pam, I'm sorry. I couldn't turn Doug away. He's a good guy, and you both belong together."

"Whatever! You still betrayed me!" I retorted.

"I'll buy you a drink later," Pete answered calmly because he knew by letting Doug in the house there was a good chance it might bring us back together.

There was something about being on Shore Drive in Virginia Beach and the bay's breeze filling the air with the smell of fresh salt and surf. It was the last weekend of the summer, and Guadalajara's was packed with both locals and tourists. The restaurant was Mexican in cuisine, but had a unique bar filled with a variety of slush machines. Each machine carried its own mix of extremely strong slush drinks; rum runners, margaritas and piña coladas were among the choices. One slush drink was dangerous enough to put a 200 pound male over the edge.

The three of us arrived at Guadalajara's at a good time with available seats close to the front door of the establishment. We couldn't help but talk about Doug and his antics. Lisa was sure he was up to something. "Pam, you two are not over, and you know it. He can't let you go because that man loves you."

Just when Lisa was finishing her statement, Pete whispered in my ear, "Don't look now, but Doug just walked in the front door."

I quickly responded by talking to Lisa more intensely and pretending as though he didn't exist. As he passed our group, I noticed from the corner of my right eye his head was tilted down and his back was slouched over. I could tell from his body language he was hurting, but I tried to pretend I didn't care anymore. I turned my back from him while Pete and Lisa kept me informed on his exact location.

"Okay, he's standing to your right, and they are moving toward the front door. He just looked over at us, and he's headed out the door."

"Thank God," I responded.

"He looked pretty upset," Pete said.

"That's his own damn fault! I didn't break up with him over the phone!" I yelled.

Pete responded, "I know. He made a bad decision, but I can't help it. I like the guy."

The three of us greeted the rest of our friends, and I tried to pretend as though the entire "Doug" incident never took place. However, reality haunted me the entire evening with thoughts of him and how much I missed him. I missed everything about him, and I didn't have the choice to call or see him because he hurt me, and I was a proud and strong woman. How could I forgive him for this one?

It was difficult putting on a show, and I couldn't wait to get home and go to bed. My pillow was my savior, and on it I could rest my body and tell my mind to try to move on with my life. I fell asleep instantly, but was abruptly awakened by knocking at my window. At first, it was a soft thud, and then the thuds starting coming more quickly. I was forced to look out my window, and my heart dropped by the sight of a dark shadow looming by the tree in the front yard. I checked my clock. It was 4:30 A.M. and out of the darkness stood Doug. I tried to ignore him, but he kept throwing pebbles and saying in a whispered shout, "Pam, please come to the front door. I need to talk to you."

I opened the window and said no, but he wouldn't stop, and I was forced to open the front door. I noticed he was dressed in winter gear with a black cap covering his head. He looked like someone who could be arrested for breaking and entering. If I didn't love him so much, my better judgment should have been to call the police. Instead, I looked at his face and noticed the sorrow in his eyes.

"What do you want?" I asked.

"I had to see you. Can we talk?"

I retorted, "There's nothing to talk about. You broke up with me over the phone after you gave me your word you would never do it again. I thought your word meant something."

"Wow, that hurts. My word does mean something. I didn't plan on breaking up with you. I made a mistake. I miss you. Can we just look at the phone thing as a bad fight?" he replied.

I was silent for a long time. We just stared at one another in silence. I didn't know what to say or do. My pride was saying no, but my heart was saying yes. I quickly rationalized how good we were together. We never fought, we just broke up. Maybe I could pretend so my pride would be satisfied.

"What are you thinking?" he finally asked.

"I'm thinking you should come in the door before my neighbor calls the police."

Doug walked in my front door. We embraced each other while his touch sent chills down my spine with his kisses like heaven. I couldn't help it; I was completely in love with him. He made a promise to me that night which was different from his last promise. He admitted his fear of marriage and assured me if he ever felt nervous about our future together he would tell me instead of running.

CHAPTER 17

ALEXANDRIA, VA, AND VIRGINIA BEACH, VA, 2002-2003

"As soon as forever is through, I'll be over you."
Toto

As the summer of 2002 came to a close, Doug and I were once again happy. I was more cautious this time, and he could feel my hesitation. It was a good thing because my holding back made him work harder. We spent the weekends alone together and took advantage of our precious time. My weeks felt like months, but every Friday Doug would come to Virginia Beach or I would travel to Alexandria. Our relationship grew stronger, and this time, he wasn't holding back. We would cuddle together and share our most intimate thoughts about life, our dreams and our goals.

Doug included me in every decision he made, and I felt as though he was finally working toward our future together. His plan in the Marine Corps was to get stationed at Camp Lejeune and become a rifle company commander. It was his dream to lead fellow marines on the ground into battle. Doug always wrote his dreams down because he believed they would never be goals until they got recorded. He said to me on many occasions, "Babe, goals need to be written down. If you don't write down your goals they are merely dreams." He recorded all his goals in journals and shared them with me on numerous occasions. He let me read a few of his entries one day. "Write down your daily goals, tasks and write down information that needs to be passed on to others, and then pass it! Write down what you did during the day so that you can reinvent it and what needs to be done." His words amazed me and gave me inspiration.

My career began to flourish because of Doug's insightful and fruitful thoughts. I would think many of the same things, but I never wrote them down. Doug helped me by sharing his ideas like, "Consider the possibility there might be a better way, or that you may have been doing something wrong. Don't be satisfied with the status quo." We were both never satisfied by the status quo. Because of our beliefs, we shared the same passion for life while never settling and our intimacy grew; every hour, every minute and every second of each day I could feel us getting closer. At times, I felt like I could read his mind as I took great pleasure in laying my head on his chest while he brushed his hands through my long blond hair to flickering candles and the soft, romantic music of Diana Krall.

Although we spent our weekends bonding spiritually, we never fell short of keeping our bodies in peak physical condition, which, for Doug, meant running in the Marine Corps Marathon. Living so close to Washington, D.C., guaranteed Doug's participation, along with as many friends as he could recruit. Unfortunately, he was unsuccessful with me. I simply wasn't ready to take on the endeavor, but knew it would be something I would give in to one day. Even Doug's parents were coming for the weekend, and I was looking forward to seeing them once again. Doug prepared his body for the race by eating extra carbohydrates and drinking plenty of fluids. His goal was to clock in around 3:20. He ran the marathon the year before, and I went to D.C. to help cheer him along. Doug's goal was 3:30 in 2001, and he finished around 3:32. This year in 2002, he trained more efficiently and wanted to shave at least 12 minutes off his time.

I remembered the marathon of 2001, and it was a pleasure meeting a few more of Doug's Academy friends. Coleman and Bridgette flew in from California, Jon was running with Doug and Kap was working to qualify for the Boston Marathon. Even Anya and Jon's mom were participating in the run. I was appreciative to be around such great people, and I got the bug for running because of them. Doug's friends were all physical masterpieces; Coleman was a wrestler like Doug and Bridget; Coleman's wife was a navy swimmer. Jon and Kap were both competitive runners, and Doug would brag about Jon and Kap by saying, "Jon is a god. He is so fit he passes out because his heart rate is so low. Kap is an Ironman Champion. He is a specimen." Doug was extremely proud of his friends and never fell short of complimenting and boasting about their capabilities. He made everyone feel good, and his excitement was contagious.

I was almost talked into running with Anya, but decided to be everyone's cheerleader instead.

I had so much fun cheering everyone on throughout the race, partly because of a girl I met who knew the area and volunteered to walk me to all the "hot" spots for watching the runners. Kap ran by us at one point along the course and the girl I met said, "Holy shit, did you see that guy? He is a god." I looked at her and with a small chuckle said, "No, that's only Kap." I was so in love with Doug I was blind to the physical beauty of his friends. The girl was right, though. Kap did resemble a Nordic god, and the way his body moved in a streamlined motion was like watching the bionic man. I could almost hear the sounds of a machine when he ran by us with arms and legs moving in unison for perfect precision.

The 2002 marathon would be different because I knew the route and could show Doug's parents around the race. We left for the race at 5:45 A.M. and made our way to the Metro station. Being in our nation's capital was always exciting, but being next to Doug running in the marathon gave me such a sense of pride because he was the ultimate marine just waiting for his chance to fight for our freedom.

The race started as scheduled, and we took off to the first place of viewing on the Key Bridge into Georgetown. Doug's parents and I waited patiently for Doug while we saw Jon pass by, knowing Doug would follow shortly. Once at the Key Bridge, the runners had another 16.2 miles to go. We saw Doug approximately one hour after he started. I looked at Doug's parents and said, "He looks strong, but he is running fast. I hope he doesn't burn out too quickly." They both agreed, but we all remained 100 percent confident in his abilities.

We walked to the next area and realized the runners had already passed and figured it would be best to head back to the finish. Jo Ann, Don and I rang our cowbells for all the runners. I loved Jo Ann's sense of humor. We watched a woman run by with an extremely lean physique carrying large breasts. Jo Ann whispered, "Do you think those are real?" I laughed because I was thinking the same thing. We also saw a young man limping to the finish. As he passed us, I noticed his right calf muscle was rumpled inside of his skin. He must have torn his Achilles tendon, and the entire muscle had moved on his leg, but he went on to finish the race.

Jon came running by, and I could tell he was exhausted. I couldn't imagine how someone felt after running 26.2 miles. "Here he comes!" exclaimed Jo Ann.

I looked and saw Doug barely making his way toward the finish line, but able enough to give us a wincing smile when he noticed his mom trying to snap a picture. For the first time since we met, I noticed Doug could get tired from something, especially with a finish of 3:36. I thought it was a great time, but I knew he wanted to beat his time from the year before.

Doug handled it with class. "Hey, I started out too quickly, and I lost steam. It was my own fault." As we rode the Metro back home, I massaged his legs and fed him plenty of Gatorade. I was humbled by his accomplishment. "Honey, I want to run the marathon with you one day."

"Sure," he replied. He placed his head on my shoulder and closed his eyes.

Each year, the Marine Corps Marathon was just the beginning of the Marine Corps celebrations. Marines were proud during the month of November as they celebrated their birthday on November 10th. The legacy began on November 10, 1775, and the only reason I was familiar with the year was because Doug used it for his bank code, phone code and computer code. Since Doug was living close to D.C., we were scheduled for two Marine Corps balls: the ball for EWS and the Headquarters Marine Corps Ball in Washington, D.C.

We enjoyed the EWS Ball on Friday evening, but were more excited to attend the ball at Headquarters that was held in downtown D.C. The only way we were able to get tickets was because Doug had a connection; the tickets were highly coveted. Jon, Anya, Doug and I piled into a white stretch limo headed for our nation's capitol and the Headquarter's Ball. We were blessed by being surrounded by many great friends and Marine Corps heroes. Colonel Ripley was in attendance as well as the commandant of the Marine Corps, General Jones.

The real fun started when we left the ball and toured D.C. in the limo. We had champagne and toasted to marines who had died for our country and those still in harm's way. As we made our way through the Mall, we paid tribute to the Iwo Jima Memorial, the Washington Memorial and Arlington National Cemetery. The limo stopped each time while we honored our national monuments. The Lincoln Memorial was our last stop because Lincoln was one of Doug's favorite presidents. The entire group exited the limo and walked up to the memorial to pay tribute to our late president. I looked at Douglas and said, "I think it would be nice if I tried to sit on Lincoln's lap."

He smiled ear to ear, but didn't hesitate. "We could get in big trouble for this." Then he lifted me over the security rope, and I tried to climb up to Lincoln's lap. My high heels were in the way, and my task was cut short by the lack of traction, but not before Jon snapped numerous photos.

"Babe, I think you should get down now," Doug said. I nodded my head in agreement while Doug carefully helped me off the monument and into the safety of his arms.

By the end of November, the beginning of the holiday season approached us quickly, along with news on where Doug was getting stationed. He was sure he would get sent to Camp Lejeune in Jacksonville, North Carolina. North Carolina was a three-hour drive from Virginia Beach and would be perfect for us to continue dating and seeing each other on the weekends. Doug said, "I want you to get a taste of the 'real' Marine Corps before we get married. Virginia Beach and EWS school have been a fantasy. It is not the real Marine Corps. Babe, I will be gone for a very long time, and I need to know if you can handle it. My intuition is telling me you can, but I need to know."

I thought his words were fair. After all, our agreement was to get engaged in 2004 and get married in 2005. The time line would work out. We would continue to date on the weekends, and I would wait for him. I didn't, however, know how much longer I could wait for him to say, "I love you." He would say everything else . . . but never those words. I was patient only because I knew by his actions he did love me. We planned spending time together before Christmas, and then he would travel to New Mexico and me to Baltimore. New Year's was a ski trip for us, along with Chris and Aurora.

As Doug and Chris planned the trip, Doug called me to ask me a question. "Babe, would you still want to be with me if my legs got shot off in battle?"

I was puzzled and half-joking when I said, "Of course, I would still want to be with you. That is why you need to donate some sperm before you go away, so we can still have kids if it ever happened." I could tell he and Chris had some drinks by the tone in his voice.

"I know you would still want to be with me because you know what's inside and by the way, I can donate some sperm. That's a great idea."

Of course I would want him still, but I thought Doug knew I would never leave him. I was completely committed to him . . . but was he to me?

Doug traveled to Virginia Beach with his bags packed for our week together before Christmas. He told me he finally got word on his next duty station, but didn't want to tell me over the phone and would surprise me in person. His voice was happy, and I knew he must have gotten exactly what he wanted.

He arrived sometime after 8 P.M., and I had wine ready for our celebration.

Doug strolled in the front door with his green bag and black backpack. He walked in my bedroom, gave me kiss and sat down. "Babe, I have good news. I'm going to be a rifle company commander." I gave him a big hug, but he hesitated, and I knew something wasn't right. "Well, I have other news. It's not going to be Camp Lejeune."

"Where is it going to be?" I asked.

"I'm being sent to Camp Pendleton," he replied.

"Okay, where is that?"

"California," he said softly. "It's going to be great. I'm going to 2/1 because a general specifically asked for me. It's an honor for me to go and serve in 2/1. The marines are great, and I will be a rifle company commander."

I couldn't say anything. I just looked at the excitement in his eyes, and I knew I was secondary. I was second to the Marine Corps. This was his calling, and I accepted it, but right now, it was slapping me in the face.

"Say something," Doug said.

"What about us?" I asked.

"What do you mean? We can still be together. We will just have to travel farther to see each other."

"Douglas, I don't know if I can have a relationship with you in California without a commitment. Long distance like this will be hard, and I need a commitment."

He couldn't look me in the eyes. He lowered his head. "I'm not ready; I can't give you a ring." He grabbed his bags and walked out the door and went back to Alexandria leaving me alone in disbelief. I didn't know what just happened. Did we break up? He didn't come to Virginia Beach to break up with me. I gave him an ultimatum, and he walked out on us. Once again, he ran away.

That night, I stayed in my room and ignored my friends' calls. Pete knew what had happened and tried to console me. He was worried when I stayed in bed for hours and wouldn't answer the phone. Finally, after two days of mourning, I called my friend Cindy. She was married to a Navy SEAL and knew the type of man I was dating. She dragged me out of the house and out of my misery. Cindy was a strong and beautiful woman, and she tried to explain why Doug was running away and told me that I deserved more. She was familiar with the military life and explained how families were second when our country was at war.

"If Doug does not have enough faith in you to be a strong military wife, then someone else will." She helped me through my first week of mourning, and then I left town for the holidays where I would spend them with my family and stay with Susan for girl time. She had been through this with me before and knew how to comfort my sadness.

I arrived in Baltimore for a Christmas "not to be remembered." My family was full of Christmas cheer, and I only thought of Doug as I looked at my nieces and nephews playing with their Christmas presents. I was the only daughter not married, and my family had high hopes for Doug. They adored him and couldn't believe he had done it again. Neither could I. I couldn't help but wonder if I caused the breakup. Maybe I should have responded differently when he told me. Maybe I should have been proud of him being chosen by a general to serve in 2/1. Instead, I was consumed with our future. I was thinking about myself when I should have been congratulating him. It didn't matter now. We were broken up, and I felt like this was the end.

I welcomed the ice and snowstorms that plagued the entire Eastern seaboard during the month of January. They enabled me to seek refuge from everyone so I could try to recover. Virginia Beach was prone to ice, which made way for treacherous roads, and I was forced to stay in my home for office days during the storms. At home I didn't have to pretend I was happy like I did when making my office calls. This breakup with Doug hit the one-month mark which was a record considering the first two lasted only three weeks. We had made it to one month without any contact, and I took great pleasure in knowing that he was snowed in for two weeks when my mom gave me updates on the conditions in D.C. and Maryland and said I was lucky to be further south.

Even in the midst of my heartbreak, my life in Virginia Beach moved on. I worked hard and was doing well within my company so my manager sent me to the home office to help assist in training classes to further my career as a sales trainer. I loved helping others, and I wanted training to be my next career step. He also knew about my breakup with Doug and knew the trips would be a good distraction.

I thought about the possibility of never having Doug in my life again. Could it be possible? Would he come back this time? Would I let him back? These thoughts entered my mind on a daily basis. Douglas made an impact on my life which haunted me by knowing he was irreplaceable. I could date again, but there would never be another Doug. I kept these thoughts to myself and acted strong in front of others while I agonized on the inside.

During the end of January, I finally caved in and decided dinner with someone of the opposite sex might be okay. He was a nice guy, and I liked his company, but Doug never left my mind. I desperately tried to move on in every possible way, and even accepted a date for Valentine's Day. He brought roses, and we went to a nice dinner, but once again, my heart and mind were elsewhere.

The following weekend, my friends and I went out for a fun night, which I thought would help me, but it only lowered my defenses. All of my friends were still up and having fun, but I decided it was time to make contact so I discreetly left everyone and pretended like I was going to bed. When I dialed Doug's number he immediately answered like he was waiting for my call. "I miss you," I said in a whisper. I didn't want my friends to hear me on the phone because I knew they would be disappointed.

He replied, "I miss you too, but we can't get back together. I can't marry you right now. I'm just not ready. I have to go to Camp Pendleton. You were right. You do need a commitment because it's what you deserve."

"Douglas, I didn't say we had to get married before you left for California. I just need to know you love me. You have never said it. I know when you say it, you will never leave me again."

Doug said, "Babe, that's the problem. That's why I can't get you out of my head. I do love you." I couldn't believe it. He finally tells me he loves me over the phone and in the midst of a breakup.

I started to cry and told him I had to get off the phone. I cried myself to sleep and woke up the next morning trying to remember our conversation. Was I dreaming? Did he actually say he loved me?

I thought about my next step because I knew we weren't finished. We would never be finished. My prayers were answered when my phone rang at 5 P.M. with his number on my phone.

"I have to see you. I can't go another day without seeing your face again."

In a soft urgent voice, I replied, "I have to see you too. What are we going to do?"

He slowly answered, "Let's meet halfway in Richmond. I'll get a hotel, and we can meet and talk there. That way, no one will know what is going on."

I quickly jumped in the shower. As I got dressed, Pete asked, "Where are you going?"

I answered without looking him in the face, "I'm going to meet Cindy." I hated lying to Pete, or to anyone, for that matter. It was completely out of character for me, and I was terrible at it. I felt like Pete knew, but I didn't care and also didn't want anyone to know where I was going. I was embarrassed about how many chances I gave this man, but I couldn't stop myself from seeing him. I knew he was my destiny and never in my life had I felt so compelled to be with someone. It was the right thing to do because he was the one.

The night was clear and cold as I drove on Highway 64 to meet him. We arrived at the same time. We parked our cars, checked in and took the elevator to our room. He was standing so close to me I could feel his breath on my neck as we rode to the eleventh floor. He grabbed my hand, and we walked briskly to the room. As we entered the room, we embraced, and I could feel something was different about him. He was in love, and I knew it this time. We were in love. As I kissed his lips, I was once again home. He looked in my eyes and said, "Pamela, I love you. I have loved you for a very long time and was afraid to admit it. I can't live without you, and I will make you my wife."

CHAPTER 18

ANNAPOLIS, MD, MONDAY, MAY 14, 2007

"Today I am bringing your husband home. I am honored to escort a true American hero."
Colonel John Ripley

I awoke from my stupor at 9:00 A.M. I hadn't spent any time with my daughter, and I wanted to play with my little angel. How beautiful was Fallyn Justice Zembiec. She was so innocent and oblivious to what was happening in her home. Oh, how her eyes lit up at the sight of her father. I would never see it again. She would never know him, and that, in itself, made me sad. It was the worst thing about him dying. He would never be with her in this life, and she would never know him.

As I walked into her bedroom, her eyes were dancing. She had his eyes deep, dark and sparkling. Her lashes were so long it seemed like they might block her vision. I wanted to protect her from all of this pain. My only reprieve now was she wouldn't feel it like the rest of us. She would feel the pain in a different way at a much later time, and by then, hopefully, I would be ready to help her as my loved ones were helping me.

I was panic-stricken when I realized there was nothing in my closet suitable to wear for my husband's funeral. My sisters and mom gladly volunteered to take me to my favorite store and purchase a dress for the wake and funeral. I didn't want to go, but the alternative wasn't an option. I wanted to look beautiful for my husband. He would see me and be proud I was his wife. I believed in an afterlife, and I knew without a shadow of a doubt Doug was there. He was there, and he would be able to see his funeral and be proud of what he had done. He wouldn't have wanted to die any other way, and I would make sure he was proud of me by being in complete control of my emotions just like a stoic Marine Corps wife. After all, death was always a real possibility when you married a man in the military. Many families were especially at risk since 9/11. I was exposed to a number of friends who lost their husbands or sons, but never once considered it could happen to me. I thought Doug was different. He was invincible in my eyes and in the eyes of all those who knew him.

As I walked into the Black House White Market in downtown Annapolis my thoughts went back to the times when Doug brought me here and purchased a special outfit for me. He knew I loved the store. Everything in the shop was either white or black, and the styles were sexy, but classy. I remembered the time he took me shopping for my birthday. We went to brunch and strolled hand in hand through the historical streets of Annapolis while window-shopping in all the quaint little shops. It was his suggestion to take me into the Black House White Market. I was trying to be good, well aware of my weakness for shopping. "Babe, let's go in. I want to buy you a special outfit for your birthday," he said. I was pleasantly surprised. Doug always knew how to make me happy.

My mom and I searched in the front, and my sisters searched in the back. I was in a daze because nothing I wore would ever be good enough to show him how much I loved him. The saleslady came by to help, and I told her I was fine. I didn't want to be bothered, and I didn't want her to know what kind of outfit was on our agenda. Our search left me tired and empty-handed. Why didn't I want her help? I suddenly realized how talking with the saleslady would cause me to lose it once again, but I needed a dress. I realized if she knew, she would most definitely find something appropriate for me to wear.

When she walked over again for the third time, I whispered to her, "This is hard for me to say aloud. I still can't believe it myself, but I am searching for two dresses. My husband was killed in Iraq a couple of days ago . . . I can't find anything . . . I don't know what to do . . . Can you help me please." I started to cry.

The only thing that came out of her mouth was, "I am so, so sorry." Instantly, she began to run around the store as I got comfortable in the dressing room. One by one she brought the dresses in for me to try. She worked diligently at finding a solution to my problem, and I could tell she was doing her part to help me in the only way she could. Even though I was a stranger to her, she wanted to be there for me.

After trying on three, I was able to easily choose two, knowing I would never wear these dresses again. The dress for the viewing was cream with black roses. It was strapless and A-lined with a black sash just below the breast area. The second dress was black, strapless and A-lined. The skirt was lace with a black bow that tied around the waist. All of the dresses helped me feel as good as I could feel by wearing them. I left the store knowing that my prince would be looking down on me, and he would be pleased.

When we arrived back at the house, I noticed the colonel's vehicle. They had returned from Dover Air Force base where they welcomed home the body of my dead husband. Doug wasn't alone. He had a military escort who traveled with him from Iraq to Dover. I hesitated for a moment outside my front door. Was I ready to hear about their journey?

I entered the house, and they both came over to hug me. The colonel began, "Pam, we welcomed Doug home. It was an honorable ceremony when his casket was taken off the plane and placed in the hearse. He was treated liked a true American hero. I want you to know that he was taken care of with the utmost respect and received full military honors. I was 100 percent impressed."

"Thank you both for going. Did you see him?" I had to know if he was in the casket and this was real. If they didn't have a body, it couldn't be real.

"Pam, we saw him. He is now at John B. Taylor Funeral Home in downtown Annapolis," Kap said.

"Oh my God, I was right next to him. We just got back from downtown," I cried.

"Pam, you have to make a couple of decisions. The funeral home needs to know if you want an open casket," Kap said.

I looked at the colonel with fear in my eyes. "I don't know if I can see him like this. I want to remember him the way he left. I can't imagine seeing him without life. I don't know . . . I don't know!" I was hysterical.

"Pam, both Kap and I saw his body. There is a bandage over his left eye, and that is it. Everything else looks good. I think you should have an open casket. There will be many people who will get closure by seeing him one last time," the colonel said calmly.

"He's not there anyway! He's gone! Why do we have to put his body on display?" I screamed.

"I think the casket should be open, Pam. You don't have to see him if you choose and everyone will understand," Kap said.

I looked at Don and Jo Ann. "What do you guys think?" I asked.

"We both agree the casket should be open," Don answered.

"Okay, okay. Open casket. I don't know if I can see him. I will make the decision when the time comes."

CHAPTER 19

ALEXANDRIA, VA, 2003

"Something is better than nothing."
D. A. Zembiec

As Doug finished up school, we planned his move to California and our future together, along with celebrating several of our friends' weddings. I discovered shortly after our reunion Chris proposed to Aurora during their ski trip with a wedding planned for April. Dan and Jen were also getting married in April. Since Dan was a Navy grad, their best choice was to have their ceremony at the Naval Academy Chapel and continue the celebration at a venue along the Chesapeake Bay.

Doug, Kap, Melissa and I piled into Kap's truck and headed for the Naval Academy. I couldn't wait to see Jen walk down the aisle with her tall and lean stature. She had long brown wavy hair with piercing blue eyes, and I was certain she would be a sight as she walked down the vast aisle in the Naval Academy Chapel. Dan was also very tall and handsome with a boisterous personality and a voice most would describe as both loud and strong. Jen, on the other hand, was soft-spoken. Though her words were few, they always had depth and meaning. Doug told me once, "Dan taught me how to pick up the ladies." When Doug mentioned this to me, I almost laughed out loud; I didn't think his pickup lines were very good. By the looks of Dan and Doug, their words were probably not important considering the type of women they sought out in their early twenties. I think Doug wanted to give Dan credit for something, and I'm sure he did help Doug in a weird way.

As the "Wedding March" began to play, we all stood up to honor the bride. Jen glided down the aisle in an amazing white gown with silver embroidery. The top was defined in a halter shape, which framed her shoulders elegantly. She was breathtaking. I watched Dan as she walked down the aisle, and the look on his face was full of pride, love and admiration. Doug and I held hands and listened carefully to their vows until everyone clapped in unison as the groom kissed the bride.

On our way to the reception I asked Doug, "Honey, did you RSVP for two when you sent in the card?"

Doug was quiet, and then said, "I told Dan I was bringing you and he said it was fine."

My gut told me something wasn't right. Kap chimed in on the conversation. "Pam, we didn't have to RSVP to Dan's wedding. He knew we were coming."

I said, "Kap, he probably knew you and Doug were coming, but what about me and Melissa?"

"It doesn't matter; they can pull up two extra chairs for you guys."

I yelled, "Kap, that is unacceptable! I helped six people plan their weddings. Do you have *any idea* what it costs to have a wedding? I guarantee this wedding cost them a pretty penny. I know about this place, and it's extremely elegant. Besides, it's rude to show up without giving someone notice."

Doug kept silent; he knew he was in trouble, and it just wasn't fair how uncomfortable I felt on such a happy day.

As we entered the reception area, I looked on the card table and I was right. The place setting was just for Captain Doug Zembiec. I walked up to Dan and apologized for Doug's mistake. He said it was fine, and they were making accommodations for us. I didn't enjoy myself with Doug because of his mistake, but I made it through the wedding because I was happy for Dan and Jen, but not happy about Doug.

When we left the wedding, he apologized and promised he would never do that again. I explained to him the importance of proper etiquette. Doug was a marine and had limited knowledge when it came to attending weddings, especially with dates. He wanted me to teach him, so we sat together on Sunday and discussed different aspects of weddings. I filled his mind with how the wedding party, the ceremony and the reception each functioned to make the wedding successful. We both discussed why weddings were fun; your best friends and family were together to eat, to drink and to celebrate. After our conversation, Doug understood why an RSVP was important and gave Chris the correct response of "two" for his wedding before I left for the week.

Doug had a special job to perform at Chris's wedding. He was the best man and the least he could do was send the right response. He felt honored and privileged at being Chris's best man. He worked diligently on his speech and kept it a secret from everyone. We drove all day on Friday for their wedding, which was close to Aurora's hometown in upstate New York. Chris was so calm the night before his wedding, and I could tell he was completely at ease knowing he had chosen the right one. I realized Chris was good for Doug because he was a marine, but not from the Naval Academy. He had fun while in college and had more realistic views on civilians. Doug was extremely judgmental at times, and Chris was able to get Doug to "relax" about certain issues. He told Doug, "There will come a day when you will work with civilians and you must be able to slightly adjust your standards; not everyone has the mentality of a marine." Doug respected his friend and listened to his words of wisdom.

The wedding was held in a beautiful garden, and Aurora was stunning. Their reception was full of Irishmen and women that knew how to have fun. Doug and I took our turns on the dance floor, and each time he picked me up and swung me around like a rag doll. And when it was time for his speech, his words emanated through the crowd as he walked around the dance floor and addressed a silent audience. He spoke about the importance of friends, family and freedom. He spoke about what truly matters in life. Most important, he spoke about the love between Chris and Aurora.

Driving back to Virginia the next morning, we talked for hours about his speech and our future. He was getting ready to visit California and find another rental property to be part of our future real estate empire. The plan was for him to go by himself, and I understood his reasoning. "Babe, this is just going to be a rental. You don't need to pick out this one because it's not an emotional purchase, it's only real estate."

I tried to be positive about Camp Pendleton and California. It would be a nice place to visit, especially in the winter months. Doug was turning his dreams into reality by becoming a rifle company commander. He waited so long to take his turn in Iraq, and now his time had come. He trained his entire life for this opportunity with his body physically, mentally and spiritually prepared to go to war. Doug's battalion would go to Iraq; it was only a matter of when and how soon.

Captain school was coming to a close and all the marines gathered at Quantico for graduation. Everyone said their good-byes, along with their good lucks. Most of the marines would be going to war in the next few months, and all were excited at the prospect of seeking redemption. Some were heading to Camp Lejeune, and others to 29 Palms. The lucky ones were going to Camp Pendleton. I didn't think I was so lucky because of the distance separating us; 3,000 miles was a long way. It would test both our loyalty and our love. However, the marine base at Camp Pendleton was situated right in the middle of Orange County and San Diego. Living there would provide any marine with a fun-filled life. The weather was gorgeous, and so were the people. The Beautiful People lived in Orange and San Diego County. Everyone had the perfect body with a little help from Dr. Plastic himself. The rate of plastic surgery was the highest in the country per capita with Virginia Beach following in a close second.

Doug decided on a location north of Camp Pendleton called Laguna Niguel. I was familiar with Laguna Niguel when I lived in California a few years earlier. I remembered the town as being lush with greenery and flowers; every corner was perfectly landscaped and each street was newly paved. Doug particularly liked the condo development because it contained all the elements necessary to make it a perfect rental in future years. It had a community pool, gym, hot tub and most important, it was 3 miles from Pacific Coast Highway and Laguna Beach. I wanted him to get settled there and start his new position as quickly as possible. After all, it was just another step before his move back East and our wedding.

My thoughts revolved around him going to Iraq, but I wasn't worried about the danger. I was more concerned with the event living up to Doug's expectations. He was more than ready to fight, and he deserved this chance. I wanted him to go because it was something he had to do. Doug had to fulfill his destiny of being a marine by leading men in combat before we could continue with our future together. I loved him, and when you love someone at such a high level, you make sacrifices only you can understand. My family and friends accepted Doug back into my life, but wanted only the best for me, which was a proposal before he left for the Middle East. I hoped for the possibility, but I already waited this long and another few months seemed like nothing.

When the time arrived for Doug to leave, he packed the truck with a week's worth of clothes and his Harley. His plan consisted of driving across the United States to visit close friends along the way. I could feel his excitement and tried hard to be there for him. He was thrilled with the idea of his next duty station, and I tucked my sadness away from his view. As I slowly helped him go through his civilian clothes, I surprised myself when I was able to laugh at the Lee jeans, plaid shirts and acrylic sweaters that dated back to the 1990s. He gave me permission to rid him of any and all clothes which I thought were out of style, and he didn't have time to second-guess my choices. It was his fault he waited until the morning of his departure to let me change his civilian style.

I diligently threw out old jeans, shirts and shoes in black bags for Goodwill. It was like an episode of *What Not To Wear*. He was finally giving me the authority to officially dress him, and I really didn't care anymore. Clothes helped in generating first appearances, but the person beneath the attire was most important. I was excellent at seeing through the superficial, but Doug only sharpened my ability. He didn't need nice clothes to make an impression on others; he generated positive light and complete greatness without them.

As we went through the closet, he agreed on all my choices, but fought me on his hunting shirts. I caved in because I wasn't the one supplying the funds for a new wardrobe. I couldn't wait to go shopping with him. It would be easy to find clothes to fit his body, which was shaped like a Roman god's with broad shoulders, a muscular chest, six-pack abs, a small waist and long legs. It blew my mind that someone could eat pints of Ben & Jerry's ice cream and never gain an ounce of fat. His body was truly amazing, both inside and out. Doug did work hard to keep his body in check, but he could go weeks without exercise and be able to run 10 miles at the blink of an eye. I was in awe as I struggled to maintain a size six. I worked out hard, but gained weight when I ate with Doug. He would say to me, "Babe, your body is amazing, and you could gain 20 pounds and still be beautiful." I don't know if those statements helped or hindered me. He truly meant what he said, but I think he also wanted me to eat with him. He loved to break bread with his friends and family. The dinner table was a place where ideas and thoughts about life would be passed on through generations. We both grew up in families who ate dinner together daily and shared our days with one another. It was a tradition we would keep with our children.

We continued working on clearing his closet when my mind stopped me in the middle of the project. *He's going to be in California with a new wardrobe. What am I thinking?* California was the State of Beautiful People, especially in Laguna Beach. I tried to remove thoughts of Doug touring Laguna Beach looking extremely handsome in his new clothes. Women adored him in his '90s gear. I could only imagine what would happen with a stylish new wardrobe.

I quickly removed my thoughts of insecurity. I rarely showed them, but frequently thought them. What woman wouldn't be a little insecure with her man moving 3,000 miles away? Doug was different, though, and he did finally tell me that he loved me. We wouldn't break up again because of this reason. He took those three words seriously, and it was extremely close to having a marriage commitment. I prepared myself to wait for the ring and formal proposal until he returned from Iraq.

When we finished, the old clothes were placed at the front door of the condo. We checked every inch of the house for any remaining articles. Doug arranged for a cleaning service to finish up the job before the renters began their lease. We opened the door, walked down the three flights of stairs and threw the last remaining bag into the Ford. The moment was bittersweet, knowing how much we loved D.C., but also knowing it was time to move forward.

He opened the driver's side, and we stood together embracing each other for a long time. I tried not to cry, but the tears couldn't be stopped as they effortlessly flowed down my cheeks. He lifted my face up to his, looked into my eyes and said, "This is only temporary. We'll be together soon, and before long, I will make you my wife. I love you." He handed me a yellow piece of folded paper and got into the truck. I watched him as he drove away from Courtier Drive. Our life was changing as Doug moved forward to fulfill his destiny and I waited to fulfill mine. As I got into my vehicle, I opened the legal-size piece of yellow notepaper, which read,

"Beautiful, you are everything that is right. You are hope and truth and light. You are the stars that burn so bright. You are warmth when I am cold. You are what make me bold. You are rest when I am weary. You are happiness when all else is dreary. You are a newborn's first breath. You are life when faced with death. You are calm when everywhere madness.

You are joy instead of sadness. You are love and health and reason after a long, cold dark season.

The world may strike me to the ground, but the thought of you lifts me up when I am down. You are hope and truth and light. You are the stars that burn so bright. Beautiful, I love you. You are everything that's right."

My entire spirit lifted with his words knowing I was truly blessed to have him in my life and with those words, every thought of losing him through another left me. Doug would always say, "The written word has so much more meaning than an impersonal e-mail or a phone conversation. I will always write you poems and letters and with those the truth of my love for you." I wanted to kiss him, embrace him and love him at that very moment, but knew it was impossible. Why did I feel such a sense of urgency to marry him and have his children? Why was my patience so thin? I felt like we might run out of time in some weird way. I could never tell Doug how I was secretly scared to death he would go to Iraq and never come back to me. Instead, I put up a stoic girlfriend front to keep him at ease because he wasn't afraid of death and I would never say anything to change his mind.

Doug loved surfers and admired their strength and courage of defeating the waves on the ocean. He told me he was going to take surf lessons while in California, which wasn't a surprise to me with his thrill-seeking nature. Mark Foo was one of his favorite surfers. He was killed at Mavericks in 1994. Doug would quote Foo by saying, "If you want to ride the ultimate wave, you must be willing to pay the ultimate price." Doug wrote Foo's quote on one of his yellow sticky notes and posted it by his desk. He placed many other quotes on yellow Post-it Notes all over his house. Some were his originals, while others were from people he admired. Doug would eventually record the quotes in his numerous journals. I admired him for many things, but writing was one of his greatest attributes. This love poem was another masterpiece I would file away and keep for our children to read someday. By giving me that poem, he was giving me part of him to keep with me while he traveled to California. I knew he would call when he arrived at his first checkpoint, and I couldn't wait to tell him how wonderful he made me feel by writing the poem.

I started my car and headed back to Virginia Beach when my phone rang. "Hi, babe, what are you doing?" Doug asked.

"I was just thinking of you and how wonderful you are. Thank you for my poem," I responded.

"You liked that, huh? Well, there are plenty more where that one came from . . . babeeeee. I miss you already." Doug would always call me babe. If he called me Pam or Pamela then something was wrong. When he really wanted to express his emotions, he would pronounce "babe" in an extra deep voice and make it the longest one syllable word in history. Doug's voice was extremely sharp and deep, and his words could resonate for hours. He would also move his left leg back and forth as he drove when he was excited. Most of the time this was happening because he was usually excited about something. We shared many common characteristics and one was our ability to stay thrilled about life. Each day brought a new adventure, and Doug was exceptional at keeping each one important.

We stayed on the phone until my ear started to hurt. Our conversations never grew weary of topics; they were endless. Most important, we discussed his plan for becoming a rifle company commander and what he would do after he finished at Camp Pendleton. He tried terribly hard to make me feel better about the move. He talked about how he would be working from 6 A.M. until 8 P.M. every day and how we wouldn't be able to spend time together during the week even if he were stationed on the East Coast. Doug said to me on numerous occasions, "Don't worry, babe. We're going to make it." I trusted and believed in him, even though he ran away three times. Everything was based upon those three little words: "I love you." Everything changed since our meeting in Richmond, and now I knew our future was set in place.

Our conversation had to end when I realized I was almost back in Virginia Beach. We were on the phone for nearly 3 hours. "Honey, I have to go. My ear is falling off," I said.

"Okay, babe. I will call you later tonight or tomorrow. I love you," Doug answered.

I slowly absorbed the words. It had taken him over one year to tell me, and I would never take those words for granted. "I love you too," I responded. *We are going to make it this time,* I thought to myself. I was sad Doug left, but happy he was leaving town and not my heart. We would be together in spirit while we were physically separated. California was only distance, and we would never let the distance come between us.

Doug arrived in California safely after he visited his friends and family across the country. He was able to stop in Texas and visit with Bo and Tandi. He also stopped in New Mexico and spent time with his parents.

I remained hopeful through the initial first weeks of our separation knowing Doug had two trips planned back East for two more weddings. It seemed like everyone was getting married, which made our arrangement even more difficult to bear. Both weddings were in Northern Virginia; one in July and the second in August. Paul, Jon's little brother, was getting married on the 4th of July, and Jon's entire family would be there for another minireunion. Andre and Steph were getting married on Labor Day weekend, and since both weddings fell on holidays, Doug had extra leave and could stay for a few days.

While I waited patiently for our visits, Doug got settled in his new position. We talked on the phone every morning, until he lost cell coverage going through the base, about his new role with all its trials. He was getting adjusted, but also becoming aware of the politics involved within a leadership role. Doug talked about the large size of Camp Pendleton and how the length of it ran from the end of San Clemente to the beginning of San Diego. The land was vast with numerous areas designated for the marines to effectively train for battle.

The 4th of July came quicker than I imagined, and I picked Doug up from Reagan National Airport on Friday afternoon. We quickly retreated to our hotel room to make up for lost time.

The wedding was on Saturday afternoon with the reception immediately following in Fairfax, Virginia. Considering Paul was recently commissioned into the Marine Corps as a second lieutenant, he and his fiancée, Michelle, chose a military wedding. As the "Wedding March" began, I focused my attention on Michelle. She was beautiful in her traditional wedding gown and her bridesmaids all wore red gowns to emphasize the Marine Corps colors.

I looked down the aisle to get a glimpse of Paul's face as his bride approached him. His face was full of complete joy as tears of happiness rolled down his cheeks. *Yes, he loves her dearly,* I thought to myself as Doug grabbed my hand with his grip of iron. Once again, he never left any room for doubt when he touched me.

Attending all these weddings gave Doug and me the opportunity to discuss what we liked and what we would change for our wedding. We liked the food at Dan and Jen's wedding, but wanted a night wedding. We liked the bar at Chris and Aurora's wedding, but wanted more guests. We liked the red color theme of Paul and Michelle's wedding, but didn't like the full mass. Each wedding gave us insight to what our wedding would be like someday. I tried to be a good sport during the weddings as Doug's girlfriend because I didn't want to be just a girlfriend anymore. I wanted to be a fiancée at the least. Doug knew my patience was wearing thin, so I kept it to myself and didn't ruin our time together.

We arrived at Paul and Michelle's reception as the sun was setting on the evening. The hall was beautifully decorated, being a traditional Catholic wedding and was simply elegant. Doug and I sat with a nice group of people, but missed Jon and Anya because they were present at the head table. We enjoyed our

105

conversations, but something was missing from the evening. After all, it was the 4th of July. This was our second 4th together, and we both were disappointed at not being able to see the D.C. sky in lights.

Doug whispered in my ear, "Let's slip out for an hour and catch the fireworks at Ft. Belvoir. I bet we can make it to and from in one hour and no one will even miss us."

"Don't you think that's rude?" I asked.

"Babe, Paul and Michelle will never miss us, and if they do, we'll tell them the truth. Paul is such a patriot he will probably be ecstatic we left to see fireworks."

I scanned the room. It was dimly lit with all the guests either mingling or dancing and the first toast speeches had already been given. "Let's do it," I said.

Doug and I slipped out from our table and walked out the front entrance. We got in our car and drove quickly to Ft. Belvoir. The base was packed with cars, and everyone was camped out on the grass with their picnic baskets and drinks. Doug parked the car in an isolated area, and we hurriedly jumped out of it. He leaned on the back bumper, and I wrapped my arms around his waist while resting my head on his chest. We both just stood there in awe as the fireworks exploded with fury over the night sky. It was the best place in the world with both of us completely content. We watched the entire show embraced in each other's arms. It was our nation's birthday, and Doug was getting ready to defend its honor. He would be in Iraq the next 4th of July, and there was no way in hell we were going to miss the fireworks show tonight. We didn't say a word to each other, but were thinking the same thing. This could possibly be the last show we would watch together. The thought drifted in and out of my mind so quickly I could hardly address it, but it was there. I would get used to being supportive of Doug's destiny, even if it might cost him his life and mine. As the fireworks ended, we returned back to Paul's wedding. No one ever missed us.

CHAPTER 20

ARLINGTON, VA, 2003

*"Can miles truly separate you from friends . . . If you want to be
with someone you love, aren't you already there?"*
Richard Bach

Doug returned to California and to his marines of Echo Company 2/1. He was thrilled at the adventure of being a leader to his marines, and each day he would share the successes, along with the failures, of his men. Doug always considered failures as a means of learning, and with Doug as their leader, his marines would learn and move forward.

Labor Day was approaching, and he would once again be traveling east to attend Andre and Stephanie's wedding. Andre asked Doug to walk his mother down the aisle, and Doug was both honored and humbled. Their wedding was being held at the Army Navy Country Club in Arlington, Virginia, and it would also be a Naval Academy Class of '95 reunion.

Once again, I witnessed an incredible display of love and admiration when Stephanie walked down the aisle. She couldn't have been more stunning with her strapless dress gathered into her slim waist. Stephanie had a voluptuous "Marilyn Monroe" figure. Her hair was pulled up in an elegant style, and she glowed with happiness. Andre was dressed in the navy's finest, and his face was in awe as she approached him. Their wedding at the Army Navy Country Club was exceedingly elegant in nature.

As we walked in the appetizer area, glasses of champagne with raspberries were awaiting every guest. Doug and I quickly placed the raspberries and champagne on our like list. With a huge reception area, there were probably two hundred guests in the seating area. I was pleased to see my name on a guest card and was sure Doug learned his lesson from Dan and Jen's wedding. This time, I enjoyed fine drinks, food and conversation with Kap and Melissa without any stress, and the night seemed to fly by because of the joyous time we were having. It was one of those weddings where you didn't want the night to end or the weekend to end, considering Doug would be back to California the next morning. This was our last scheduled trip, and I felt uneasy about him leaving, not knowing when I would see him again.

The trip back to Virginia Beach was a difficult journey when all I wanted to do was get on the plane with Doug and be with him in Laguna Niguel. The weekend was too short, and I could tell his job was consuming most of his mind, but there was no other choice for him. This was his dream turning into reality, and he wouldn't be satisfied unless he was the most respected rifle company commander in 2/1. Doug would always say, "Respect is most important. Not everyone is going to like you, but they must respect you as a leader." I agreed with him. It was most important to be respected; especially in a life-or-death situation. His men had to believe in and respect him in order to follow him into battle. I supported every aspect of his new position and supported him even more when he invited the Mendoza family into his home for an indefinite amount of time.

CHAPTER 21

ANNAPOLIS, MD, TUESDAY, MAY 15, 2007

"One more day, one more time, one more sunset, maybe I'd be satisfied, but then again, I know what it would do, Leave me wishing still, for one more day with you."
Diamond Rio

The decisions were made, and my entire family prepared for the inevitable. Today was the viewing at John B. Taylor Funeral Home in downtown Annapolis. I was familiar with the place, but never expected to have my husband be the guest of honor at such a young age. We were only supposed to be in Annapolis for three more years, not end our lives here. Sometimes things don't go as planned.

I arrived one hour before the first scheduled viewing to pay my respects to the one person I loved more than anyone in the world. The last time I saw a dead body was several years prior when my grandma died. I remembered telling her how much I would miss her, but knew she was in a better place. This was different.

There were no words to describe my heartache on this day, and I wasn't about to tell Doug he was in a better place. I wasn't ready and had no idea when I would be. Doug's parents and I lingered around the front entranceway, but I didn't want to go inside. It was my strong will that projected my body forward and Doug's parents. They convinced me to go into the chapel to see the body of my dead husband, assuring me I would get closure from seeing him, but I wasn't convinced. I respected and loved them dearly, so I took their words to heart and slowly walked forward to the casket. Yes, it was true. Doug was dead, lying there with his white-gloved hands holding his sword. He was dressed in Marine Corps Blues. They weren't his Blues that he wore to every Marine Corps ball and every social event. They weren't the Blues that he wore on the day we were married. I could tell because they appeared too new. Doug's Blues were worn, and they had a small stain on the left lapel. He acquired the stain from the icing on our wedding cake.

I approached the coffin and knelt on the stool. I noticed his face. There was a brown bandage covering his left eye. I could see how the long lashes of his right eye swept under his socket even with the eye closed. Reaching for his gloved hands, I slowly discovered they were so cold, frigid even. It was like winter in Sun Valley during the blizzard of 2004. His touch was never cold. Why did they cover those magnificent hands? I wanted to see his hands. We held hands always; even while we slept.

I started to lose control, and my body began to shake. Kap was forced to take me to the seating area in the chapel. I sat for a few minutes, and then I had to leave. It was enough for me. The case had been solved. It wasn't a lie. I entered the public area and was overwhelmed by the number of guests that were arriving. I noticed the collage of photos my sisters put together. It was wonderful. There were pictures of Doug at every stage in his life: husband, father, son, friend and warrior, but the crowds of people were too great. I had to escape. I was escorted to a private room where I stayed with my family, and friends came in to see me one by one. There were so many, it was a blur. All I cared about was when I could leave this place and became obsessed with the clock; praying for the viewing to end. I was physically, mentally and spiritually exhausted and wasn't able to voice another word or see another familiar face. I was done.

Finally, the afternoon session came to an end and the entire family took a break at the Annapolis Yacht Club, which was within walking distance from the funeral home. Tom Ripley was kind to help get the luncheon organized. He was a godsend during the entire process. In fact, all of Doug's friends, all of my friends and all of our families were godsends. The support was there, and I was grateful, but obliviously, I just needed my husband.

The Annapolis Yacht Club furnished food and drinks for my entire family and some close friends. The location was perfect and exactly what we needed as we sat outside along the water in the beautiful sunny May weather. The sky was so clear and mild I could sense Doug's presence surrounding us. He wasn't in the casket at John B. Taylor; he was with us.

He was all around me, especially when I walked alone on the dock. It was a place we had been together on previous occasions. I stared into the tranquil water. The water appeared calming, and I wondered if I jumped in, if I would be able to find Douglas. It reminded me of a movie I once saw where the husband jumped into water to find his dead wife, but when he did, she wasn't dead any longer. He found her as he swam, and they ascended to the surface together.

My thoughts were interrupted when two of my friends came barreling down the dock. They brought me a glass a wine for an excuse. I wondered if they thought I might jump in the water, but my friends knew me very well and knew I would never leave my daughter. She was part of Douglas, and I would have her every day to keep me alive.

The sun started to set along the Severn River, and the entire group headed back to the funeral home. It was a slow process for me considering the only thing I wanted to do was escape and return to the sanctuary of my bedroom. However, it wasn't an option. Doug's coworkers and the governor were coming to pay their respects.

As I passed the chapel entrance, I completely avoided the opening when I went to the ladies' room because I wasn't going back in there. Doug wasn't there, and I wanted to remember him as the man of all men. He was a wax figure in the casket. Where were his sparkling eyes? One was shut and the other was blown away by gunfire! He was wearing those ugly gloves which he never wore. I don't think he even owned a pair of his own. His hands were so incredible and masculine. Why hide such wonderfulness?

I slowly went back into my private room. The crowds were greater this time. There was a line outside of the doorway, and the visitors were endless. I sat on a flowered couch while listening to everyone's condolences that never registered; they were like waves of air filtering through my head. I held back tears with the unfamiliar, but when the ones I loved came in, I couldn't hold back. I needed a break, but there wasn't going to be one, and I would never disappoint my husband. He would want these people to pay their respects to his family, and I was a fighter and a Marine Corps wife. I pondered my thoughts as the men Doug worked with came to pay their respects. I met a few of the men on previous occasions, but I was only familiar with two, Ken and Jason. It was difficult to get to know these men because they were away fighting for our nation. Doug would have parties and invite some of his coworkers when they weren't deployed. I think one of the reasons Doug went on deployments was because he respected the guys and they respected him. All of the men were wonderful, but my conversations were limited due to my lack of cognition.

While conversing with Doug's teammates, we were interrupted by a representative from the governor's office. She told us the governor was waiting outside to pay his respects. I apologized to the representative, but told her the governor would have to wait as some of these men in my presence were with Doug the night he died. I wasn't about to ask these men to leave. I felt closer to Doug, and I wanted to hear what they had to say.

I wasn't sure how long I made the governor and his staff wait, but when they entered, I could feel the irritation and annoyance. I said, "I'm sorry about the wait. Thank you for coming." I quickly glanced at the governor. He looked completely bothered, and I saw his eyes roll like cues on a pool table.

"Rolling of the eyes is the most disrespectful gesture a person can make," Doug would always say, and the governor of our state rolled his eyes because he had to wait. He approached me, and I almost walked away. However, I gave him the benefit of the doubt and allowed him to pass along his condolences. I thought to myself, *My husband just died for this country. You had to wait to see his family. Big deal! My daughter and I will have to wait forever to see Doug again!* I could tell Doug's parents were feeling the animosity as well. We were on the same wavelength. The lieutenant governor, on the other hand, was a pleasant surprise. He was superb, being prior military. He knew what it meant to serve and had experienced sacrifice and loss. Both Doug's parents and I were moved by his heartfelt words, and when they left, the night was over. As I drove back to my house, I was empty. This day drained any life left in my body, and I needed to rest because tomorrow would be the burial, Wednesday, May 16th, 2007. It would be the most painful day of my life.

CHAPTER 22

CAMP PENDLETON, CA, 2003

"The best way is to come uphill with me and have our fire and laugh and be afraid."
Robert Frost

Ray Mendoza was a marine who attended Captain School with Doug at Quantico. Like Doug, Ray was a wrestler, and the two of them became close immediately. When Ray and his family were stationed at Camp Pendleton, their home was not yet available, so Doug offered his to Ray and his family. Doug was completely selfless and was always there for his friends in any situation. I met the family once before and knew I would do the same for my friends. It would take away from our privacy, but I could care less. Doug's nature to "do to others as you would have them do to you" was another quality of his I loved.

Doug and I agreed my first visit would be toward the end of September, and we tried to keep our visits at the four-week minimum. The Mendozas would still be living at Doug's home, but I was excited to spend time with Ray, Karen and the kids. I hadn't been to California in over three years and was thrilled to be in a new town with Doug. He had the entire weekend planned for us. We would have dinner with the Mendozas at home, and then go explore Laguna Beach. Doug wanted to take me to the Ritz Carlton in Dana Point for drinks during sunset.

I arrived in Long Beach to a large grin, a huge bouquet of roses and my heavy heart. Just looking at him waiting patiently for my arrival was all I needed to know he was definitely it for me. Doug lifted me up and embraced me with the intensity of twenty people, showing his usual high emotion and zest for living each day as though it was his last. The drive to Laguna Niguel took us 40 minutes, and we arrived just in time to have dinner with everyone, but not before he showed me every last inch of his new place. The neighborhood was alive with pink, purple and yellow tropical flowers encased inside neatly manicured sidewalks. All of the buildings were crisp and white. The development housed seventy-five different units and contained two floors. Pulling into the gated community, I could see the beautifully kept pool and Jacuzzi that called our names as we drove by.

The weather was a dream in Southern California. The nights hovered around 65 degrees with low humidity, and the days stayed in the high 70s. I understood why the state was completely overpopulated. Who wouldn't want to live in paradise on earth?

Doug's unit was on the second floor and the entire area was so clean you could eat off the ground. He couldn't wait to introduce me to Ray, Karen, Keana and Alec. I met them briefly on a prior occasion, but nothing this personal. There was no doubting Ray was an extremely large man. He was an inch taller than Doug, but his build was almost double in size. His grin exposed beautiful, straight white teeth and his mannerisms reminded me of Doug's. His skin was the color of light brown cocoa, and when Ray spoke, his voice was deep but soft. I liked him instantly, and I could tell why Doug shared such a strong bond with him.

They were similar in many ways; both were marines and champion wrestlers. They understood the meaning of sacrifice and shared the same mental toughness. Pain wasn't in their dictionary, and they were more like Grecian gods than men. When Ray and Doug stood side by side, all you could see were muscles and strength. I could only imagine the two of them wrestling. Who would win? It didn't matter because both were completely humble and selfless. I stared in admiration as I watched Ray with his wife and kids. He was an excellent father and husband. The respect and love he had for his wife Karen was immeasurable.

Karen reminded me of myself in many ways. She was stoic, a true Marine Corps wife and athletic. I could tell she worked out all the time. Her body was trim and fit, and she had the most beautiful long, dark shiny hair; her hair extended past the middle of her back. She was cooking dinner for everyone, and I could smell the aroma as we talked about the kids and life. The entire area was filled with smells of garlic, oregano and rosemary. She was making some type of

Italian dish. Doug had mentioned she was spoiling him with her cooking, and the smells justified his comments.

Keana and Alec were two of the most well behaved children I had ever met. Keana was extremely respectful and kept to herself by reading, and I loved this about her. She was reading instead of watching television; a girl after my own heart. She was also a champion in judo, and her body looked fit and muscular as she demonstrated some of her moves. Alec was a few years younger, but respectful and intelligent all the same. They were a wonderful family, and I could tell why Doug enjoyed their company.

We all sat down at the table together and enjoyed Karen's pasta carbonara with chicken while enjoying a nice dinner conversation among the family. Doug and I were extremely grateful to Karen for cooking, but we had our own private agenda to attend to that evening. We graciously excused ourselves and got ready to view the sunset. It was a perfect night to take the Harley to Dana Pointe.

The sun was nestled on the edge of the horizon with the evening hues of pink, orange and purple. We hurriedly got on the back of his Harley and began our evening stroll to the Ritz. As I rode on the back of the bike, I felt home again as I held onto Doug while feeling the cool breeze of the day about to become night. We sat at the Ritz overlooking the Pacific Ocean and enjoyed the calming affects it had on the soul. I asked, "Honey, this place is completely tranquil. Is this our reward for all the sacrifices of our men and women overseas?"

Doug answered, "This is why I do what I do. Americans have all of these luxuries because of what our Founding Fathers accomplished. It gives me purpose and meaning in life to be a marine. I sacrifice for you and even for people who don't appreciate our country. Some people will never understand the true meaning of a democracy, but I will do whatever I can to keep it alive."

I replied softly, "I love you." We toasted to a beautiful weekend as the sun disappeared off into the Pacific.

During the next couple of months, Doug and I planned our Christmas vacation, and the holidays were going to have special meaning this year with him leaving for Iraq shortly thereafter. We would spend time in Laguna Niguel with Doug's parents and have Christmas dinner with many of Doug's friends. For New Years we were off to Sun Valley, Idaho for skiing and for Doug to get my seal of approval on the state. He loved Idaho's conservative nature and realized this when he visited the area with his father on a previous vacation. He even bought a book about the state's history which we read together on numerous occasions. Doug wanted me to love Idaho as much as he did so I would agree to move our family there after he retired from the Marine Corps.

He arranged the entire event by inviting all of his best friends to come with us. Even with all the excitement surrounding our trip, my mind still wondered about my Christmas gift from Doug. Would it be a ring? My hopes were up, but my intuition told me differently. We had heated discussions on the phone during the last couple months about getting engaged. Doug told me he was going to propose after he returned from Iraq, but I wasn't happy with his response and decided to buy my own house in Virginia Beach. I told him, "There is no guarantee you will give me a ring when you get back. Seven months of you being gone is a long time. Are you going to change your mind about us over there? I'm not going to wait for you to buy a house. I will buy it on my own, and if you give me a ring as promised, then we will own three houses when we get married."

Doug responded angrily, "I give you my word I am going to marry you when I get back. My word is greater than any ring I could buy. Besides, I want to save money over there and get you a rock."

"Douglas, you could give me a piece of plastic before you go and I would be happy." I could tell he was upset.

"I can't propose before I go. I need to have a clear head so I can protect my marines. I promise you I will marry you when I get back."

After several discussions like this, I knew we wouldn't officially get engaged before October of 2004. However, we did come to a compromise. I would buy the house, and he would get a date reserved at the Naval Academy Chapel for April 30, 2005.

Buying the house was a good distraction that would keep me busy in the upcoming months of Doug's deployment. The town house was located only 1 mile from the ocean, but could use a little work with some paint and new carpeting. In fact, every room in the house needed a fresh coat of paint. It was a cute two-bedroom town house with cathedral ceilings and a small backyard that would eventually be used for our yellow Labrador. Our future was being set in place with the chapel date and the dog. Doug was really trying to convince me of his loyalty to our future. He burned me on three prior occasions, but I knew it wouldn't happen this time.

CHAPTER 23

LAGUNA NIGUEL, CA, AND SUN VALLEY, ID
CHRISTMAS 2003 AND NEW YEAR'S, 2004

"Sometimes loving someone means letting go. Letting go of fears and challenging life."
Pamela Zembiec

I couldn't believe the holiday season was already here, and we made sure it was going to be a lasting memory for Doug to take with him overseas. Our family and friends gathered in Laguna Niguel for Christmas dinner while Doug made the decision to share his Christmas presents for me in front of the entire crowd. What did he have up his sleeve? I knew it wasn't going to be a ring, but what could it be? He handed me a brown envelope to open first, but I read it to myself.

Dearest Pamela, I love you in the afternoon,

When you come home from the gym sweaty, with your hair pulled back and smiling Showing off your beauty and firm, but soft-in-all-the-right-places gorgeous body.

I love you in the evening when you smell like perfume with your hair done up,
Dressed in a fancy outfit and your eyes sparkling like diamonds.
I love you in the morning when I run my hands through your tangled hair,
Hold your warm body close to mine and kiss your soft lips.
I love you all day, every day, beautiful! Merry Christmas.

There was a second letter attached that was dated December 24, 2003. The letter read *Dearest Pamela,*

> *You brighten my life the way the sun ripens the endless orchards of heaven. I love you the same way. I am grateful for your presence in my life—ETERNALLY. My life is wonderful with you in it, and we are spending Christmas and New Year's exactly the way we should . . . together.*

> *Love, Doug.*

When he handed me two small boxes wrapped in green Christmas paper, I knew for sure they had to be jewelry. As I opened the first one, my heart dropped. Could this be my ring I had waited for so patiently? My heart slowly sank when I saw a pair of earrings that were white gold and in the shape of the eagle, globe and anchor with a small diamond located within the setting. I was disappointed, but amazed at how much I loved them. I quickly placed them in my ears and knew I wouldn't take them off until Doug returned from Iraq.

The look in Doug's eyes was full of hope and anticipation. He was waiting for my approval, hoping the gifts would be sufficient until the ring was delivered. I looked at him without an ounce of displeasure and watched his eyes soften. I could tell he was relieved I would be okay until his return. I did want him to go to Iraq and fight with a free mind. But, what was a free mind? Did a ring symbolize he was free from leaving me behind if he didn't return? We did have a date at the Naval Academy for April 30, 2005, and his word was stronger than any ring. I asked Doug on a number of occasions to explain his mental reasoning behind the official engagement, but he couldn't, not understanding it himself.

I accepted my gifts with gratitude and moved forward with our Christmas celebration. I wasn't going to let another argument take hold on a subject that was fruitless. We were going to have an amazing Christmas and New Year's together, and I wasn't going to let anything destroy it.

My visit only intensified over the next few days while we prepared for our trip to Sun Valley, Idaho. His excitement was contagious, but I was consumed with the idea of skiing in the west when I was a complete novice. I had skied only one other time prior to our trip, and it wasn't a positive experience. The trip was on much-smaller mountains, and I tried to ski, but was unsuccessful, so I decided to take off my skis and walk a mile down the mountain. As I trekked through the snow, the crowds on the lift overhead were shouting demeaning statements at me. It was comical at the time, but the experience left a sour taste in my mouth, and I was determined to never ski again. Doug released my anxiety and promised he would teach me the basics. Of course, I believed in him. Doug had a way about him that brought me up to another level. When I was with him, I felt like I could conquer the world, but unfortunately, conquering the world with Doug was always on his time line, which was usually late. He was late to every party, dinner or movie. The root of all our fights began with his constant tardiness. So, when we arrived 20 minutes before our flight departure to Sun Valley, Doug was forced to beg the ticket agent to let us board the plane. He was invigorated at the challenge of being late, the challenge of convincing the agent and the challenge of making it through security. I looked at him and could tell he loved every minute of this charade that killed me with anxiety. When the ticket agent reluctantly agreed to let us on, his face was full of victory; he won the first battle.

As we rushed down the aisle and through security, he once again had the victory look on his face. Luckily, the plane did wait for us to board as we both hurried to our seats, sweating and out of breath. There was no need to say anything; Doug knew he was in trouble. He kissed me on my ear. "See, babe, I told you not to worry. We made it!"

As the plane took off down the runway, my anger dissipated with Doug sitting next to me, sleeping like a baby. I didn't understand how he could fall asleep so easily after all the stress of getting to our plane. He had a gift of being able to release all elements of stress at the blink of an eye and kept true to his word of always staying calm under pressure. I remembered reading a quote out of his journal, "Always maintain your levelheadedness, especially under pressure and especially in life-or-death situations." I guessed missing a flight wasn't a big deal to Doug.

We arrived in Boise, Idaho, on schedule and were greeted with the most genuine people I ever met in my life. Doug was right; the people in Idaho treated everyone with respect and courtesy, and I felt completely at ease here. It felt like we were home. Idaho had everything we wanted for our family; a low cost of living, conservative mind-set and a tremendous school system. Mountains that were great for skiing in the winter and biking in the summer also surrounded the town. The Snake River ran through the middle of the city and many locals and visitors alike enjoyed the wealth of this river for it's salmon fishing and power boating. Oh how I immediately loved this place! Even breathing the air was invigorating so I took in long, deep breaths that refreshed my lungs.

We quickly got in our rental van to see as much of Boise as we could before our friends arrived. We drove past quaint little shops, the town hall and various restaurants. The more we saw, the more our minds were made up. This would eventually be the place where we would raise our children together. We stayed put at a local sports bar for some dinner and drinks.

Ray, Kap, Andre and Stephanie planned on meeting us downtown where we would all make the drive to Sun Valley together. Doug could barely wait for his friends to arrive. We sat in the booth and both his legs were moving back and forth in anticipation of their arrival.

We were both excited to see Kap, Andre, Steph and Ray arrive, especially when we noticed snow pouring out of the sky. It was well past midnight as the minivan drove north into the mountains. The snow was pelting the van while large gusts of wind pushed us off the road. Doug was trying hard to keep the van on the road, but calmly drove as though the snow didn't exist, with a speed well over 70 miles per hour. Instead of asking him to slow down, which would have caused a fight, I moved to the back of the van and went to sleep. The drive was stressful, but I trusted Doug to get us to Sun Valley in one piece.

When I awoke, we were still 2 hours from the ski resort. I soon discovered that we were lost as Ray and Doug backtracked to find the correct road. The snow was piling higher on the roads, and Doug began to ease off the pedal as the van slid back and forth on the dark and winding road up to Sun Valley. I could tell Doug was a little nervous, but he focused on staying calm, cool and collected. We kept moving forward through the downpour of flakes from the sky, and then finally, off in the distance, I could see a small light with many more following. We made it! The entire van cheered as we saw the sign for the resort. At last, we had reached our destination.

We pulled up to the rented house and noticed Chris and Aurora were already there. Chris was standing on the lighted porch as we made the right-hand turn down to the house. The hill was very steep, and the van seemed to glide down the hill on the slippery surface. It had been snowing for hours in Sun Valley, which made it perfect for our first ski day. At last our vacation was here!

Doug pulled all the suitcases out of the van, and we tried to settle in the house for an arrival toast. Aurora was waiting inside, not drinking champagne, and we were all excited to hear she was expecting their first child. We had several items to toast about on this snowy evening in December.

We were pleasantly surprised at the house, which was two stories tall with a loft and four bedrooms. The front door opened to a mudroom, which housed all the ski equipment. Walking up the first level of stairs, a hot tub was to the right, and up the next level there was a great room with a kitchen, dining room and living room. The master bedroom was on the first left as you walked down the hallway and another bedroom was located immediately behind the master. Doug and I were given the honor of staying in the master suite since he planned the entire event. Even so, this surprised me because Doug always gave to his friends and family before himself. In the living room an enormous stone fireplace monopolized the sitting area with a hearth large enough to seat at least three people. The most incredible element to the house was the huge windows in the living room overlooking the entire valley.

The view from our den was mind-blowing. Looking out the large bay windows I could see the most incredible snowcapped mountains as the morning sun rose from the east. Fog was settling over the Sawtooth Mountains as the sky glistened with the first hints of sunshine. The day would be outstanding for any skier, beginner or advanced. I listened to Doug, Kap and Chris talk about their plans to ski down the black diamonds, and I wondered what the experience would be like. I had never skied down a green diamond, much less a black. The thought made me shiver as I stared out the window up to the top of the highest mountain. Doug, Kap and Chris were talking about going there for their day after Doug gave me lessons.

"Babe, we will go get fitted for our boots and skis, and then I will teach you some moves on the bunny slopes."

"Okay," I agreed.

Stephanie whispered in my ear, "Pam, Pam, that's going to be a mistake. You should get a lesson from an instructor."

I whispered back, "I know. I have a feeling Doug's lessons aren't going to work, but I will let him try to see what happens. Let's hope we don't break up over this one." We both started laughing at the thought of Doug trying to teach me how to ski. He was an excellent skier, but lessons learned from other couples in the past made me hesitate on him trying to help me. I would give him one chance, and if it didn't work, I would take some lessons. Doug was an excellent coach and mentor in many ways, but we would have to see about skiing. An alpha male and alpha female could butt heads at times during challenging situations. Doug and I shared the same belief system, but didn't always agree on how to perform certain tasks. I think I would purposefully question his authority because I didn't want to seem like a yes-girl. I kept him guessing, and it made him crazy at times. What man didn't like a challenge? I would, however, let him know when he was right, if, in fact, he was.

As we drove up to Bald Mountain, which was officially in the town of Ketchum, I felt nervous and excited all at the same time. Doug made me feel like I could do anything, but horrible thoughts kept entering my mind from my past ski experience. Would I walk down the mountain again? Since Doug was an optimist, we bought the lift tickets for the entire day, but I didn't think I was going to last that long. The mountain was immense, and the greens looked like reds, the reds like blacks and the blacks were surely unattainable to even an experienced skier. Even the bunny slope looked challenging. What was Doug thinking? How could I learn how to ski on such a difficult course? I eyed up the ski lodge and located my spot at the bar for hot toddies. I just knew I would be there sooner rather than later.

Andre, Steph, Ray, Kap and Chris made their way up the lift to start the skiing adventure while Doug and I maneuvered over to the bunny slope. I could barely balance myself on the skis. Damn, this was hard and all of the bad memories were returning to me.

"Babe, use your poles to help balance you and your upper body to push your body forward. Watch me."

I watched and quickly tried to follow him from behind. As I tried to push myself forward with the poles I lost my balance and bit the dust. Doug hurriedly came over to help assist me.

"Lean your body to the right and place both your poles on the right side while pulling your body up," he insisted. I tried diligently to do this move, but was unsuccessful. My upper body strength was not my best feature, and skiing certainly proved how much I needed some push-ups. Doug came over and helped me.

Once again, I tried to move forward in the snow, and this time made it three paces before I fell. I was able to lift myself up this time, and I finally made it to the bunny slope rope. The rope pulled you up the hill, and at the top, you let go and tried to ski down. Doug demonstrated, and it looked so easy. I thought to myself, *I can do this*. I grabbed the rope, and it tugged at my body and moved me up the hill. It wasn't so bad after all. I let go of the rope at the top and tried to ski down. *Wham!* I ate it once again.

Doug came over to the rescue and guided me up once again. He was patient but getting frustrated. Andre and Steph came over after their first run and let Doug know how great the snow was on top. I could tell he was anxious to get skiing with the guys. I looked at him and said, "Honey, go with your friends. I'll be okay." He refused, and we worked the bunny slope a few more times. It was getting easier, but I was thinking about how nice and cozy the ski lodge looked. I imagined myself sitting by the warm fire with my aching feet propped on the stool and sipping a hot toddy. Skiing was for the birds . . . or maybe I just needed a lesson from a professional.

Doug and I ventured off to the lift, and I agreed to take one run down the easiest trail. I felt nauseated as we moved up the mountain on the lift. My legs were dangling with the 14.5 inch skis, and I couldn't help but wonder how the hell I was going to get off of this lift. I barely knew how to stop or stand up. My stomach was aching, and my legs were weak. The higher we rose, the more I felt like vomiting. The scenery was beautiful, and I tried with the best of my ability to focus on both, the beauty around me and the security of Doug next to me. After all, he gave me his word he would help me off of the lift.

As we traveled, he coached me, "Babe, place your skis on the ground and let the ski lift guide you as you glide your butt off of the lift."

"Okay. Whatever you say," I replied.

As I jumped off the lift chair, his words were emanating in my head: "Skis on the ground, let the lift guide you." I did as Doug said, and sure enough, I made it off the lift. "Babe, you did a great job!" Doug shouted in excitement. I was excited too.

"Okay, what's next?" I asked.

"Watch me."

I watched Doug move his body with the poles and followed from behind as he started down the mountain. Andre, Steph and Ray were with us, and they helped guide me as well. I started down the mountain and began to go so fast I couldn't control myself. "Move your skis together!" Doug shouted.

I tried my best, but couldn't stop and wiped out hard. Doug came over to my rescue and proceeded to give me another lesson on how to stop. I watched and started down the mountain. As soon as I began to move, I slowed down. I continued this way, frustrating Doug. "Leave me!" I yelled.

He hesitated for one moment. "I'll see you at the bottom." He took off down the hill lightning fast. I kept my turtle pace, but didn't care. At this point, my legs were sore, my butt was sore and my feet were aching.

Forty-five minutes later, I saw the lodge. "Praise Jesus," I said to myself. I let my body glide into the lodge. Faster and faster I sped down the hill until I crashed into the ski holder, which ultimately made me come to a screeching halt. Everyone stood up and clapped. I made it down a ski run for the first time in my life. I thought I had successfully completed my first day at Bald Mountain and decided to call it a day. Thank God the girls had the spa on tomorrow's schedule. The guys would ski all day, while the ladies enjoyed massages and facials at the Sun Valley Ski Resort. Doug had the entire trip planned for everyone. He surprised me with the Spa Day because I truly believe he wanted me to love Idaho as much as he did. He filled my every need by supplying me with the spa, gym and friends. It was a treat to spend alone time with Aurora and Steph. It felt good finally being accepted as not only a girlfriend, but also a "wife-to-be."

Our day at the spa was heaven, and I opted for a "hot rock" massage and a European facial. Stephanie and Aurora both had Swedish massages. Steph and I talked about the slopes, and she agreed they were quite challenging for the beginner.

While we enjoyed lunch at the Sun Valley Resort, we casually mentioned the slopes to our waitress, hoping she would recommend another place better suited for beginner skiers. She suggested we try another mountain called Dollar Mountain as it was less challenging and would be great for a beginner like me. I knew Doug would be excited about our discovery, so Steph and I decided to sign up for lessons at Dollar Mountain. When the guys returned that afternoon, I shared the news with Doug and he seemed relieved I might actually learn how to ski from a professional.

As we snuggled in our bed during the morning hours, I shared with Doug my excitement about finally getting some real ski lessons on an easier mountain. I told Doug how I desperately wanted to learn how to ski so we could both teach our kids one day. My parents weren't skiers, and my sisters and I didn't ski until later in life, and I was determined to get better for my children's sake. We tried to finish our conversation before we got out of bed, but were rudely interrupted by Kap exploding through our bedroom door. He ran over to the bed and tried to jump on it and on me. I screamed, "Get out, Kap, I'm not dressed!"

Doug and Kap were laughing as I hid under the covers. "Okay, Pam, I'll leave," Kap said casually.

I yelled at Doug, "Honey, you have to talk with Kap. He enters our room whenever he pleases and has zero respect for our privacy. I don't feel comfortable changing in my own bedroom."

"All right, babe, but I don't think it's a big deal. He's family and is like my brother."

"Do you see Andre, Chris or Ray barging into our room without knocking? I don't think Kap understands the magnitude of our relationship. I think you better have a talk with him and let him know I'm not just another girl. You need to tell him we're getting married."

Doug answered, "Kap does know I'm going to make you my wife. I'll talk to him about barging into our room. Don't worry."

The moment I met Kap, we developed a love/hate relationship. I loved him when he was being respectful and fun loving, but I hated him when he tried to monopolize Doug's time. Doug relied on Kap like a brother and vice versa. They had been through many things together; the Naval Academy, Force Recon Training, Armed Forces Eco-Challenge, etc. The list could go on and on. I tried to keep my cool when it came to Kap, but he was different from the rest of Doug's friends. He wanted Doug to himself when we were all together. They had an interesting "brotherlike" friendship. Every time Kap had an ensuing thought about life, which challenged him both morally and spiritually, he would question Doug about it. Doug would always give him the right answer because he lived his life doing the right thing every day. In a way, Doug was Kap's moral compass and a moral compass for many other people. I decided to let the incident slide and moved on with my day.

Stephanie and I packed up our stuff and headed to Dollar Mountain while the rest of the crew went to Bald Mountain with a possible attempt at "heli-skiing." Steph and I picked an instructor who was around 65, but anyone would think she was much younger by viewing her on the slopes. She taught me how to get up properly, fall down correctly, push myself with poles diligently and ski down the mountain easily. I skied down Dollar Mountain without ski poles and balanced myself without relying on them. I knew if I could ride a mountain bike for 52 miles, I could ski down a mountain. I couldn't understand why we didn't start on Dollar Mountain in the first place. The resort and the mountains were much smaller and better for beginners. Knowing Doug, I didn't have to ask why he didn't suggest the mountain. He believed in me and thought I could learn how to ski instantly—even on an expert slope.

Steph and I worked with our instructor for 2 hours, and then went off on our own for a while. We were climbing on the ski lift when I told Steph about the Kap incident. "Steph, why do you think Doug lets Kap intrude on our privacy all the damn time?"

Stephanie just smiled and said, "Pam you are just a girlfriend right now. When you become a wife, and you will become Doug's wife, you will always be first. Friends always come second after you are the wife." I took her statement to heart, knowing I wouldn't be a girlfriend for much longer.

I left Dollar Mountain with absolute confidence I could ski on Bald Mountain, but not getting the chance because Doug and I were scheduled to leave the next day. As I drove back to the house, I wanted to talk to Doug and see if we could stay a couple more days so I could show him my new moves. After all, he was leaving for Iraq in February, and we wouldn't get the chance to ski again for a long time. When I talked it over with him, he jumped at the chance to make the change.

As New Year's Eve approached, the entire group agreed we would have a nice dinner at home, and then go out to a local bar to ring in the New Year. Sun Valley, Idaho, was one of the best ski resorts in the country. We thought about going to Bruce Willis's bar down the road, but driving was a problem considering everyone wanted to drink. Another problem would be the blizzard on its way ready to bombard Sun Valley with several inches of snow that was supposed to begin just before nightfall. The weather channel predicted at least 20 inches of snow before dusk on January 1st. Andre, Steph and Ray had planned on leaving in the morning and hopefully would beat the biggest punch of the storm. I secretly hoped they would be forced to stay a couple more days.

With dusk came the first few snowflakes of the storm. We ate our dinner overlooking the valley as the snow fell in blankets. We didn't care how much snow piled on the ground; we were still going to ring in the New Year somewhere, which ended up being a local pub with a small dance floor and all the usual stuff: party hats, dancing and drinking. As the New Year approached, I ran over to Doug and made sure I was next to him. It was the first New Year's we were together as a couple, and I had to be in his arms at the stroke of midnight just like his letter read to me: "We are spending Christmas and New Year's exactly the way we should, together." Everyone counted together as the ball dropped, "Five, four, three, two, one! Happy New Year!" It was 2004 and finally we were together, but I knew this year was going to be the hardest in my life. I also knew that together, we could conquer anything, even Iraq.

The snow continued to pour out of the sky when Andre, Steph and Ray left on New Year's Day. Andre had to get back to D.C. for work, and they were forced to leave in the midst of the storm. I was worried, but Doug reassured me everything would be okay as the rest of the group packed their things and headed to Bald Mountain. At first, we weren't sure if the lifts would be open because the snow was coming down so heavy. But Bald Mountain Ski Resort certainly wasn't closing because of too much snow. Even with the snow, I remained excited to test out my new skiing abilities, but did get a little nervous when I could barely see as we walked to the lodge. *If I can't see walking, how am I going to see when skiing swiftly down a mountain?* I secretly thought to myself.

Kap and Chris headed for the lifts while Doug and I went to the ski shop and rented new skis. The snowfall continued getting heavier and heavier, and I noticed the resort already closed the red and black runs, leaving only the greens; if snow was falling like this in Maryland or Virginia, the entire state would be closed for a week. The lift tickets were the last thing we needed to get on the mountain so I stepped up to the ticket counter to buy our lift tickets for the day.

"What run would be best for a beginner in weather like this?"

The man at the counter gave me a quirky smile. "I wouldn't recommend any for just a beginner. The conditions are terrible up there."

Doug pressed in front of me and quickly interrupted. "We need two half-day lift tickets." He then turned to me and said, "We'll be fine, babe." I couldn't say another word and trusted Doug's judgment, but was also scared beyond belief.

When I put my skis on, I immediately realized something wasn't right with the boots and skis. I said nervously, "Honey, something's not right. My skis seem too long or wide. Are you sure he gave me 14.5-inch skis?"

Doug looked at my skis and said, "No, babe, those look much longer, but you'll be fine."

"I need to get them changed. I'm not ready for long skis!" I exclaimed.

"Babe, calm down. You'll be fine. Longer skis are more difficult, but you'll be fine. Tell her, Kap."

Kap was waiting in line with us for the lift. "Pam, your skis are going to be fine. Longer skis work more efficiently in the deeper snow. They'll be perfect for these conditions." Kap assured me I would be fine, but deep down, I knew something wasn't right.

As we worked our way up the ski lift, the snow pelted us in the face, and visibility was extremely poor. At this point, I couldn't see ten yards in front of me as I tried to breathe with snow filling my nose instead of air. However, when

I got off the lift, I was fine, and I slowly made my way down the mountain. The snow was deep, but I was skiing through it without my poles. I made it to the bottom of the hill with the skills I had learned on the previous day and was so impressed with myself that I got back on the lift for another run. This time, Doug waited at the top and went down with me.

As I accelerated forward, something was amiss. I lost control of my right ski, and the tip got stuck in the deep snow. My body twisted, but my boot didn't twist with it. The ski was stuck in the deep snow, and my ankle felt like it snapped. Doug rushed over to help. "Babe, are you okay. I saw the entire thing. You might have a broken ankle."

I didn't know what I had, but whatever it was, it was painful, nonetheless. Doug took my boot off, and my foot was extremely swollen. The ski patrol came rushing over and notified the lodge of the incident. They placed me inside a warm wool blanket on top of a medical sled and proceeded to pull me down the mountain. I could feel the snow moving under my back and legs as the ski patrol hurriedly rushed me back to the lodge. The ski patrol carried me into the lodge while the crowds stared and wondered about my injury.

"Babe, I'm so sorry. I was wrong and made a big mistake," Doug said. He looked like a puppy dog that had just been scolded. That was enough for me to know he was truly sorry.

I was required by the ski resort to fill out an incident report so they couldn't be held responsible for the accident. After all, it wasn't their fault. I could only blame myself for not following my incredible intuition. I knew deep down Kap and Doug were being dishonest about the skis, but I didn't want to back down from their challenge. As Doug would always say, "Take responsibility for your actions." I was taking full responsibility for believing something I knew was a lie. Doug would be the one to pay in the end; he was flying home with me and my crutches. Chris quickly ran in 20 inches of snow to retrieve the minivan, and I sat with my swollen leg elevated and iced while watching Doug agonize over his mistake. Kap entered the ski lodge with regret for his decision. I could see he felt bad as well.

"I'm sorry, Pam," Kap said. I looked at him and laughed. We all laughed, knowing it would be another funny story we could tell our kids one day.

Chris calmly approached us. "Guys, I have both good news and bad news. The good news is the van is parked out front for easy access. The bad news is it's running with the keys locked inside."

"Holy shit, the story just gets better," Doug said with a grin.

Chris spoke again, "It's going to get even better because there is so much snow outside, I don't know how much longer the van will be able to make it on the roads. I already called a locksmith, and they're on the way. Aurora has the other car, and she can take the rest of us back to the house while you take Pam to the emergency room."

It only took a couple of minutes for the locksmith to do his job, and we slowly found our way to the Ketchum Hospital. We pulled into a completely empty parking lot with only two cars parked outside the entrance to the emergency room. The lot was filled with snow that was packed well above the sidewalks. Doug quickly retrieved me from the car and carried me over to the entrance in snow well past his knees. The amount of inches accumulated was hard to understand since we had never seen this much snow before in our lives. Thank goodness the staff was warm and welcoming, and we were taken back almost immediately. The nurse placed me in a room, took all my vitals and looked at my swollen leg. When the doctor first came in, she thought that it was a bad sprain, but wanted to x-ray it to be sure. We both made our way to the x-ray room, and the tech placed all the proper equipment on my body to block the harmful effects of the radiation. Doug asked the tech, "Are you sure this stuff is protecting her reproductive parts because we are going to have babies one day and I want them to be healthy." The tech laughed at him and assured him it would be okay.

Outside, the storm was raging as we felt the effects inside when the hospital lost electricity and the generator had to go into full swing. Eventually, we found out the leg wasn't broken, but just badly sprained. The doctor warned me about the effects of a sprain and to expect pain, which could be worse than a break. She gave me some pain killers just in case, but Doug, being Doug, told her I wouldn't need them because I was a stoic woman and could handle the pain on my own. She looked at him and simply shrugged her shoulders as she wrote the order. I kept quiet during the conversation and gladly accepted her recommendation.

Things changed the moment Doug discovered my ankle wasn't broken; his sorrowful attitude disappeared, he seemed less sympathetic and acted as though I was completely recovered. "I've seen marines run a marathon with a sprained ankle. You'll be just fine," Doug retorted. I looked over at him and shouted, "I'm not a marine, Doug, and don't you forget it!" We fought in the van about the magnitude of my injury and the fact that I should "suck it up" since it wasn't broken.

The snowfall was ridiculous on our drive home. We couldn't drive the van down the hill to the house and were forced to park at the top. I had a sprained ankle with crutches and because of Doug's horrible attitude, I ignored any attempt for his help and tried to crutch myself down the hill in two feet of snow. He didn't try to stop me and kept walking while leaving me at the top. I wondered if this was how he was going to treat me when I was old and disabled. He would always say, "True character is revealed under pressure." Was this *his* true character? I guess Doug figured out how difficult it was going to be for me to make it home and decided to come to my rescue. I wanted so badly to push him away and show him I didn't want or need his help, but, unfortunately, I did. I hesitantly climbed into his arms and closed my eyes as he carefully walked down the slick and steep hill to the house.

I removed myself from his presence as soon as we entered the house, went to our room, closed the door and started crying. Aurora came to console me and couldn't believe Doug's actions. He was always the gentleman and worshipped me, but maybe it wasn't me at all. Maybe it was he lashing out because of his guilty conscious. I guessed he thought it was partly his fault this happened, but I certainly wasn't blaming him. Doug eventually figured out his issues and apologized for being an ass. We never fought for long, but when we did, fireworks exploded at both ends. Even still, I spent the night with my leg aching because I refused to take the pain medication. There was no way I would lose this challenge; it was too easy, but I sometimes wondered if my fear of losing would one day get the best of me.

We left Idaho not thinking about my sprained ankle, but cherishing all the good times. The mountains were beautiful, the people were wonderful and the lifestyle was conservative. There wasn't a doubt; Doug and I were going to live there someday. He would retire from the Marine Corps as a colonel, and we would make our home in Boise, Idaho, with our three children. We would buy our dream home for little money, our kids would go to excellent schools and I would go back for my master's while Doug started his own business.

On the drive home, we planned our life together which would start as soon as he returned home from Iraq. Iraq. I hated that place. It was always in the way, but it was a necessary cause. Our country made a commitment to help the Iraqis, and Doug was going to help complete the commitment. I would always support the mission because I would never forget 9/11. The year 2004 was here, and I felt as though some Americans were beginning to forget. How could they? Terrorists killed innocent Americans, and Iraq was a breeding ground for them. Iraq harbored the criminals who hated America. The country needed our help so they could be free of the hatred and start their own democracy.

Every day, I thanked God I was an American citizen and was born into the best country in the world. I would tell Doug, "Honey, if I was born in the Middle East, I would have been killed because of my strong willed nature. Thank you, God, for letting me be an American citizen."

CHAPTER 24

NAPA VALLEY, CA, AND LAGUNA NIGUEL, CA, 2004

*"I waited for you for an eternity; seven months
is the blink of an eye."*
Pamela Zembiec

I was devastated when I had to go back East after our return from Idaho. I wished I could take leave from work for the next two months until Doug left, but that was impossible. I was in my new house and had a mortgage to pay. My only saving grace was knowing I would return to California for one last trip before his departure. We planned a long Valentine's Day weekend to Napa Valley with Dan and Jen and were being hosted by Doug's uncle Anthony and aunt Lois.

Before I could blink an eye, I was on my Jet Blue flight headed back to Doug, where we traveled to Napa Valley together. We wanted to start our wine tasting bright and early the next morning with our first stop being Opus One. The winery was known for producing the finest wines in Napa Valley. It was a joint venture created by Robert Mondavi and Baron Philippe de Rothschild that began in the 1970s. Their first vintage was released in 1981. The winery was located on a 50-acre ranch on Highway 29 in Napa Valley. The name Opus One was generated from Latin and had the meaning of a "musical analogy denoting the first masterwork of a composer." The wine was a masterpiece design as every taste filled your senses with cherry and oak that ran through your blood with warmth and smoothness. Opus One wine was truly amazing, and the winery itself was a masterpiece. The building design was based upon the expression of the wine that was made there; subtlety and grace. I read from the brochure, "Opus One doesn't rush to reveal itself, neither does the winery." The building looked as though it rose out of the earth with colonnades on either side of the entrance. It was a combination of both new and old architecture, which represented the elements of combining "old" French wines with "new" California wines.

Our tour and tasting in Opus One were phenomenal. All of the wines were aged in oak barrels that were discarded after each vintage. Uncle Anthony and Doug's cousin Adam joined the four of us on the tour. By being from Napa Valley, Uncle Anthony and Adam were well versed on the wines, and we all learned many new things from them. We didn't leave Opus One empty-handed, with Doug and Dan both buying bottles of the 1995 vintage commemorating their graduation year from the Naval Academy. We continued on to several other wineries, such as Cakebread, Duckhorn and Mumm's. Mumm's was our last stop, and we enjoyed sparkling wine along with decadent chocolates as sunset fell upon the luscious green valley.

The weekend ended way too quickly being around great family and incredible friends, but Doug and I were looking forward to our alone time in Laguna Beach before I left for home. He was leaving for Iraq the following week, and it would be our last visit for seven months. After our exciting weekend in Napa Valley, we sought refuge in Doug's two-bedroom condo. We had the house to ourselves and wanted nothing more than to be with each other on our last night together for seven months. But first, Doug was compelled to go to the music store for a song he wanted to play for me before I left. The song was by 3 Doors Down, and after he bought it in two different versions, he played it over and over again on our drive back to the condo. Doug had that habit; if he liked a scene from a video or a particular song he would play it again and again. I remembered our visit to New Mexico where he continuously replayed a scene from the movie *Conan the Barbarian*. He must have played the scene at least ten times before his dad finally said he had enough. Doug took his dad's request as meaning he had enough of *Conan the Barbarian* and repeated the same action for the movie *Red Dawn* instead. He finally stopped his shenanigans when his mom and I removed our selves from the TV room. When he began the same process with the song "When I'm Gone," I just let him do what he needed to do and listened carefully to the words. *"There's another world inside of me that you may never see. There's secrets in this life that I can't hide, but somewhere in this darkness there's a light that I can't find. Maybe it's too far away . . . or maybe I'm just blind, maybe I'm just blind*

. . . So hold me when I'm here . . . love when I'm gone . . . hold when I'm scared . . . love me when I'm gone."

The words resonated inside my head, and I didn't need to ask him why he was playing the song. I would love him when he was gone, and I didn't need anything else in the world but him. Doug was leaving to fight the war he trained to fight for his entire life. He was full of exhilaration, but he was a realist. The possibility of him not returning was clear, but that type of thinking never entered our minds. Doug said time and time again, "If you think it, then you shall become it." We never talked about him not coming home; only when. We went home and snuggled close in each other's arms as the Pacific winds whistled in the window among a bright full moon as we shared one more night of love together.

The drive to the airport the next morning was silent. I think we had already covered everything at least a hundred times and there was nothing more to say. He walked me to check-in, and we kissed good-bye. I was stoic until I knew he couldn't see me, and then my emotions took over when I realized he was gone and would be gone for a very, very long time. The tears started streaming from my eyes, and then I began to hear myself sobbing. At first, I thought it was someone else, but no, it was me. I quickly ran into the restroom and tried to gain control of myself. Why didn't I let him know how much I was going to miss him? Did he know I loved him with all of my heart and soul? Surely he did, but why had I been so calm and cool? I quickly called him.

He answered on one ring. "Babe, I knew you were going to call me."

I quickly interrupted. "Honey, I'm sorry. I couldn't bear to think of you leaving me for so long. I love you, and I would wait for you forever if I had to . . . just like a Spartan wife."

"Babe, I know you would. Why do you think I'm going to make you my wife when I return? Don't worry. I will come home in one piece, and we are going to live happily ever after," he said.

"I know. I have faith in you, and I love you," I answered.

"I love you, too," Doug replied.

I got on the plane and headed east, thinking how in two weeks, Doug would be on his way to Iraq and finally fulfilling his destiny.

CHAPTER 25

ANNAPOLIS, MD, WEDNESDAY, MAY 16, 2007

*". . . When everything was still, I listened to the bugler play
and felt a sudden chill. I wondered just how many times
that taps had meant 'Amen' when a flag had draped a coffin
of a brother or a friend. I thought of all the children, of the
mothers and the wives, of fathers, sons and husbands with
uninterrupted lives. I thought about the graveyard at the
bottom of the sea. Of unmarked graves in Arlington . . . NO,
FREEDOM IS NOT FREE!!"*
Author Unknown

The morning birds chirped outside my window. It was just another day for them. They chirped while I listened in the darkness of my lifeless bedroom, reminding me I was still alive. Kap knocked on my door. "Beautiful, if you want to see Doug one last time, we need to leave in one hour. The hearse has to leave for the Naval Academy by 8:00 A.M."

Kap was a good friend. My sleep was very uneasy, so I heard him typing the eulogy all night. I guessed he didn't get much sleep last night. I doubted anyone did. "Okay," I answered. When I woke up, I wasn't sure if I wanted to see him again like that. His body was so still and cold, just like a wax figure. However, after hearing Kap say, "one last time," I jumped out of my bed and hurriedly got ready for the funeral. My adrenaline was pumping, making it difficult to get ready. My hair was all wrong. I curled it and wanted to wear it up, but Doug wouldn't like it that way. He loved my long hair, and I compromised by pulling just the sides up to keep some of it out of my face and eyes to see everything of this day as clearly as possible. Maybe then I would believe this was true.

We raced out of the door at 7:30 A.M. I was frantic and wasn't sure if we would make it to the funeral home before they prepared Doug's body for the funeral. My stomach was sick with the thought. After I made the decision to see Doug's body, I would die inside if I wasn't able to do it now because I was late. They were going to close his casket, and it would never be opened again. I had to say good-bye to the magnificent shell of my husband one last time.

The traffic was horrible, and I was going crazy on the inside. I could see Kap perspiring next to me as he drove; he wanted to see him again as well. We arrived 5 minutes before 8:00 A.M., and they waited for us, knowing we were coming. I walked briskly down the aisle of the chapel, hoping something might be different, but the same body was there. It was Doug, but it wasn't. I noticed the marine standing next to him. He was different. The marines took turn standing guard over his body throughout the last 24 hours. I didn't touch him this time because I already knew what he felt like: stone-cold ice. He was definitely gone. I left the funeral home before they loaded his casket in the hearse and because I couldn't bear to see it any longer.

The drive through Gate One of the Naval Academy forced me to relive my past. Doug and I drove through these gates only on happy occasions. We were engaged here and married here. Our daughter was baptized here. How was this happening? It was too soon, and I wasn't ready to let go or believe, but how could I not? I just saw his dead body. My mind was in a tailspin. On one side, I was ready to walk into the church to honor the life of my husband and be the strong woman who Doug married. On the other side, I wanted to run and hide and pretend this wasn't happening.

I slowly walked into the chapel with Kap, and he helped support me down the aisle. As I made my way, I remembered the last time I took that walk. It was on my wedding day. How could this glorious place harbor such happiness and sadness at the same time? It was too soon to be experiencing the saddest . . . too soon. I robotically took my seat next to Doug's parents, and Kap and waited.

The distressing music began to resound through the building, but I didn't look back. I already knew what was happening; they were bringing the casket forward. When the pallbearers arrived next to the altar, I looked to my right and could see the casket draped with the American flag. It was hard for me to watch, and I recognized many of the pallbearers, but I could only remember Andre's name. I knew the rest, but I couldn't remember their names. What was going on? My memory was gone, and I felt as though part of my mind had gone with it. The music in the chapel was so loud and unnerving I couldn't concentrate on anything and wanted to run away. When was this nightmare going to end?

I sat there on the bench going through the mechanics of the mass; I felt like a puppet moving without emotion and strictly by the pull of strings. As Kap got up to give the eulogy, the view of the casket on my right became unhidden, and I refused to look over my right shoulder. I avoided the casket like the plague as I watched Kap approach the altar and over to the right podium. What was he doing? The right podium was reserved for those who speak the Gospel and give the homily. He walked to the microphone and began to speak.

"Okay. Today we are going to do a little exercise. Marines in the back, stand up. Now, raise your arms to the side and start circling. Sun gods are what they are called. Let's begin counting together, 1, 2, 3, 4. Okay, enough. Please be seated. The reason for our exercise was to honor Doug's workout ethic. He would do 100 sun gods, and with everyone joining in together, I calculate that we just accomplished that. Thank you, Father, for letting me use your podium."

The start of the eulogy was good. Kap was able to lift the spirits of the audience for just a moment. He moved over to the podium and began . . .

> "Good morning. I am Eric Kapitulik, one of Doug's very good friends. And he had many. This is my life's greatest privilege to speak to you today in remembering him, and I would like to thank Pamela and Fallyn for giving me the honor to do so.
>
> "I have done numerous public speeches, and typically, I wait till I finish before I gauge how good a job I have done . . . I do not need to do so today. Before I even begin, let me start by saying that I'm sorry. This eulogy just isn't very good. Please believe me when I tell you that it was not from lack of effort. Simply, it was from lack of imagination and a very limited lexicon. And although I am sure there are others who may have done it better, I am equally confident that no one would have gotten it just right. It is a tough task to explain who Doug Zembiec was. His name became a descriptive word unto itself.
>
> "For those poor and timid souls who know neither the glory of victory nor the agony of defeat, specifically, exactly the type of people that Doug did not associate with, they might describe a larger-than-life event or individual as

'crazy,' or 'ridiculous,' or even 'unbelievable.' I can't, however, use those words. Those descriptions would not do Douglas justice. They simply do not begin to adequately convey what or who he is. Rather, for those of us who knew him well, when describing Zemmie or one of his many accomplishments or adventures, we, instead, used simply 'Zembiec.' Nothing more was needed. And everyone knew exactly what you meant.

"But let me tell you what 'Zembiec' meant to one young enlisted marine: Shortly after returning from Iraq and the battle of Fallujah, Mr. and Mrs. Zembiec went out to visit Doug. Mr. Zembiec and Doug went to the base for a visit, and one of Doug's marines who was with him in Fallujah, the bloodiest battle during the entire war, was manning the main gate checking IDs of cars that were entering Camp Pendleton. When the marine saw Doug, and then saw the gentleman sitting with him, the marine asked if he were Doug's father. After replying yes, the young marine looked at Mr. Zembiec and said, 'I was with your son in Fallujah. He was my company commander. If we had to go back there, I would follow him there with a spoon.'

"Today, as I have said, I am the most privileged man in the world. Not only because I have the opportunity to tell you what he meant to me, but, seeing the warriors who are assembled here today to honor him, I realize how lucky I was to call him my best friend, if only for seventeen very short years. As I have already said, regardless of how hard I have tried and how much time I have spent in writing this speech, it has still proven to be quite a challenge. And as I have also already mentioned, this is quite a congregation to eulogize in front of. Maybe not since Gettysburg, or Normandy, Hue, or more recently, Fallujah, has there been a commiserate number of American war heroes in one place. Of course, unlike those battles, but still equally impressive, is the number of Naval Academy demerits represented here. This is a regular 'who's who' of Smoke Hall: Dan Morris, Big Daddy Kane, Jimmy Loreto, to name only a few. And those three alone represent well over 1,500 restriction musters!

"Father, as you can see from the company that Major Zembiec kept, he was our hero, but he was no saint. And, Father, I'd also like to say that I offer my sympathies to you. Through no fault of your own, you might be the only man in this chapel that did not have the opportunity to get to know Doug Zembiec. And you missed the opportunity to know a legend.

"Colonel Ripley, the only man that Doug held in the same esteem as his own *father, he and I have spent a lot of time together this past week. Sir, as always, it has been my honor. To quote Colonel Ripley, 'Doug has done the one thing that very few people have ever accomplished: he has made himself into one of the few people that, regardless of people involved or agenda, eventually the conversation will turn into Zembiec stories.'*

"Father, although you may not have had the opportunity as the rest of us, let me, however, try to describe him to you. As the congregation will attest, Doug had this annoying habit of writing down everything that you said. He was going to put it all into a book on leadership that he was going to write when he retired from the Marine Corps. And apparently, according to his many filled notebooks, he was going to write this book in his free time between starting a leadership consulting business, climbing Denali and, I quote, 'take Pam on an African safari.'

"Now, some may say that this act of writing down your thoughts on leadership and life would be the highest form of flattery, and, I guess, maybe it would be. But, Father, I have been a captain of a team or held some other leadership position for almost my entire thirty-four years. I have known Doug for seventeen of them, and we have had ample opportunity to sit around and talk for hours. Over the past week, I have read every single notebook that man has ever filled . . . And I have exactly one, ONE entry to my credit. And it has to do with massaging your scalp to stimulate your hair follicles! Further, for all of us who ever saw Z without his shirt on, and that was a regular occurrence, we all know how well that worked! The only place that warrior didn't have hair was on his head!

"Although his physical presence was undeniable, it is also documented, and there is little reason to tell anyone here that Doug Zembiec was the toughest man in the house. So let me, instead, touch on other parts of Douglas's life. The description of me that I hold most dear is simply: 'Zembiec's best friend.' And to be Zembiec's best friend, you have to be a pretty confident person. However, #1 on Doug's priority list was, and always has been, his family. Originally, that was Mr. and Mrs. Zembiec and John. When we were seventeen and we met, all of Doug's friends will attest that wrestling was securely #2. And outside of wrestling, Zembiec only associated with two other people: Bo Mansfield and Ray Lipsky. Doug chose his friends wisely. When we graduated and entered the Marine Corps together, I fell even further on the priority list as the Marine Corps inserted itself into the #2 position.

"Following Basic School and Infantry Officer's Course, Doug took his first command of men, and if he led a 21-man platoon, then, as they should, all 21 of those men would now occupy 21 positions above the best friend's rank. But, truthfully, all of this was OK by me. As Doug was going through this time period, my life was mirroring his. Like Doug, I love my family. When he was wrestling, I was playing lacrosse. We both entered the Marine Corps together, went through Marine Corps training together, entered the Fleet Marine Force together, took command of our respective platoons together, etc. And Zembiec and Kapitulik's best friendship rolled smoothly along. But then . . . Doug met Pam. And although I do believe that Doug and I are very similar people, we do differ in at least one way. I am not a man of superlatives. I don't say I'm starving, I say that I am hungry. I don't say that I am freezing, I say that I am cold. Zembiec, however, lived his life way out on the superlatives. And if we were talking about cold or hunger, it wouldn't be so bad for a best friend. But when after years of talking about battle tactics and bench press workouts for dinner conversation turns into stories about his 'Nordic Ice Princess,' a best friend, even with a girlfriend, can quickly become disillusioned.

"But, Pam, I am glad that he blew me off. I know that he made you, like all of us, a better person. But you made him a better man too. And not that I should play the fashion police, but you also turned him into one hell of a better dresser. Finally, little did I know that my priority ranking was about to fall even further, and it would fall like a meteor. But as soon as Fallyn Justice Zembiec entered Doug's life, I could have been King Leonidas, Reagan and Dan Daly rolled into one, ringing his doorbell, and if he was playing with Fallyn, that door was not going to be answered.

"One of the many great things about Doug, though, is that we were all Doug's best friend, and Doug's enthusiasm and limitless positive energy allowed him to play the role for all of us. I may have been more fortunate than some, in the amount of time I spent with Doug, but that is a wasted measure when talking about him. Four minutes, four months or thirty-four years, you would leave him knowing exactly who Doug Zembiec was and what he represented. Although, I may have been quoted both wrong and rarely, let me read you one of Doug's quotes that he got right:

"Be a man of principle. Fight for what you believe in. Keep your word. Live with integrity. Be brave. Believe in something bigger than yourself. Serve *your country. Teach. Mentor. Give something back to society. Lead from the front. Conquer your fears. Be a good friend. Be humble, but self-confident. Appreciate your friends and family. Be a leader, not a follower. Be valorous on the field of battle. Take responsibility for your actions."*

"It is the most fitting description of Doug that I have ever read or heard. And it should be. He knew its author the longest.

"Some quotes in Douglas's books had people's names that the quotes belonged to, some did not. After this quote simply, Principles my father taught me.

"And having had the pleasure of reading many of Zembiec's writings this past week, I have really just got to share a least a few other Zembiec thoughts. No one could describe Doug, other than maybe Pam, or his mom, as well as Doug can for himself, so I would like to take the opportunity to share some of Doug's quotes, goals and favorite sayings with you.

"First, some of his friends' favorite quotes:

"You can't feed a lion lettuce" (Jon Sanchez).

"God throws curve balls. You've got to learn how to hit them sooner or later" (Chris O'Connor).

"Boundless motivation and enthusiasm are a leadership trait. Think about it" (Tommy Donovan).

"Where a goat can go, a man can go. But a man can bring a rifle" (Captain Fischer, SPC TBS).

"If you don't love your wife, someone else will" (Anonymous).

"Never forget those that were killed. Never let rest those that killed them" (Col. George Bristol).

"As we all know, Doug was also, hands-down, the most positive-energy person in any room, crowd, city or state to others and for himself. As such, he was also a huge believer in the power of positive affirmations. Here are a few:

"Prepare as if no one will ever help you."

"Every day, look forward to it as if you are about to embark on a great adventure."

"Desire challenge and thrive on adversity."

"If it doesn't make you stronger, it makes you weaker."

141

"I'd rather live one day as a lion than 100 years as a dog."

"And this is Doug we are talking about, 'Alpha males get what they want from life . . . And in a wife."

"Finally, and my personal favorite by Zembiec, 'I want to be like Dr. Salk and the polio vaccine for Muslim extremists."

"Doug also had lists upon lists of goals: Goals of the day, goals of the week, month, year and life. Here are some of them:

"Celebrate faith in life, God, your marines, your friends and yourself."

"Live with honor, integrity and honesty."

"Work out religiously."

"Become the greatest husband and father ever!"

"Then, three lines down, as if he had a follow-up thought, 'who compliments his wife."

"Read an hour a day."

"Sleep at least 7 hours a day."

"This next one even surprised me, 'Eat as least 4,000 calories a day."

"And just to show that the little kid was never lost in Douglas, 'Eat breakfast, lunch and dinner . . . and a snack."

"I would like to thank you for showing so much support for both families during these very difficult times. I can not even begin to tell you how much Tom Ripley, Chris O'Connor, Major Hart and Hoffman and Colonel Ripley did for all of us. I would also be remiss if I did not thank John Fleet and so many other men and women who provided so much care. Further, the families know that these men were simply the ones privileged to be close enough to be able to help, and that everyone here was standing by to provide whatever assistance was necessary. You all have shown great loyalty to Doug through your support of his family during this grieving period. But now and for the rest of our lives, I hope that we all show him our honor.

"Late last night, after dropping my family off at their hotel, I went back to the funeral home to visit with Zemmie one last time and to say, uh, 'See ya later' to him. When I was there, I did not want to and could not look at him lying in his casket. It is not Doug's body that I loved. Admittedly, although

his body and physical presence were without peer, I wanted to visit with what you love and I loved about him most; his spirit. And you do not now see Doug's spirit in his body, but you do see it in the pictures of him. And the spirit you see in those photos manifests itself in each one of us that he touched. Last week, Friday, Doug Zembiec sacrificed his life for our country and for each one of us. But he did NOT sacrifice his spirit!!! Only we can do that. And shame on us if we do.

"Instead, 'Be a man of principle. Fight for what you believe in. Serve your country. Be brave. Teach. Mentor. Give something back to society. Conquer your fears. Be a good friend. Appreciate your friends and family. Set goals and accomplish them. Tell your friends 'I love you' before getting off the phone with them. Live as if you are getting better or getting worse, and not just 'maintaining.' Compliment your friends and compliment their girlfriends and wives even more. Cry while toasting loved ones, and lead your men, not by the rank you wear on your shoulders, but the one you wear in your heart.

"And if we do, we will have done him our honor, and though he may no longer be with us in body, he will surely not be dead either.

"A few years ago, I lost some very dear friends of mine. At the end of one of the marine's funerals, I stood behind the parents of the fallen warrior as the congregation filed out. My parents had attended the service and as my father stepped in front of the fallen marine's father, he shook his hand and said simply, 'Congratulations.' The father, startled, looked up and said, 'For what?' My dad, never losing eye contact or the firmness of his grip, replied, 'For raising your son to be a man.'

"Marines, Warriors, Friends and Family, Mr. and Mrs. Slunt, Mr. and Mrs. Zembiec and John, and of course, Pamela and Fallyn . . . Congratulations."

143

CHAPTER 26

PAM, VIRGINIA BEACH, VA, 2004
DOUGLAS, FALLUJAH, IRAQ, 2004

"There is nothing stronger than the written word."
D. A. Zembiec

After Doug's departure, I waited patiently for his letters. I was prepared that phone calls would be few and far between, but I missed them and the sound of his deep, masculine voice. His words would brighten up my day and turn my rainy days into sunshine. I missed my daily cheerleading sessions, and it was showing in my work. My funk would have to go away or I might not have a job. I worked on my new house and tried to keep busy. Doug and I agreed I would start planning our wedding in private until he officially proposed on his return from Iraq. Both of our parents knew we scheduled a date at the Naval Academy Chapel, and I was prepared to visit Annapolis and begin the search for a reception site. It was all very exciting, and I finally realized being an "official" fiancée truly didn't matter because I had the man and his word.

The days went by without hearing from Doug, and it felt completely foreign; yet, I had faith he would write to me soon. March was a busy month with my National Sales Meeting for work, and I was diligently searching for a yellow Labrador to start our family. I searched all over Hampton Roads and found a reputable breeder in North Carolina. She was an independent breeder by the name of Pamela Lassiter. I contacted her via e-mail, and she informed me of the upcoming birth of her yellow lab pups. They were expected to be born in early April. Pamela said she would contact me when the pups were born, and I could pick one after four weeks and come back to pick her up after six. I couldn't wait to write Doug and tell him about our upcoming edition, but I had to wait for his first letter in order to get the correct APO address. Then one day it happened; the letters started arriving one by one.

March 3, 2004

Dearest Pamela,

We are in Kuwait, getting ready to cross the line of departure. The marines are psyched, ready to hunt. You and I might want to think about retiring here. The mail is free, and think how much money we would save! We are about to get very busy, so I wanted to take the time to write the woman that I love. Forgive me if my prose is not very colorful. I feel it more to fire off a letter when I get the chance than to labor over the perfect sentence. I have been thinking of all the places I want to take you in the world. I would like to go to the running of the bulls in Pamplona with you. We could alternate "roughing" it with staying in nice places. How about it? How about Italy, Germany, Iceland, Budapest, Portugal, Hawaii, Alaska? I love you. We are ready. I miss you and can't wait to see you. I will write more when I get the chance.

Love, Doug

It was magic with the exhilaration I felt when I opened my mailbox and saw the envelopes. The base of the envelope was white with light blue shadowing framing the borders of each corner. On the left bottom corner there was a picture of marines behind a machine gun. The size of the envelope was strange. They weren't the ordinary standard envelope and were much smaller in size. The width was 3.5 inches, and the length was 6.5 inches. The return address had an eagle, globe and anchor where Doug had scribed his APO address. He also drew a rectangle box and inside wrote "free mail" where the postage stamp was normally placed. I guessed Doug wanted to make sure the U.S. Postal Service knew the military received free postal services while on deployment.

It was extremely easy to know when I had a letter. The mailman knew what I was waiting for and made sure he told me when one had arrived. One day he said, "Pam, you have two letters today." His statement made my day. I hurriedly ran inside, put all my things down, grabbed a drink and sat comfortably on my sofa. I wanted to be focused on every word he wrote. His writing was like Hemingway's in many ways.

March 19, 2004

My Dearest Pamela,

Yesterday, my key leaders (platoon commanders, platoon sergeants, squad leaders) and I did a left seat ride with Bravo Company, 1/505, 82 ABN Division, as they provided security for the Fallujah Provisional Authority Council (FPAC). The FPAC is a bimonthly meeting of local Iraqi leaders from the town of Fallujah in an effort to get the town running again. Army and marine commanders meet with the leaders and try to help the situation. Bravo and Charlie Company of 1/505 has been giving us a turnover, as they have been operating around Fallujah for the past seven months.

At around 1323 local time yesterday, the insurgents mortared us. The first round impacted about 100 meters away from me. The next one landed 100 meters behind me. The next three landed in a mosque and some civilian houses, killing three Iraqi civilians and one baby. The next one landed near the first. The 1st mortar round landed directly on top of building Bravo #4 where a large number of soldiers and marines were pulling security. Unlucky for us. The 82 mm mortar round injured 13 soldiers and 3 marines. Sgt. Miller and Lt. Solis from my 1st platoon asked if they could go check it out and make sure our marines (none from Echo Company) were OK. I said, "Go for it" and hopped the wall myself. I didn't think, or rather didn't know, if it was a direct hit.

I ran to building #B4, and then I heard screams. Running up the ladder well (stairwell) I told Lt. Solis to give the army a hand moving the wounded down the 3-story house. I dragged a big paratrooper down the stairs. He was covered in rich venous blood and had a head wound where some shrapnel hit him. The ladder well was packed with wounded soldiers. I dragged the soldier to a courtyard, set up a casualty collection point. As I ran back up the stairs, I looked at the soldier. Thick red blood ran through his blond hair and all over his face. Blood bubbles formed on his lips. I thought he was dead. I dragged another trooper out. The stairwell was coated in blood. I had never seen that much blood in my life. I waited for the medevac vehicles for about 1 second before realizing nothing was being done about getting them to Bldg. #B4 (B4 was separated from the FPAC compound by a six foot wall). I shouted to the soldiers on the other side of the wall. "Get the medevac vehicles!!" I hopped the wall back into the compound, rounded up my marines, a few soldiers and some other marines from 2/1. I told my company gunny, Gunny Jonas, to commandeer two army vehicles. I said, "I need a few [men] for security. Let's go."

As we left the compound, I gave my CO (Lt. Col. Olson) courtesy as to where we were going. We rushed out. Gunny Jonas is a good driver, drives 4-wheel ATVs back home in Arizona. We pulled into the walled compound of B4. I told my gunny to pull around back on the east side of the building, because I had already reconned the route. The west side had palm stumps and an air conditioner that would've made it hard to get a hummer through. We pulled around back. I asked a marine to help me untie the center line bench so we could make room for the wounded. The marine said, "It's pretty tight." I pulled out my Benchmade that my dad gave me (it has the words Semper Fi engraved on the blade), and I cut the strap holding the bench. I passed the knife off to the marine, and he did the same on the other ropes. I scooped up a trooper in a bridal carry (Jesus, these paratroopers are big!) and another soldier helped me carry him to the hummer. I looked at the first soldier I carried down and saw a sight that made my day. The soldier I thought was dead had his blue eyes open and was breathing! Thank God for good army medics!

We loaded up the wounded and staged around front. All this time there is army machine-gun fire and AK-47 fire going off. I told the gun trucks out front to stand by to move. I pushed the medevac vehicles out and followed in a caat hummer. I knew the convoy was going to get hit on the way out (I didn't), and I wanted it to be there when it did. The convoy pushed out. My hummer didn't. I looked at the driver, and he said, "It's not in gear." I said "Well, get it in gear." He tries it again and says, "It's in gear." I say, "Well, let's go then." He revs the engine, it doesn't move. Meanwhile, the convoy is gone.

The machine-gun fire from the army is going on overhead, several hundred rounds and an AT-4 rocket at only about five or six gunmen. I look at the lance corporal driver and say, "Take two deep breaths and get this in gear, relax." He tries again. No joy. I said, "Do you realize we're a big target out here?" as the staccato of an AK-47 fires to my southwest toward building # B6. He tries again, nothing. I said "Listen, motherfucker, put it in neutral, we're going to push it into the compound" (B4 had concrete barriers and Jersey barriers which provide cover). We pushed it back to B4. I said, "You shut this off, wait 5 minutes and get it started. Do you hear me?" He did. I hopped back over the wall and talked to my company. The 2/1 marines were going to head back to Camp Volturno, our base we shared with 1/505 for the next few days before they leave back to Ft. Bragg. We pushed out. The Battalion QRF had secured the cloverleaf. The QRF (Quick Reaction Force) was my 30 platoon, Lt. Chandler and his men. Army Kiowas with rockets escorted us back. Thirteen army wounded and five marine wounded. Most of them were "just" shrapnel wounds and will heal up quickly. Two soldiers had to get evacuated to the States. One of the two had his femoral artery nicked. All 18 wounded will be fine. All the time we pushed it, you could hear the soldiers and marines duking it out with the insurgents.

What I didn't tell you yet was that Sgt. Parks, USMC, a sniper from my battalion, was on the rooftop when the mortar round exploded, only a few feet away. Miraculously, he only picked up a little shrapnel in his thigh. He shook it off, got behind his M-40 sniper rifle and killed two RPG gunners! That is the Marine Corps! Shake it the fuck off and get back into the fight! That is why I joined, to serve with men like him! An army sniper killed an insurgent with an SR-25. My 1st sgt. spotted for him and told him to shoot. Two other marines killed two more insurgents. One of the marines shot an insurgent with two bursts from his M-240G machine gun! Of the five confirmed kills (higher checked the hospitals that evening), four were from marines, and we were just along as guests to observe how the army does business! All of the marines have been returned to duty, but they will get a few more days to heal.

One of the LAR lieutenants (USMC) got hit in the thigh and drove back to our compound with his men before being treated. Like cancer that doctors cut out, there are evil people in the world that need to be killed. I hope our sons grow up strong and have the opportunity to feel honor of leading warriors in harm's way, to feel the exhilaration of watching the valor of young men patch up their buddies and shoot 5.56 mm and 7.62 mm into the fucking chests of our enemies. I wish every American could've seen the stairwell of building B4, slick with the dark crimson blood of their sons, could've witnessed the determination of those five young marines and soldiers. It was an incredible effort of teamwork, and they met the challenge. The public needs to know how these insurgent animals killed 4 of their own people with their own mortars that day, how they murdered a little boy who sold chickens to coalition forces just because he cooperated with us.

When we got back to the compound, 1st Sgt. Skiles said, "You motivated me, watching you hop over the wall and . . ." Gunny Jonas, who drove the wounded back to the compound said, "Sir, you inspired me today. I don't know if they (the army) ever would have got the medevac vehicles over there (building B4 where all the wounded were) if you hadn't." Hell, Gunny, you motivated me with your bad-ass driving. Most days won't be like this. There is a threat out in Fallujah, but this fighting doesn't compare to what our forefathers in our corps went through. Look at Belleau Wood, Guadalcanal, Iwo, Okinawa, Inchon, Chosin, Hue City, Khe Sanh. I gave you the major parts of the action. I am going hunting tomorrow (B 1/505 is going to show us how they do a cordon and search). I won't have time to write everyone, so I will only write you.

Dearest Pamela, Please call my father and read him the letter, but don't let my mom hear, as it will make her nervous. My knuckles are still stained with the blood of American soldiers as I write this, and the left leg of my utility trousers is soaked with the blood of the wounded soldiers I dragged and carried to the medevac vehicles. Princess, the marines will square away this town, as we have done with so many others in our 228-year legacy. Nothing can stop us. This storm will pass, and when I return, I will make you my wife. I love you, Doug.

I finished reading the letter, and it sent chills down my spine. It was such a dangerous place. How could I have been so naïve to think he wasn't going to be in harm's way? It was worse over there than I thought, but for some reason, I had complete confidence Doug was going to make a difference over there. His strength and courage would somehow motivate all that surrounded him and help save the innocent people in Iraq. I looked in the envelope closer and I noticed another sheet of paper sticking out from within it.

My Dearest Most Lovely Princess Pamela,

I love you. Often, I think about how wonderful our lives will be together, when you and I are married, about all the places and events we will experience together. I think about our wedding day, about our reception, about our little lion cubs we will raise into men of courage and integrity. I think about looking into your beautiful princess eyes and holding your warm, firm but soft in all the right places, body next to mine. I love you, and I am so fortunate to have you in my life. You are a gift from heaven. I'll be home in only a couple more

149

months, to bathe in your confident, positive outlook.

Love, Doug.

The second letter was dated March 27, 2004.

Dearest Pamela,

On March 25, 2004, a marine convoy (not a 2/1 convoy) was ambushed on its way through Fallujah. 1st MARDIV was passed. 2/1 stood up and Echo Company seized a highway cloverleaf east of Fallujah in order to provide an area from which the battalion could operate into Fallujah. We got the order at 2100 on March 25 and by 0600 that morning, we had secured cloverleaf.

At 1000, E Company was tasked with taking security patrols into the city. At 0800, I finished up establishing our last blocking position #50 in Fallujah when the insurgents attacked our BP#50. I immediately turned around and took a hummer to BP#50 and dismounted. Rocket-propelled grenades (RPG) impacted within 100 meters all around us. I watched an RPG skid and bounce twice only 20 meters away 60 feet. The fins broke off from the warhead, and the fins and warhead slid right on by, a memorable sight watching RPG fins skip down the road. Sweetheart, an RPG is the type of weapon the Somalis used to shoot down the helo in Black Hawk Down. I noted mentally how the warhead hadn't exploded. The next two did about 75 meters away. An RPK light machine gun opened fire, and I could hear the sonic crack of the bullets as they snapped through the air about 10 meters away.

My marines were tactically dispersed and in gun positions. We returned fire. I could see the muzzle flashes of the enemy AK-47 a couple hundred meters to our west. Then we got mortared. An air burst exploded just in our south about 50 meters away. I informed higher and sent 1st and 2nd platoon from their defensive positions at the cloverleaf to clear in zone west of BP 90. When they reach me, I accompanied 2nd platoon, and we went hunting. I called up weapons platoon (which I turned into a provisional rifle platoon for these types of ops) to follow in trace of 2nd platoon as they cleared north of the MSR, Highway 10. 1st platoon cleared south. Both platoons attacked west. We received sporadic mortar, RPG and small arms all morning into the early afternoon; some of it pretty close. Babe, I swear, had I been a few feet taller, I could have grabbed one out of the sky! I had never seen marines take cover so quickly in my life. Any of the other fire didn't even faze them. My marines fought like lions. The enemy would shoot at us, and then immediately flee. It was difficult to get a good site picture on the cowards.

All morning and into the afternoon we took RPG, mortar and small arms fire. I personally lost count of the RPG fire I saw explode, about 15 rounds of it. Echo Company probably had 20 RPG rounds fired at it and twice that many 82 mm mortars. The anticoalition forces (ACF) mortared several civilians in the process of trying to get us. We treated a civilian, but he died about 15 minutes after we found him.

Marines in combat are magnificent. They are the greatest Americans. Lance Corporal Elrod got shot through both ass cheeks, probably from an RPK. We loaded him in a hummer and medevaced him to the rear. The bullet passed through his body and nicked his bowel. He has a temporary colostomy bag, but he is fine. My 2nd platoon commander, Lt. Wagner, was hit in the lip by enemy small arms, but he is OK. He continued to lead his men. It wasn't a deep hit, but it made him bleed all down his flack jacket. Wagner's radio operator, Corporal Fernandez, received shrapnel in his ass when an RPG exploded next to his platoon about 15 meters away. The marines were incredible. Squad leaders and fire team leaders and platoon commanders never hesitated and led from the front. The marines remembered what I told them, "Marines own the ground we step on."

Corporal Pierce killed two enemy with his M-16. Later that afternoon, we linked up with some soldiers from a different unit and conducted a cordon and search mission. The soldiers were from a unit similar to Joe's, but in the army. Real professionals. No one was at the objective, but we recovered some information. When we returned to our defense, four Abrams tanks were at our position! We were pulling out our gloves! During a security patrol, some Iraqi kids warned two of my marines of impending danger. Corporal Hill and LCPL Christmon were moving away from the area the kids warned them about when a vehicle-borne improvised explosive device blew up, perforating their eardrums. God bless those little kids! The kids around here are beautiful. Too bad they grow up to be terrorists.

Unfortunately, PFC Sandoval, from Fox Company, was killed by small arms fire on March 26, 2004. Echo Company has had 14 people wounded in action, but no one killed in action. That's a quick summary of March 26, 2004. We've been here since March 16, 2004, but it seems like two months. It's great! I have never felt more alive, felt more honor, than when leading men in harm's way. Your senses become so acute and sharpened. The marines love it. Cpl. Rettenburger killed an insurgent with an AK-47. Cpl. Place, a sniper, killed another. The marines have landed, and the situation is well at hand.

Princess, I love you. I am not afraid of making a bad decision and failing a mission or getting my marines hurt because the worse a situation is, the better decisions I make. I am not afraid of dying. I am not saying that to sound macho because I do feel fear. I am saying that because I understand what it means to lead. Before I go out on a mission, sweetheart, I look at your picture. I look at your picture because if I am blinded in combat, I want the last thing I see to be something beautiful, something that is positive and confident and faithful, something that is near perfect. That last sight is you, Pam.

I love you, Doug.

My heart dropped as I read the last part of his letter. Doug was making me feel wonderful thousands of miles from me, but this time, in his letters. He was my true hero. He was the one who would be in my heart forever and the one I would marry. The fact that I was able to inspire him in any way through the battles that he was enduring made me feel like I was part of something bigger than myself. I now understood why military spouses and families were so pertinent to the success of missions; they gave the men and women in battle something to come home for one day. The wonderful thoughts of coming home kept them inspired to push forward and make our country safer for those they cherished dearly. Doug's letters were appearing in my mailbox on a daily basis. He was journaling all of his major battles and sending them to me to keep in a safe place. I assumed it was for a purpose one day and was sure he would tell me when he returned home.

March 29, 2004,

Dearest Pamela,

My little Princess from Valhalla, when I return, I will probably have to stay in California a few days to submit awards for the marines, which I will already have written, and wrap up items, then I will fly back east to be with the one person I love most in the universe, you. We can spend a few days in Virginia Beach and go to Zia Marie's, eat good chow, drink wine and have chocolate for dessert. After that, head to Maryland, visit your parents and your fabulous sisters and go out in Baltimore. Then go down to Annapolis, stay at a bed and breakfast, see the colonel, go to the chapel where we are going to be married, eat more good chow, look at places to rent for our wedding reception, look at places to buy when we move there in May of 2005, watch Navy football, tailgate, watch our dog practice retrieve, walk along the Severn, make love, look into your beautiful eyes, hold your warm, firm marathoner little rocket ship race car body next to mine, talk to Carmen Bailey's dad about catering our wedding, make more love and get up in the morning and go to Starbuck's so you can get a cup of gourmet joe. Then we will go party in D.C. with Ray, run the USMC Marathon, party in D.C. during Halloween, talk to Joel and Jamie, party, eat, drink, sleep, make love, worship your body and visit Mike and LuAnn and drink the bottle of 95 Opus One (or shall we keep it for ourselves?).

Lover, being out here only makes me appreciate my marines, you, my life, my family and friends even more than I already do. I look forward to the day when you and I go somewhere on the weekend for a date, as husband and wife, while my dad takes our sons hunting and fishing and teaches them how to be men. I look forward to the empire of courage, integrity, valor, determination, justice and love that we are going to build with our family. I look forward to loving you eternally, of skiing with you and our children, or waking up in the middle of the night when it is snowing in Boise and taking our kids sledding. Sweetheart, we have so much to look forward to! I look forward to fulfilling your dreams of being the greatest husband who gives you three healthy children, raises them to be healthy warriors and leaders and love you more every day!

Love, Doug

How could I ever doubt him again after the letters he was sending to me? Doug and I did have many things to look forward to, but we still had six more months to go. One month felt like twenty months during this deployment. My friend Cindy had been through numerous deployments with her husband, and she gave the advice to stay as busy as possible. I was trying my best, but my thoughts were consumed with Doug coming home again. She also said that the first two months and the last month were the most difficult. I was a strong person, but the separation was extremely hard. A couple days passed and I received yet another letter.

153

March 31, 2004,

Dearest Pamela,

I received your letters and first care package today! You can't imagine how good it feels to receive your mail. [Oh yes I could.] Princess, I am sitting here watching the sunset, missing you. We just had three mortars and/or rockets fly over our compound and slam into another marine compound down the road. I hope everyone is okay. Just before the army left, an army surgeon was killed along with another soldier while he was on the phone. I hope he wasn't talking to his family, as the rumor had it. We (Echo Company) medevaced two marines who were in a convoy and were ambushed yesterday. The marines dismounted their trucks and attacked! They threw a grenade. The insurgent picked it up and tried to throw it back, but didn't get it far enough away. The grenade killed him, but wounded the two FSSG marines (first service support group). FSSG marines are not grunts; they are support guys. The enemy is not used to having the support convoys fight back! The two marines I saw were okay, but busted up. One was missing about half his nose and about half his upper lip.

I took out a night ambush last night. The marines did a fine job but no joy on enemy killed. Babe, it is like hunting season. Some days you see them, some days you don't. Today, the cowards killed, burned alive CPA workers and their two vehicles. It's all over the news. Our enemies are thugs. We spoke with some Iraqis. The insurgents are literally criminals. They are not locals. They care nothing about the people of Fallujah. They prey on the defenseless, like the victims today. People in Fallujah are afraid to go out after dark because they are robbed and mugged. Babe, I am writing this in the dark. Our generator broke. It might be days before it gets fixed. It doesn't matter. I am amazed how good we have it here. The only thing missing is you! Babe, I don't want you to ever have to see or live like these people. They are lawless and care only about themselves. They have no sense or justice (at least very little) and no national sense of pride. They are cowards and animals. We can't kill enough of them. This letter wasn't supposed to turn out this way, but those 3 rockets just hit the compound near us. I write this letter in flack and helmet in case one lands close. We are required by higher to wear flack and helmet after 1800 on base.

I love you, Doug

I was thrilled Doug received my care package. I carefully wrapped all his favorite things in a box and mailed it to the APO address. Doug loved MAC III razors and Hint of Lime Tostitos. He also asked for deodorant and candy for the locals. The marines loved to give out candy to the local kids because they were helpful in warning them about impending danger. It was my pleasure to send him and his marines anything they wanted. They were over there defending our freedom, and they deserved much more than I could ever send.

It was all over the news about the four Americans who were brutally murdered and burned. Their bodies were disgracefully dragged through the city of Fallujah, and every station was covering the story. I could only wait to see what was to be done about the extreme violence against our countrymen and women. Doug's group battalion would be part of the plan. I wasn't sure in what capacity Echo Company would get involved, but it was going to happen. Doug's parents received word from Karen Mendoza that 2/1 was going to retaliate against the violence. I didn't receive word directly from the Marine Corps because I wasn't Doug's wife. His parents were the closest next of kin, and they forwarded any information they received directly to me. Doug's parents were wonderful, and we were trying to support each other through this difficult time.

Fox News began broadcasting the retaliation, and I couldn't stay away from the television. Even while at work, I watched Fox News in physician's offices and asked if I could change the station if necessary. I received word Echo Company was indeed in the heart of the fight. My stress levels were very high, but I kept the faith. Doug would always say to me "Keep the faith." I was keeping the faith, but couldn't stay away from the news. My heart was stuck on Fox News because the reporting was the most accurate. Other stations such as CNN and MSN were more liberal and focused on reporting the news on that end. I wanted the truth, or something close to the truth, and Fox News was my choice. The television remained on throughout the evening and into the morning hours, but when Doug got a short interview from one of the media stations, I missed it. My friends, my parents and sisters all called to tell me they saw Doug on the news.

April 2, 2004,

Dearest Pamela,

In a short time, U.S. Marines will avenge the brutal murder of four Americans who were burned alive two days ago in Fallujah, Iraq. Young marines will be killed and injured, but we will fight with courage and valor. Our heroic deeds

155

will be immortalized in the history books. My marines fight like lions. They won't quit ever, and they will die before they dishonor their fellow marine. When it all boils down, that's who we fight for, each other. True, I believe in our cause and always will. We are fighting to make the world a safer place, to bring freedom to an oppressed people, to destroy the enemies of our nation and our way of life. This I will die for but I fight for my men and the honor of our corps. War brings death and suffering, but it also releases valor and courage and brings peace. Combat only makes me love and appreciate you more. My love for you was always eternal, always strong. Now it is so focused, so intense that I can clearly see our long, healthy, happy love-filled future together. Clear as day! I love you and respect you. I will never forget when you told me, "I would leave you too if you were ever a coward like that," referring to the main character in the movie The Four Feathers and how he refused to go on a campaign with his fellow soldier. You understand that our country needs rugged, violent men willing to fight for the principles of our great nation. Americans need men, warriors, who will defend what they love, to the death. Any society that forgot that has crumbled. Not on my watch.

Sweetheart, I love you for that. We share the same values. We will accomplish our mission. I will look at your pictures before we go on our attack, and when we get back, I will look at them again! Everything is going to be great, the men will conduct themselves like U.S. Marines, and I will make good decisions when the going gets tough. I can't wait to see you and love you and make it official, forever, when I ask you to marry me!

Love, Doug

The letter was written right before his company was sent to the violence. Doug was okay, but I wanted to hear from him. It was impossible because the company was in the city of Fallujah and not in their compound. Doug promised in an earlier phone call that he would call me on his birthday. I was sure it wouldn't happen because of the circumstances.

The violence was getting less severe, but we were informed of a casualty in Fox Company. I was sorry for the loss to the families, the marines and the country. My house became a Fox News sanctuary. The television was on in both my bedroom and in my living room. My townhome was only 1,300 square feet, but I wasn't taking any chances.

It was April 14th, and I waited for his call all day. I already expected the severe possibility of him not calling, but he said he would try his best. At about

2200 Eastern Standard Time, my cell phone rang, and my heart dropped.

"Babe, babe, can you hear me?" Doug asked.

The exhilaration of the call filled my entire body, and I jumped up in bed to make sure I could take in every word. "Honey, oh my God, you called like you promised! I love you so much and Happy Birthday!" I responded.

"Babe, it's not really my birthday today; yes, I was born today, but my real birthday is on November 10, and I love you," he said.

"I don't care what day it is, I am just so happy to hear your voice, and now I know you're okay," I replied.

Doug asked, "Did you see me on the news?"

"No, but everybody else did. I'll wait for a recorded version. I heard you looked handsome in your helmet and flack jacket," I answered.

"Nothing better than a marine in uniform. I can't talk long, but I wanted to call as promised. It is crazy here, but my marines rock. They fight like lions, and their courage is unbelievable," he said.

"Honey, I have all faith that you guys are going to get the job done. Did you get some of the bastards that killed those poor Blackwater guys?" I asked.

"We got a few of them, but not sure if they were the ones, but they are all the same, criminals," he answered.

The phone began to get muffled, and I could barely hear him say good-bye. I was relieved that I said I love you at the beginning of the conversation. He knew it, but we made a pact to never end phone calls or leave without saying "I love you." He was teaching me how to not take anything for granted as it could be the last time you are given the chance. He was teaching me how to live life to the fullest each day as it could be your last. He was teaching me how to love unconditionally, and that love was eternal.

April 12, 2004, Doug, while in Fallujah, wrote this letter. He and his men were staying (had taken over) in some former Ba'ath Party member's house, and he was short on paper so it was written on what looked like some kid's homework tablet . . . probably some future terrorist.

Dear Mom, Dad, Pamela, Family and Friends,

The marines of Echo Company and I are doing incredible. We are currently strong pointed in Northwest Fallujah. A few marines have been wounded from enemy rocket-propelled grenades, bullets, and grenades, but they have all been minor. Echo Company has the highest number of wounded marines in the battalion, but we have had no marines killed in action. I am proud

157

of this fact and attribute it to the aggressiveness and esprit de corps of my marines. Like Colonel Ripley says, they "press the attack." This offensive mind-set saves lives.

Our lack of marines dying at the hands of the enemy is not from luck or not being in harm's way. Echo Company has penetrated the deepest into the city of Fallujah, and we have killed scores of insurgents that we have left littering the streets of Fallujah. 2/1 established a cordon around Fallujah on 4/5/2004. 2/1 cordoned off the west and northwest of the city, 1/5 cordoned the east and southern portion of the city. Fox Company got ambushed on their way in to setting up blocking positions there, and one marine was killed in action. Spectre was calling in at night, and 40 insurgents were whacked. "G" Company was attacked that evening as well, and Cobras were called in. CAAT Marines attached to "G" Company stopped a vehicle that tried to run a traffic patrol point with a .50-cal machine gun.

I had done a thorough leaders recon, and Echo Company set up blocking position two without an incident. The marines were itching for a fight! We soon got it. On April 6, 2004, Echo Company was tasked with attacking enemy on Fox Company's east flank, and then tying in with that company. I took tanks and tracks to a dismount point, really the only dismount point available, south of BP3 and just north of Kaluan. We dismounted behind a tank support by fire position. Our tanks and heavy machine-gun vehicles were blazing away. The marines advanced south toward town, using available cover and concealment. RPGs and enemy small arms fire whizzed and snapped by our heads, fired by the approximately 50 enemy about 150 meters to our south from parapets and balconies on buildings. I identified an enemy position, watching the muzzle flashes of his rifle before I fired four times. His firing stopped.

My battalion commander wanted Echo Company to attack further to the east, as he believed, incorrectly, that Fox Company had penetrated further east than they actually had. I moved my marines behind the cover of the railroad tracks, and we cleared east to an assault position. We conducted a night attack south into Fallujah at around 21:30. My marines killed two insurgents with AK-47s on the way in. We took two RPG shots near us as well, with no effect. We cleared 6 buildings with two platoons reinforced with machine guns and assault teams, and strong point four. One building had an Iraqi family that we put in one room.

At 23:00, the insurgents tried to counterattack. Spectre Gunship picked up two groups of twenty insurgents 300 meters to our south, and killed them all. My FAC (Forward Air Controller) Capt. "Oprah" Martino did a great job talking on the gunship. In the morning, Echo Company cleared west toward Fox Company's east flank (1,500 meters away!). We cleared a building just east of a mosque and found IED materials, then we cleared a big mosque where we found shell casings and bullets from where the enemy had shot at us the day prior.

We crossed through a cemetery and strong pointed four buildings and from my current location, we started taking fire. Two RPGs slammed into the minaret on the mosque we had just occupied. Both platoons linked up, and the enemy attacked us again. I watched one insurgent shoot an RPG at us before marines suppressed. The rocket went over our heads. Another RPG gunner shot, but marines were already shooting at him. The enemies' round hit a house 50 meters in front of the point he launched from.

We moved further west, strong pointed four houses, tied in by fire with the one platoon Fox Company had south of BP3 (2nd Lt. Jamison, "He's got it."), and expanded our battalion foothold. The enemy counterattacked with a squad-sized element. The enemy fired multiple RPGs, small arms, and had one gunman, probably a sniper, shooting about a foot from my marines and me. I called Black Six/Capt. Mike Scaggs, from EWS, and his three tanks. Then I ran outside to his tanks and tried to talk with him on with the tank phone. Rounds were cracking by overhead from both sides. The tank phone talk-on wasn't working, so I hopped on the turret and talked directly to the vehicle commander. The marines watching loved it! Mike and his marines smoked three problem buildings with the 120 MM main gun! Outstanding. The buildings caught on fire and burned for 3 hours.

While we used tanks, my fire support team called on two Cobras (the helos that Bo flies) and whacked enemy that were 150 meters to our south. 20 MM shell casings from the helos fell on our roof! That is close air support. (At 0330, Oprah talked on Spectre and killed 10 insurgents 400 meters from our position armed with RPGs and AKs.)

On April 8, 2004, we took accurate but ineffective fire from gunmen 250 meters to our southeast. I sent a reinforced squad led by Lieutenant Chandler and his first squad leader to eliminate the threat. They got into a pretty good fight, took some RPG fire and small arms fire. I pulled them back, and then mortared and bombed the enemy positions. Later that day, I watched two BM 21 rockets smash into the train station to our north with huge explosions. Later that evening, we received more rockets and gunfire from our troubled neighbors. I called up Lt. Sayer from "C" Co., 1st tanks, and led a platoon down into the neighborhood. We got into a great fight! RPGs bounced off tanks, and bullets cracked close by our heads. The streets were littered with enemy bodies that my rifleman and snipers (mostly snipers, CPL Place has killed over 22 enemy) had killed. We loaded one body on the tank, for Intel purposes and withdrew back to our defensive position. Turned out the enemy was a mortarman, loyal to Saddam Hussein. We are fighting former Ba'ath Loyalists, a lot a Syrians and foreign fighters. We turned the body over to higher. Things quieted down after that patrol. That night, Oprah ran Spectre at the location where we received Dragunov sniper fire from the preceding days. Spectre killed six at that location, then 12 more from the RPG gunners at 0300 who were trying to flank us. Spectre is great.

On April 9, 2004, I sent Lt. Chandler back into the neighborhood. He made contact with the enemy and three of his marines sustained minor injuries. I pulled them back, then bombed and mortared the enemy. LCPL Jennings received a grazing bullet wound in the left arm, LCL Playo received RPG fragments to the neck, head and hand, and CPL Hampton got shrapnel in his upper arm. He begged to stay! CPL Place and his sniper team continued to kill many enemy and the 8th and 9th of April. LCPL Cruz machine-gunned two BP2. On April 9, 2004, Doc Rousseau sustained a minor mortar injury in the vicinity BP2.

Tuesday, April 10th was more of the same. BM 21 rockets all day and some 200 meters to our north. Nothing compared to the 10 or 12 RPGs a day over the last few days, some missing us by only feet. On April 11, 2004, I finally linked up with Warhammer 2, my second platoon that was a BP#2 the last few days. We moved into new positions. Cats and dogs feasted on many enemy bodies. We held Easter service at a strong point building with a reeking dead insurgent on the road out front.

April 12th, 2004, was a rough day. While I was at a battalion meeting, one of my marines called in a mortar mission. The round landed short, killed two of my marines and wounded four at 2nd platoon's position. I jumped in the hummer and drove straight to the scene and assessed the situation. I ran up and guided the medvac vehicles to the casualties, calmed my marines down and made sure we loaded all the casualties, as many marines were excited. I helped load one of the casualties, made one last sweep, then sent the last MEDVAC vehicle to the battalion casualty collection point. The position was soaked with blood. I don't like having American blood on me. I scrubbed my clothes when I got the blood of one of the dead scumbags we shot on me, but I don't want to see any more American blood again. Unfortunately, I probably will. We will prevail. Marines always accomplish the mission. I love you.

Combat only makes me appreciate my marines, family, friends and life even more. I am grateful for the way you raised me, Mom and Dad, because it is keeping my marines alive and helping us kill the enemy. It makes me appreciate Pamela even more. I intend to marry her when we return.

Love, Doug

P.S. Please send a copy of this letter to Pam.

Doug's letter was frightening. All of the reports on Fox News seemed to correlate with his letters. I watched the news and noticed the green spectre lens as the marines fought against the insurgents well into the night hours. When were they sleeping? What were they eating? I was concerned for Doug's welfare, but my gut told me he would be fine. I hurt for him when I read about the two marines killed through friendly fire. Doug loved his marines like he would love his sons. His marines would prevail, but they would never forget those that had perished. His heart was breaking, and I wanted to be there for him in some way. A week went by and I received another letter from Douglas. I needed his correspondence so that I could have a small piece of him.

CHAPTER 27

ANNAPOLIS, MD, 2004

"We are only going to do this once. Choose wisely, be picky and accept only greatness."
D. A. Zembiec

I was beginning the initial stages of our wedding plans. Before Doug left, we made the choice to hold a date at the Naval Academy Chapel for our wedding and I was getting ready to go to Annapolis and search for our reception site. We wanted to host a big party for our closest family and friends. Doug and I both agreed the wedding would be more for our friends than for us. Searching for a reception site would keep me very busy and focused on our future. It was hard not to worry, especially when I received his letters that described the danger in extreme detail. It was Doug, and he would not miss a beat. I opened up my mailbox one day and found an odd piece of cardboard paper. On the front was Doug's handwriting. He had written a postcard from Fallujah on the back of an MRE box. I wouldn't wonder what he ate on April 13, 2004, because the box read "Ham and Shrimp Jambalaya." I wondered how they made the MREs for a second, then I read his postcard.

April 13, 2004,

Dearest Pamela,

Greetings from Fallujah! We are here doing what marines do best; killing our enemies. My men fight like lions, no matter how bad the situation becomes. I love you, and I am going to make you my wife when we return.

Love, Doug.

April 17, 2005,

Princess Pamela,

Enclosed is a psychological operations speech written by our Kurdish interpreter, Peshi, that we actually played. I sent a copy to my parents as well. We are getting ready to go deeper into the city and crush more of our enemies. I love you. I have our whole leave period planned out and 99.9 percent of it involves me around you! Speaking of which, how about you and me eating dinner at Mie N Yu? I love you. The thought of you makes my spirit smile. Thank you.

Love, Doug

Babe, several cans of smoked oysters and a big bag of hint of lime Doritos would make our day. I love you, Doug.

Life was good when I received his letters. Almost every letter ended with him writing "when I return I am going to make you my wife." Doug was holding up to his word, and I started my search for our reception. Life was also good when I was not witness to reports of casualties in Fallujah that spread across the bottom of the television set. A cease-fire was ordered in the city of Fallujah while leaders of both the U.S. and Iraq negotiated on the terms as to how the violence might end. It seemed that all was quiet for at least a couple of days. To keep my time occupied, my sisters, mother and I visited Annapolis on a bright and sunny Saturday to look for our reception site. Doug requested a place within close proximity to the chapel, and I made appointments with three within 5 miles of the chapel and one over the Bay Bridge. We both wanted our guests to be able to park at their respective hotels and not worry about driving too far. The plan was to have the best of everything.

Our first visit was to the Fleet Exchange Room. The Fleet Exchange Room was an exclusive club for the military. It was located in the heart of downtown Annapolis and next door to the Marriot Waterfront Hotel. I made the appointment out of respect for my future husband, but I was not pleased with the looks of the club. The outside entrance was brick with big bold letters stating "The Fleet Exchange Room." The front entrance consisted of two glass doors which were locked to the public. I was forced to ring the doorbell for entry into the club. The parking lot was black-topped with bold parking spaces. There were not many available, which might present a problem. The Exchange was already proving to not be the location for my dream wedding. It reminded me of an old VFW hall, which wasn't close to the glorious reception site I had in my mind. I wanted elegance and beauty; the Cinderella fairy tale. I was going to be Doug's princess, and he would be my prince. I couldn't imagine entering this place after my walk down the aisle at the Naval Academy Chapel. I was sure it would be appropriate for a couple that wanted a casual wedding.

An older gentleman answered the door and kindly escorted us to the bar area where we would meet with the manager. He walked over to us and introduced himself.

"Welcome, ladies, my name is Tom. Nice to meet such a beautiful group of young ladies, and who is the bride-to-be?"

"I am the bride-to-be. My name is Pam."

"Well, welcome, Pam. Let's go outside and talk about your plans. Would anyone care to share a lunchtime cocktail with me?" Tom graciously asked.

"Sure," I said.

"I'm having a vodka martini. What would you ladies like?" he asked.

"I'll have what you're having," I responded.

My sisters looked at me in shock. I was more of a red wine drinker, but I felt like having a martini. So my sisters joined me, and we all enjoyed our cocktails. We sat outside on the water and discussed my ideas, the prices and the date. He was able to accommodate everything and at a reasonable cost. I was polite and took the information, but knew it wasn't the place. I already decided beforehand that I would know the place as soon as I entered the front door.

The next three locations all brought the same feelings, and I wasn't about to settle. I was getting married once, and it had to be at the right place, but we already exhausted the venues close to the chapel and the only one left was located over the Bay Bridge. Doug explicitly asked me to stay away from the area, but I needed to go. There was something about The Kent Manor Inn that drew me to its Web site, and I wasn't going against my feelings. So I made an executive decision to go against Doug's wishes this one time. I felt like I was being called to this place, even though I agreed with his reasoning. The Bay Bridge was always crowded and was a longer drive for our guests. On this particular day, we sat in traffic for nearly an hour making us over an hour late for the appointment.

When we finally crossed over the bridge, the Kent Manor Inn was the first exit off the bridge, making it highly accessible without traffic involved. As soon as we began driving down the road to the manor, I noticed beautifully manicured lawns and trees surrounding the roadside; it was already breathtaking. The inn appeared in the distance among the greenery and flower beds. It was near the end of April, and the lawns were amazing. Flowers of red, yellow, purple and pink adorned the entrance to the inn, which was behind an antique pair of restored white stairs. The exterior was painted bright white with black shutters surrounding large picturesque windows.

The inn sat along the Thompson Creek with water views everywhere. I didn't need to go inside, I already knew this was the place. My family and I walked in the front entrance, and I could feel the energy. The inn had been completely restored, but I felt as though I walked into a plantation from the 1800s. I imagined all of our friends dressed in their finest, wandering around the yards. The uniformed men would feel at home because of the Civil War history lurking among the walls of the plantation.

We walked around the property and were taken to the reception area. It comfortably housed 150 people, but wouldn't be big enough. The host looked at my face. She didn't have to ask me another question. "For larger parties, we can set up a tented area outside on the lawn and the greenhouse can be used for the cocktail area. Your guests can sit for dinner under the tent. Dancing can take place in both areas."

I could picture my wedding here, and I knew Doug wouldn't be upset with me. He would want what I wanted, especially after I found out guests could stay at the inn for the night. "Okay, I want it. I'm having my wedding here!"

My sisters jumped up and down like schoolgirls. I said, "You guys were excellent at hiding your excitement before I made up my mind."

Kimmy said, "We liked the other places, but we loved the inn from the moment we drove up. We didn't want to alter your opinion because this is your wedding, not ours."

"Thanks, guys. The Kent Manor Inn is it. This was emotionally exhausting. Can we go home now?"

I was elated and didn't doubt my decision once. Doug would be happy. The host mentioned the owner could order extra Jack Daniels for our wedding. The chapel and the reception site were now in place. My mind was at ease for the wedding, and now it was time to pick out our dog. I arrived back in Virginia Beach the next night and was blessed with a letter from my love. It was the perfect ending to a perfect weekend.

April 23, 2004,

Dearest Pamela,

My love for you grows even stronger every day. Just as I find you even more beautiful every time I see you. We are going to breed some warriors! Congratulations on your raise. You deserve it! You are so talented and industrious and hardworking, all character traits that make you even more attractive in my eyes. I received Kelsey's and your mom's Easter cards, and I sent them a reply. I sent both of them to Kimmy's address as I couldn't read the return address to your parents. Your family is in my thoughts and prayers, and I can't wait to join it!

Sweetheart, I looked at the wedding gown advertisements, and I visualize you in all of them, looking like the princess from Valhalla that you are! You could wear a potato sack and look gorgeous in it, because you are a beautiful person by yourself. *I sent Kelsey a quote from Sir Edmund Burke written on the memorial for my two marines killed. She will understand it when she is older.

The McClintock dress looks classy, appropriate for a dignified lady like yourself. The cake with the roses looked especially elegant, and the Harley bride figurine will look perfect on top! Sweetheart, don't worry about finding a place for the reception. Don't listen to the people that say people won't rent out their house, as they don't know the people we do or have our force of personality. I can ask the colonel to help us when I get back in October. The Samples' neighbors to the west of their house with the big lawn sloping gently to the Severn River might be a good spot, or the marina over in Eastport. There is a restaurant, a few restaurants, actually, in Eastport that we could rent out. Babe, there are so many good places to have it! I want to have the reception where you want it, but I don't want to have it across the Chesapeake Bridge so our friends don't have to worry about driving a distance after they have been partying. It is going to be such a great day! All of our friends will witness our union, before God, and then we can get busy making you pregnant with our healthy, beautiful children.

I dream and fantasize about the life we are going to have together when we are married. We are going to have such a happy, fulfilling, lifelong marriage. I dream about the month of leave I am going to have, spending it with you. We can spend a fall weekend in Maine at Kap's parents' house on the shore eating lobster, drinking wine and making love. We can visit Uncle Tom and go to New York. I'll wear my Alphas, and we won't buy a drink all night!

I look forward to going to the Red Maple and just talking to you. I look forward to going to the Great Argentine Restaurant in Columbia with Jon and Anya, feasting on red meat and being naturally high from being with great friends! I can't wait to run the USMC Marathon with you (if you still want to) that will be the longest distance you have ever run and a great accomplishment, hauling those big mamba jamba 36D breasts around for 26.2 miles! A few days later, we will party in D.C. for Halloween!

Sweetheart, I can't wait to be married to you, raising our children in Annapolis. I am honored to be fighting with 1st Marine Division, but that is the only reason I am on the West Coast. I need to be on the East Coast, with the love of my life, the woman who I will forever be in love with, you, my dearest Pamela.

I took my company into Fallujah two days ago. We got into a pretty big fight. One of my marines got shot in the neck, LCPL Gonzalez. He is going to live, but he has some nerve damage on his left side. Another warrior took some RPG shrapnel under his left armpit where there is a gap on our body armor. His call sign is Valhalla. No shit! He is fine and with us today. The shrapnel will work its way out. His grandpa fought in the Chosin with Chesty Puller, and his grandpa would be proud of his grandson.

The news reported that we killed 36 insurgents, and that is about right. Just got interrupted by enemy RPK fire. We can't kill enough of them. It is either we fight them in the streets of Fallujah or in the streets of Baltimore, New York, London. Thank you for keeping in touch with my friends, our friends. Please give Elliot a call and give him a summary. If his number is no longer in service, you can try and find him in D.C. where his parents live.

How wonderful is the Marine Corps Ball going to be this year, with you and all your beauty. Even better than all the rest combined! I can't wait to take you to Mei N Yu in Georgetown and have a wonderful night out with you. You are the most wonderful gift in my life, and there is no one person who I love more in my life.

I love you,

Doug

"Oh shit!" I said out loud. Doug was adamant about keeping the reception from being on the other side of the Chesapeake Bay. I didn't sign the final contract, and I would talk to him before I make the final mark. Once I spoke with him about the Kent Manor Inn, he would agree with me. I couldn't go completely against his wishes, but my dreams would be fulfilled if we chose the Kent Manor.

I woke up the next morning with thoughts of negativity. I desperately tried to get them out of my head, but I couldn't. I dragged myself to work, feeling sick the entire day. Even the weather was dreary and dismal. Something was wrong, and I couldn't shake the feeling. My stomach was sick, my head hurt and my mind was racing. I tried to push my feelings aside thinking it was Monday, and Mondays were always difficult, especially since I was drained from traveling over the weekend. I continued to push the thoughts out of my mind, but I knew it had to be something about Doug. I wondered if he was in trouble or hurt. Doug and I had a connection that spanned over thousands of miles, and I could feel him.

I went to the gym and tried working the feelings out of my head. It was only a temporary fix because as soon as I entered my home the feelings returned, but only stronger. I turned on the news. The reports on Iraq hadn't been posted. After dinner, I settled on the couch with the news blaring when the phone rang. "Hello," I answered.

"Good evening, ma'am. Is this Pamela?"

"Yes, it is," I answered with my heart about to jump out of my chest. I knew the caller was military as soon as he called me ma'am. Something had to be wrong.

"Ma'am, this is Sergeant Miles from the 1st Division Marine Corps. I understand you are Captain Zembiec's fiancée."

"Yes," I replied as tears began to stream down my face. "Please don't tell me Doug is dead."

"Calm down, ma'am. Captain Zembiec was injured today when his rifle company was ambushed by insurgents in the city of Fallujah. His injury was classified as a category five. He was treated for injuries and is now with his rifle company. We usually don't call fiancées, but Mr. and Mrs. Zembiec requested I call you. Do you have any questions?" he asked.

"No, just knowing he's back with his rifle company makes me feel better," I answered. Thank God he was okay. For the first time since I met Doug, I realized how risky it was being a marine and how strong I would have to be if something ever happened to him.

The news finally reported the ambush in Fallujah with one casualty. Doug would be devastated once again. My only hope was another letter in the mail. I waited patiently for his call or a letter and nothing came. Each day, I listened to the news and kept my cell phone next to me at all times. I knew I could answer in front of a doctor if he called while I was working. When my manager rode with me, he understood the situation. Joe was a good man and was the first to tell me I was going to marry Doug. Doug would call my cell phone over and over again while Joe rode with me. I would apologize, and Joe would say, "Pam, you are probably going to marry this one. The way he acts is the way a man acts when he's in love." I laughed at Joe and admired his acute perception of the situation. Finally, two weeks after Echo Company was ambushed in Fallujah, I received a letter from Douglas.

April 30, 2004

My marines and I got in a big fight on the 26th of April. My men fought like lions and killed many insurgents. The valor and courage of the marines was magnificent. The marines fought with such ferocity that any marine who went before us would have been proud. We had no less than 30 rocket-propelled grenades fired at our position and no less than 4,000 rounds of enemy machine-gun fire shot at us in the first 12 minutes of the fight. The enemy closed within 15 meters of our position before my marines forced them back. An insurgent fired at me from 20 meters away with an AK-47. His bullets whizzed by and between my legs. A bullet or a piece of shrapnel hit my left knee and a bullet ricocheted onto my dick plate (groin protector). It is our company standard operating procedure to wear them, and now you can see why. I threw a grenade at the enemy who shot at me. Sweetheart, when I ran over to the northern building we held to check on my marines at that position, I said, "Everything's going to be OK." The squad had a lot of injured and one marine who was fighting for his life, LCPL Austin. Later, two of my marines, LCPL Payne and PFC Sleight, said "Sir, you motivated me. When you showed up in that room I knew everything was going to be all right."

I wanted to stay and fight, but I have four seriously wounded marines, so I told Warhammer 2 to fall back. The tanks requested showed up and really helped out. I am writing up two of my marines for the Silver Star, one posthumously as LCPL Austin didn't make it. Many more I am putting in for the Bronze Star, and these are Marine Corps Silver Stars and Bronze Stars. When it was all said and done, 13 marines and sailors were wounded, and one of my marines killed. My marines killed at least twelve insurgents, and after we pulled out of our positions, we called in Cobras and mortars and killed many, many more. My men deserve official recognition of their battlefield valor. I couldn't be more proud of my men. With men like the marines of Echo Company defending our nation, we will live free, forever.

The marines and corpsmen who medevaced our wounded, under fire, are true heroes. The marines who fought down in the alley, under fire the whole time, are heroes. The marines who fought on the rooftops are heroes. You would have to ask my marines how I performed that day to get an unbiased opinion. I think you will find that I made good decisions from the front, the only place I know from where to lead. I was unashamed when I shed tears for Austin. I told my men Austin was a warrior, and we will honor him by slaying more of our enemies, that his death will only strengthen our resolve. He died a warrior's death, throwing a hand grenade at the enemy.

Thank you for all your letters. You couldn't imagine how happy it makes me to receive your mail. My soul lights up when I see your name on the return address of an envelope. Pamela, it was divine intervention that we met. You are an angel from Valhalla and the most wonderful person in my life. You know, I am looking forward to so many events we will share together. I can't wait to ask you to marry me, and you are going to love the way I am going to ask you! Thank you for keeping in touch with Colonel Ripley. Please send me his address. Please tell your family I said hello. Please tell Kelsey that she is a good little angel and plant the seeds of internal motivation! Please tell my future brothers-in-law hello. Tell Jon Sanchez that he and Anya, Little Jon, Paul and the rest of his family are in my prayers. I want to keep writing and taking the luxury of thinking about you, but I must get back to writing awards. My thoughts for you are an internal paradise, a refuge, a well cool and clear from which my soul drinks. I love you,

Doug

My instincts were correct. The insurgents' force was only made stronger by the American cease-fire and more American blood was shed as a result. The only positive was General Conway's decision to pull the marines out of the city because the offensive wasn't an option. I didn't understand why the marines were not allowed to take over the city of Fallujah. The Iraqis would benefit, and the marines would have been able to do their jobs. However, it was better for the marines to be out of the city if they were not going to be able to take it over with force.

The news was quiet over the next few weeks, and I wondered constantly about Doug. Since the marines were taken out of the city, I was not being updated by the news and was forced to wait patiently for another letter.

CHAPTER 28

VIRGINIA BEACH, VA, 2004

"Lo, there do I see my father. Lo, there do I see my mother, my sisters, and my brothers. Lo, there do I see the line of my people, back to the beginning. Lo, they do call me. They bid me take my place among them in the Halls of Valhalla. Where the brave may live forever."
The Vikings—The 13th Warrior

On Memorial Day weekend, I picked up our dog. I waited six weeks after her birth date of April 4, 2004. She was a purebred Labrador retriever with white fur mixed within yellow hues. She had the most incredible "Egyptian" eyes, brown in color with thick black liner around them. Her disposition was stubborn, but outgoing, which I liked. I knew from the moment I picked her she would be a challenge, which was probably the main reason I picked her in the first place. My personality thrived on challenges, and my dog wouldn't be an exception.

Doug and I talked about a few names. Quanti, which was short for Quantico, or Vahli, which was short for Valhalla. Quantico was the headquarters for the Marines Corps and the name would have been appropriate for a male dog. Valhalla just seemed to fit her perfectly. Valhalla was called the "hall of the slain" in Norse mythology. It was a majestic hall located in Asgard and ruled over by the god Odin. Half of those that died in combat traveled to Valhalla upon death, while the other half went to the goddess Freyja's field, Fólkvangr. In Valhalla, the dead joined the masses of those who died in combat, and they would all prepare to aid Odin in afterlife battles. The legend was fascinating, and by naming our dog after this place, we would be honoring all those that had gone before us in battle. Many marines would talk about Valhalla, and Douglas would often refer to me as his "Princess from Valhalla."

From the moment I took Valhalla, or Vahli (her nickname), home, she was trouble, but a good trouble. She challenged me at every angle. I enrolled her in obedience school, and the instructors warned me of her mischievous ways. The dog had a mind of her own and wasn't about to let another female control her. Doug would have to put her in her place when he returned from Iraq, but in the meantime, her place was by my side being just Vahli.

I was successful at potty training the wild beast, and my affection for her grew as each day passed. She was my baby girl, and I was solely responsible for her until Doug returned home. Taking care of Vahli, in some way, was beginning my journey toward motherhood. I was prepared to have three kids after compromising with Doug about the decision. Two would be plenty for me, but for some reason, Doug was stuck on three. The number three was important to him and the Marine Corps. They performed every task in groups of three: three companies, three platoons, etc. Doug believed three of anything was a good balance that harbored many successes and having three children would guarantee the same.

Having children wasn't our only topic of discussion as Doug wasn't one to take things lightly, and marriage was certainly not an exception. He discussed every avenue of our future together, and at times, it felt like he was interrogating me similarly to the way Robert De Niro questioned Ben Stiller in the movie *Meet the Fockers*. Another woman lacking in self-confidence and self-respect would never have been able to deal with Doug's ways. She probably wouldn't have lasted more than a week. I was certain his challenging demeanor was yet another test to see if I could "cut it" as a Marine Corps wife.

From the beginning, I was his number-one fan after I accepted the fact that I was in love with a marine. Falling in love with a marine meant the Marine Corps would always come first, and I would have to sacrifice many things. I was willing to sacrifice because being with Doug was worth the price. Yes, I would be second to the Marine Corps for another ten years, but it was an honor. Doug was a man who gave his all at everything. When he was fighting, he led from the front, and when he was with me, he treated me like a princess. Doug was the exception, a diamond in the rough, and he was going to be my husband.

I noticed his letters slowing down while e-mails picked up. The battles were going on daily, but Echo Company was out of the city of Fallujah and wasn't at high risk for being ambushed. I still waited patiently to get a special envelope, but nothing came for weeks. Finally, the end of June brought good news.

June 16, 2004,

My Dearest Pamela,

A long time ago, I misled myself into thinking I was in love with someone I had met. I was in a relationship with a woman who was untrustworthy and disloyal. Rather than understanding that my situation was not an uncommon and very real part of life, I allowed a small part of my heart to be shattered. I vowed never again to open my heart up like I had to her, that I would never be able to completely trust someone. I resented her for destroying that initial, pure, almost naïve feeling of bliss I thought I was experiencing because I thought I was in love. Then I met you, and I learned what true love means, what it truly means to want to dedicate your entire life to someone. Your beautiful spirit healed the wounds that I was unable to mend. You gave me a new lease on life, for without love, there can be no life. Because of your love and patience, I can now trust another human being and open up my heart. You created what I had allowed to be destroyed.

For the first time, I truly feel love, and the complete bliss and strength and hope for the future that accompanies it. Thank you! Pamela, I love you. I loved you the first moment I saw you. I just wouldn't admit it to myself. I am going to ask you to be my wife shortly upon my return from my current deployment, and I am going to dedicate my life to you. You and I are going to make our dreams come true. I will love you, protect you and appreciate you for the rest of my life. I love you more every day.

Love,

Doug

My heart melted with his words. "*I love you, I loved you from the first moment I saw you.*"

My intuition was right, and I was fortunate I listened to it. My pride would have never taken a man back into my life after three breakups, but I knew it was right. He was the one. I was told from an early age that when "the one" shows up in your life you will know. My dreams were telling me from the beginning of our relationship he was indeed the "it" I searched for my entire life. Being soul mates, our love would stand the test of time and distance, even with this deployment putting us through the ultimate test. I yearned for his touch, his voice and kiss because life was without life when Doug was gone.

June 24, 2004

My Dearest Pamela,

On the battlefield, I witnessed healthy, handsome young marines become mangled, writhing masses of pulp and blood. I have seen young men, who, minutes before, had strong, muscled legs that let them sprint like deer, legs that were splintered and shattered like matchsticks when mortar fragments pierced their bodies. A young warrior, a machine gunner, who, on the day before, stacked sandbags in a window in order to protect his comrades from enemy fire, was crippled by an enemy. Machine-gun bullets that spilled pints of his blood atop a rooftop he defended. I have seen enough bloodshed and shattered human beings to last a lifetime. Out of the darkness of this conflict, I have also seen moments of valor that will withstand eternity. Magnificent moments where young marines withstood a hailstorm of enemy machine gun, rocket-propelled grenade, grenade and small arms fire, and then smashed their enemies into retreat fill my memory. Young men risking their own lives to save their fellow warriors under intense enemy fire was not uncommon during our firefights in Fallujah. True, young men died, but they died fighting for what they loved, for their country, for their corps, for each other. Young Americans made the sacrifice for our freedom, for liberty, for our way of life. With men like the marines I serve with, America will be free and strong forever.

I did not just see valor and honor, I saw beauty. I saw the most beautiful sight I have ever seen. I saw you, Pam. Out of the darkness, I saw you shining like a ray of light straight from heaven! Combat has given me a new lease on life, and I have only grown more appreciative of your love. In my darkest hour, the memory of you gave me refuge, a vision of truth, of light, of love. I left for deployment knowing we will marry, but now, that fact shines more clearly than ever before, like a beacon for a ship lost at sea. I will get my men through this storm, to safety. I will hold you in my arms again, and forever. Pamela, you are the light of my life, the one ray of pure joy. I love you.

Love,

Doug

The summer moved by like murky waters of a swamp, slow and sticky, wet and hot. I kept busy trying to tame our wild beast, but wasn't successful. She was determined to give me her most stubborn attitude, and I would deal with it until Doug returned. He was able to call more frequently, and I was able to get my spirits lifted around once per week. During the calls, we discussed our wedding, the dog and his return. 2/1 was due back during the last week of September, and I was counting down the days.

In the meantime, work was getting complicated, and I was forced to seek employment with other companies. My wonderful biotech company was being bought out by a larger pharmaceutical firm. My manager was confident I would be kept on board, but I wasn't going to sit around and wait. I searched for jobs online and landed an interview with a company within two weeks. The timing was excellent because my parents were visiting and they could watch the dog for my interview in Atlanta.

The job market was good, and I was fortunate to get an offer on the position. However, the hiring manager put me in a quandary because they gave me a choice between Virginia Beach and Northern Virginia. I told them I would consider both and get back with them. I waited patiently for Doug to call so I could discuss the opportunity. Our next plan was to move north and live in Annapolis. With this opportunity, I could get moved to Northern Virginia with the company for the time being, and then move to Annapolis after Doug I were married. It was a perfect plan, but I wanted approval from him. He was going to be my husband, and I wasn't going to make this decision without him. I was being tested once again as I waited before making a life-altering move. Military wives were faced with these problems on a daily basis and sometimes waiting wasn't an option.

My mind continued to race until the phone rang with the strange number I knew would be Doug. He always seemed to call when I needed him. He told me to take the job in Northern Virginia. I was going to make the same choice, but it made me feel good when we both agreed, knowing I could make the right decisions without him, and he would agree. The military wife role was going to be a piece of cake! I forced myself into believing this, but deep down, I knew it never would be easy.

The move was happening so quickly my eyes were spinning. I would be in Northern Virginia before Labor Day weekend and off to training during the month of September. My new manager was well aware I would be in California to welcome Doug home. Steve was a true patriot and admired Douglas for his service to our country. Training would be completed the week before Doug's return. My only problem was marathon training. I was scheduled to run the Marine Corps Marathon with Doug, and it was quickly approaching. I wasn't training efficiently and thought about withdrawing. Between the dog, the move and the work training, I wasn't able to run. I tried my best to keep up with the schedule, but I was considerably behind.

The Rock 'n' Roll Half Marathon was during Labor Day weekend. My long runs were close to 6 miles, but I was supposed to be at 12 miles. How was I going to do this? I decided it wasn't an option to quit. Quitting wasn't in my nature. I would train as much as I could and run slow; that was my plan. I was going to run the Half and the Full, no matter what. Doug was counting on me, and I would never let him down.

July 26, 2004

Dearest Pamela,

I am the most fortunate man in the entire world to have found you. You know, we were destined to meet again, after our first meeting, as I would have gone to the ends of the earth to encounter you again! As many times as we broke up, we always returned to each other. I could not resist you! It was your patience with me and loyalty that allowed us to start over each time, ahead of where we were when we left off. I thank you, and I thank God for the second chance to make things right.

The pace of the battlefield slowed down since we left the city in early May, yet every day, it is a fight to keep my marines and myself alive and uninjured. Every day, our positions take mortar fire. Every couple of weeks, we'll be in a firefight. The insurgents are poor soldiers and most are poor shots, but you must respect the fact that they have the ability to kill and injure your marines. The battlefield is about free will, but there is an element of chance to it. No matter how well trained or decisive of a leader you are, your men or you may still get hit. It is a battlefield reality that my men and I have accepted and where we function magnificently, in my estimation.

On a daily basis, my marines throw the idea of self-preservation out the window and regularly risk their life and limb so that their comrades may survive. I have seen it on countless occasions. It is a magnificent sight, "For there is no greater love that this, than he who lays down his life for his brother." Pamela, I will gladly lay down my life, make the ultimate sacrifice, for our mission, for my marines, for the eternal principles of valor, integrity, fidelity, duty and honor and our country and for you. I will lay down my life for you, Pamela, and not just out of duty, but out of love, true love. Princess, I love you. Don't worry, my marines and I are coming home, alive and in one piece. I am just articulating my commitment to the men I am entrusted to lead, and my love and devotion to you.

Upon my return to the United States, I will turn over my command to a deserving marine captain, and I will focus my life on loving you. You are a gift from heaven. You are a selfless person who understands our freedom requires men willing to go into harm's way to fight and slay our enemies. You know that my decisions and actions literally affect the lives of the marines and sailors whom I lead. You know that I am not romanticizing or glamorizing when I write of this reality. I appreciate your maturity, patience and unselfishness, and you show me yet even more reasons why I love you. I love you, because, deep down, you are a principled person who I am fortunate to ride the river of life with and be able to challenge and reward. My love, combat makes me appreciate you even more than I already do. You are the reason why I am coming home, alive. Being so close to death (inches, and on many occasions, even closer) makes me appreciate life, life with you, even more. Thinking of you makes me want to live, live so hard and so well and be a good person and help others. I thank you for that, as you fuel my personal will to survive.

I get angry thinking about the enemy trying to take me away from you! I will not let that happen. I will fight to the moment my remaining marines return safely, and I am holding you, my little princess, in my arms. And hold you I will, strongly, gently, firmly and lovingly. For a mere mortal like me to love a goddess like you will be a gift from God, especially after being in the desert, literally and figuratively, for all these seven months. Babe, it is your being, your loyalty, faith, love and optimism that attracts me to you.

My love, thinking of you is a source of motivation for me to live, but it is also a tease. We have another two months to go before I see you. Sometimes, it seems like two centuries, but I will see you and love you again. I am dedicating my life to you shortly upon my return, my princess, and I look forward to riding the river of life with you! My dreams center around you, center around loving you and making you happy. We have so many options of what to do and where to live, but I want to buy a beautiful home for you in Annapolis while I work in D.C. How divine will it be to come home to you after working, to see your smile! My love, the thought of you makes my soul smile. "Life is about free will, but who you marry is divine intervention." Remember who said that? How true it is! Pamela, I love you with all my might and my spirit grows stronger every day because of you. I love you!

Doug

The following days brought my thoughts back to Doug's many letters of his promises. He promised he was going to marry me when he returned, he promised that he was coming home alive and he promised to dedicate his life to me. I waited so long to hear his words and finally I could be free with him in every emotion, on all levels. Every step I made was for our future and the future of our family.

I was asked to make a special trip to Bethesda, Maryland, and visit Doug's injured marines. I visited Bethesda once before with Doug before he left for California, and I remembered how humbled he was as he walked from room to room thanking all the marines for their service and bravery. I stayed back in his shadow; a little intimidated by my emotions. These men were heroes. I was honored being in their presence and simply didn't know what to say. Now I was taking this journey by myself. What was I going to see? What was I going to say? These men were heroes who stood by Doug's side and probably, in some way, saved his life. I would figure it out, and I guessed Doug did as well. All I knew was that I was honored my future husband trusted me enough to give me this task. I planned the visit to Bethesda on a Friday afternoon. That way, I was able to head straight to Baltimore afterward for the weekend.

I arrived around 2:00 P.M. wearing a nice skirt and jacket to pay my respects to the marines. The grounds at Bethesda were vast, and I followed the map to the appropriate building. The hospital entrance was surrounded with navy and Marine Corps flags placed next to the American flag, which made the information desk easy to locate. I was directed to the Marine Corps office, where I met with a lance corporal.

"Hello, ma'am, what can I do for you?" he asked.

"I would like to visit with three injured marines from 2/1," I answered.

He looked at his watch and said with a sigh, "I'm sorry, ma'am, but those marines have had so many visitors today. We are not permitted to let anyone else up to see them."

"I see. I guess I will come back on another day." I turned and walked out of the office but before I made it to the door, I stopped and thought to myself, *I'm not leaving here that easily. I need to tell the lance corporal who sent me and why.*

I walked back to the office with confidence. "I'm sorry for coming back, but I didn't make myself clear as to why I am here and who sent me. My fiancé, Captain Doug Zembiec, sent me here to visit his injured marines from Echo Company. He is still fighting in Iraq, and he sent me here to give his marines a message. Is there any way you can get one more visitor up to see them today?" I pleaded.

"Ma'am, let me see what I can do."

A few moments later, a major walked out to greet me.

"I'm sorry. We can definitely get you up to see Captain Zembiec's marines. I'm sure they would love to hear from their leader."

"Thanks."

I followed the major in the elevator, and he proceeded to take me to each room. One of Doug's marines was sleeping. He was seriously injured, and I was able to relay the message to his mom. He was a young man, around eighteen. His mom was extremely grateful, telling me to thank Doug for sending me on his behalf. I felt honored to be in this young man's presence.

I was able to speak briefly to the two other marines and noticed a spark in their eyes when I relayed their leader's message. These men were like Doug . . . believing in something bigger than themselves by making a difference in the fight against terrorism. I wasn't shocked by their wounds or sad when I left the hospital. Instead, I glowed with admiration and was extremely grateful we had warriors like these men to keep our nation free.

I walked back to my car and began my journey to Baltimore. When my phone rang, I already knew it was Doug calling from Iraq. He was aware of my visit to his marines on this day.

"Babe, did you get to see my marines?" His voice was full of excitement and anticipation.

"Honey, of course. I promised, and I made it. I spoke with two and relayed your message of positive affirmation and gratefulness. You should have seen their faces. They were glowing with pride. One of them was sleeping, and I spoke with his mom."

"Babe, you have no idea how grateful I am. I love you so much. I will tell all of my marines about your visit. They will be pumped up about it." He spoke with happiness.

"Honey, when are you coming home?" I asked.

"Soon, baby, soon. Before you know it," he answered.

CHAPTER 29

ARLINGTON, VA, WEDNESDAY, MAY 16, 2007

"I'm proud to be on this peaceful piece of property. I'm on sacred ground, and I'm in the best of company. I'm thankful for those things I've done. I can rest in peace. I'm one of the chosen ones. I made it to Arlington."
Trace Adkins

Exiting the chapel, I followed slowly behind Doug's casket, embracing my daughter as tight as she would let me while I buried my face in the small of her neck to feel her warmth and smell her sweet scent. As I moved my face away from her, I watched her stare blankly at the men in uniform struggling to carry the weight of the steel casket with the body of her father lying inside. Thank God she didn't understand what was going on! One day I would explain and keep her daddy's memory alive for her, but for now, a tiny part of me was happy that she didn't comprehend the magnitude of this loss. It was a hard blow to bear. For those that knew Doug, they would suffer for a very, very long time. I, being the wife, would suffer until my death. The thought of learning to live without him made me ache inside. It was like an incurable illness that was slowly debilitating me, bit by bit.

The entire family shuffled into the black limousines. I picked a spot next to the door and a window opening. My stomach was sick, and I felt as though I might vomit. But what would I vomit? I hadn't eaten anything for days. I was drinking water, but food was still not an option.

The limo slowly moved, following the hearse immediately in front of it. My

182

eyes began to close while we drove; it was my only out. I tried to shut the world away and imagine where Doug was. He wasn't in the hearse in front of us; he was in the afterlife looking down on us. I hoped he approved of the funeral and his eulogy. I was pleased with Kap's words and extremely proud how he presented my husband to the crowd. There must have been over one thousand people housed in the chapel. I remembered glancing around the church as I walked out and noticed every row was filled. Doug was being honored as a true American hero. I called him my hero constantly, and he was to humble to just say "thanks." He would always respond, "Babe, I have done nothing when compared to those that fought in World War II and Vietnam. Now, those marines and soldiers are the ones I want to be one day."

I would simply shake my head and say, "No, you are a true American hero already." He was, and now he died in the only way that would suit him. I was beginning to realize this, but I still wanted him back. I would always want him back.

As the limo entered the 50 freeway, I noticed a number of police officers on the highway. The police escorts to Arlington were many, but something was strange about the setup. I noticed they were blocking traffic from entering the freeway, and it was closed to oncoming traffic. The 50 freeway was closed. There were hundreds of cars following us to Arlington, Virginia. Doug would certainly be impressed. My vision was blocked from the tinted windows on the limo, but I could see past the windshield, and I was in disbelief. My husband was being followed by hundreds of cars. It looked like a funeral procession fit for a king!

We drove slowly to Arlington National Cemetery and arrived well before the scheduled burial time. As we entered the cemetery, I noticed thousands of white tombstones throughout the yards. I had been there before, but never thought I would be back to bury my husband. I always thought I would be the one to die first. He was stronger physically than I, and longevity ran in his family. My family was genetically healthy as well, but not like the Zembiec genes. I was okay with dying first. In fact, I wanted to die first because I knew how difficult it would be to live without Doug. Maybe that was selfish thinking, but Doug and I discussed everything, and he agreed with me. He always assured me he would come home alive and unharmed. Maybe he was trying to convince himself.

I was forced to leave my family and discuss the burial with the manager of Arlington National Cemetery. He escorted me to a separate room and talked about the specifications of Doug's tombstone. It was cryptic the way the illustration appeared to me. His name would be plastered on a white tombstone with his birth date, death date and military honors. The tombstone looked like something from my worst nightmare. Did I dream about this before? I was having a déjà vu experience.

"Mrs. Zembiec, are you okay?" the manager asked.

"Yes, I'm just not up to this right now," I said.

"I understand. We don't have to pick out everything right now. We're going to wait on finishing the stone until after The Silver Star Ceremony. I will escort you to the family room for some privacy. Are you okay with inviting Doug's parents?" he asked.

I immediately took offense. "Of course, I love them like my own parents. Why wouldn't I want them with me? Doug was their son!"

He looked at me with heartfelt eyes and said, "Mrs. Zembiec, I'm sorry. You see, some of the wives don't get along with their in-laws, and I have to ask that question. I will make sure they come upstairs with you."

"Thank you," I replied. I followed him to a separate room where I met with Doug's parents, Kap, the colonel and a number of other officials. We all sat around a round conference table and blankly stared into space.

The silence was uncomfortable, and the air in the room became stale. I reclined my chair backward to help with a growing discomfort that began to take over my body. I was preparing myself for the worst part of this day; burying my husband. We sat, and we waited. The time was ticking by slowly, and it felt as though time had stopped until the manager opened the door.

"We are ready to begin."

I walked out the front entrance and noticed the hearse waiting. Behind the hearse stood, what seemed like, an entire battalion of marines. They were dressed in their finest and in perfect alignment. The hearse began to move, and the marines began to march in unison following the vehicle. I could hear the sounds of their footsteps as they walked together flawlessly. Our choice was to walk as well and follow the marines to pay tribute to our fallen hero.

I sauntered along the hot black streets that separated each section in Arlington National Cemetery, and my pace could barely keep up with the hearse and the marines. Kap held my hand for support because I was struggling to keep my stoic façade. The sun was sweltering, but there was a slight warm breeze flowing through my hair, and I could smell fresh honeysuckle and lilac. It was like being in the botanical gardens. I hoped Doug could smell these scents. He was always the one who recognized the fragrance of a particular flower. I attributed this quality to him being born in Hawaii and having a master gardener for a mother. Doug loved flowers and always brought them to me. He began bringing me flowers on a weekly basis when we were dating, and he never stopped; even after we were married. Oh my God! How was I ever going to recover from this when NO ONE could ever take his place—no one.

The walk became relentless, but I wanted to feel everything about this day. My feet were aching, and I could feel the rise of blisters rubbing against the sides of my black heels. The blisters were already busted and the flesh of my second layer of skin was being rubbed. I didn't say a word because feeling physical pain was a sign I was actually alive. I would never wince in pain or let anyone know something was wrong with me. My mental state was so frail that my physical side was obsolete. "Keep your shoulders back and your arms at your side. Keep your head up high. You are the wife of a marine." I kept saying these words to myself over and over again as I walked through the streets of Arlington.

Where was Section 60? I noticed the marines moved well ahead of our group, and I pushed harder and harder, but my energy was wearing thin. Finally, Section 60 appeared within my view, and I felt like a runner trying to make it over the finish line after covering 26.2 miles.

The hearse came to a stop, and the marines positioned themselves to remove the casket. We walked up slowly behind them, and then they proceeded. I could see the casket inside the hearse, and it made me shiver, even with sweat falling down my back from the May heat. The strongest marines lifted Doug's coffin out into the open air. They slowly positioned themselves around the casket in ceremonial unison and began to march along the dirt road that led to Douglas's final resting place.

Once there, they placed the casket on a steel-rimmed surface that held it firmly in place. As I walked behind the marines, I imagined Doug's coffin being lowered into the ground, six feet under. He would never be seen in this life again after the dirt of Arlington National Cemetery was placed over his body. It was difficult not to think about what his body would look like in a day, a week or a year. Memories of my worst horror movie came to mind, and I tried to focus my attention on something else. Anything else was better than thinking about my husband's flawless body turning into ashes.

The realization that his body wasn't made of steel hit me like a ton of bricks. I wondered about the terrorist who killed my husband. I had nothing but hatred

185

in my heart for that person. Did he have any idea who he destroyed? I was told he was killed, but it didn't matter. Killing one or one million Al-Qaeda would never serve justice for the death of my husband. His loss was too great.

The Marine Corps hymn began to play in the background. I heard the hymn on a number of occasions, but it was being instrumented differently today. The tone was soft and without error, and the band played while the marines slowly lifted the American flag from the casket. There were six of them dressed in their finest. I watched them trace the seams of the flag with their white-gloved hands, and they handled the flag as though it were a newborn baby. Every move and every gesture was implemented with complete care and grace. These guys took pride in paying respect to their fallen comrade. I was seated in the front row within two feet of Doug's body, and I could see everything clearly. My eyes were wide open because I wanted to make sure this wasn't a terrible dream. I had seen this picture many times before, but was it *really* Doug being honored today for paying the ultimate sacrifice?

Chaplain Radetski began to speak to the crowds. "Today, I brought something with me from Camp Pendleton. It is a rock. A rock that Major Zembiec, Major Mendoza and I took from the top of the mountain at Camp Pendleton when we carried a huge cross to the top of this mountain to honor all those that had gone before us. I wanted to learn more about the history of the Marine Corps, and Doug gave me the history as we carried the cross up the steepest mountain at Camp Horno.

"This rock represents David from David and Goliath. Remember the David who conquered the huge giant? Yes, that is the David I am talking about. It was one stone that brought him down . . . one shot. The stone had an F on it. The F stands for faith. All of you are going to enter into a daily battle. A daily battle without Doug, a battle of integrity. The prayer that I am going to say today is not going to come out of my mouth. I am going to ask you to live that prayer, emulating the core values in everything you say and do. David became a king after slaying the giant, and Major Zembiec is with the King, by his side.

"Doug taught me many things. One thing was to overcome fear. There is an acronym for it . . . You can forget everything and run, or you can face everything and recover. It is your choice, and it depends on what beats in your heart . . ."

As I listened to the chaplain, I remembered him and how he touched our lives. I knew him very well because he served with Douglas and his battalion during the battle for Fallujah in 2004. Doug worshipped side by side with his company and the chaplain when they lost their fellow marines in battle. Doug had immense respect for Chaplain Radetski and asked him to marry us. He was the cofacilitator at our wedding, and he was a wonderful man. I couldn't ask for a better person to say farewell to Douglas. It took me one second to make the choice; there was never a second thought.

The chaplain finished his words, and then there was silence. The marines holding the American flag over the casket were frozen. Anyone looking at them might think they were statues. There were seven marines aligned beyond the casket carrying rifles. I could hear the movement of their guns as the commander gave orders to fire. Their guns fired three times, totaling twenty-one casings. Then, in the distance, the bugle began to play. The bugle played its farewell song to Major Douglas Alexander Zembiec, "Taps." Every military person in the fields of Arlington stood saluting their good-byes, while every civilian held their hand directly over their hearts. I placed my hand over my heart and felt a beat that was dull and listless. It was the beat from half a heart; the other half was in the grave with Doug.

Suddenly, the statuesque marines began to move. They began to fold the flag ever so carefully. The marines moved with finesse as the ends creased perfectly together in alignment creating the ceremonial triangle. The triangle only revealed the blue background with white stars. I waited patiently for my flag as the assigned major walked over and placed it in my arms. I grasped it tightly, hoping I could feel some part of my husband. The major was saying something to me, but I couldn't comprehend a word; I wanted to caress the flag and somehow find Doug somewhere beneath the folds. I sat there clutching Doug's American flag and was oblivious to everything and everyone around me. I heard the manager of Arlington announce the end of the ceremony. He asked everyone to give the family "private time."

My family and I sat there for a few moments of silence. As everyone got up to leave, I ran forward and collapsed over the casket. I began to cry uncontrollably as I grasped the hard steel structure, trying, once again, to feel some part of my husband. But he wasn't there. He was gone.

CHAPTER 30

CAMP PENDLETON, CA, 2004

"If you wait for me, then I'll come for you. Although I've traveled far . . . I'll always hold a place for you in my heart. Remembering your touch, your kiss, your warm embrace. I'll find my way back to you, if you'll be waiting . . ."
Tracy Chapman

It was over. Seven months of waiting for him had finally come to an end. I was overwhelmed with joy and the anticipation of being with him. The wait was so difficult; I couldn't bear another second from seeing his soothing face. Doug was coming home from a land of terror and violence in one piece like I always knew he would.

My flight across the United States was daunting and uneventful, and I tried hard to sleep on the flight, but it was hopeless. My anxiety levels were at maximum force. I felt like I could run 100 miles, but I was stuck in a tiny commercial airline seat for 5 painful hours. All I could do was imagine what our homecoming would be like. My body yearned for him like a desert yearns for rain. I missed everything about Doug, and finally, for the first time in my life, I was completely in love with someone. I thought I had loved before, but it was never like the love I had for Doug. We were already one without being married, but we would soon make it official.

My plans for his homecoming revolved around a five-star hotel room in Dana Pointe overlooking the Pacific Ocean. We drove past the hotel before his deployment, and Doug made a suggestion about how nice it would be to stay there when he returned. The hotel had exquisite rooms overlooking the peaceful ocean and was known for breathtaking views of Pacific sunsets. I was hoping to stay sequestered in our room for three days, with only room service knocking on our door. After reading Doug's letters, I was sure he wanted the same.

I arrived in Long Beach, California, on schedule and had forgotten how beautiful the weather was in Southern California. Blue skies hovered within the comfortable temperature of 70 degrees without an ounce of humidity. No wonder the state was crowded. I would have loved to live in the weather, but not with the people. Doug and I both agreed upon settling on the East Coast. The weather wasn't as nice, but we would enjoy the seasons and raise our children around a society not fixated by appearance and material objects. Doug would always say, "It's not about what you have, it is about who you are. And if you are a good person who works hard, then good things will come to you." People in California seemed superficial and consumed with material possessions. Of course, we didn't want our children raised in that type of environment.

Driving on the I-5 was miserable with road rage and bumper-to-bumper traffic. I could hardly wait to get to our hotel, shower and wait patiently for my phone call. Karen Mendoza was going to call me when the battalion had made its way back to Camp Horno. Camp Horno was a camp within Camp Pendleton where 2/1 was stationed. I had visited the area with Doug on prior occasions and was familiar with the directions. Karen was going to call me so I would have plenty of time to drive from Dana Pointe and be waiting for Doug. I wasn't a wife and therefore wasn't privy to direct phone calls from the Marine Corps. In six months, I would be a wife and would never be neglected again.

I arrived at the hotel around six in the evening and began preparing for Doug's arrival. I couldn't believe he was finally coming home. My mind was full of anticipation and nervousness. I bought flowers, champagne and wine for our room. The room service menu was filled with delicious food items that would satisfy Doug. He loved mozzarella and tomatoes, and I made sure it would be available for him. Doug savored many types of food, but I knew he would be happy with just about anything after eating MREs for seven months. I made sure our room had a beautiful view of the Pacific Ocean, and I opened the blinds on the windows to view the sunset. It was perfect. As the sun began to set, I could see the purple, pink and orange haze along the Pacific shore from our window. Everything was in place, and I began to relax on the bed as I waited for Karen's call.

At nine o'clock P.M., Karen finally called. "Pam, sorry, but the plane was delayed. 2/1 is scheduled to be back at Horno around one in the morning."

"That's fine, Karen. I waited seven months, I can wait another 4 hours. I might take a nap," I responded.

"Good idea. You should head over to Horno around two and I'll call you when the guys are ready to march on," she suggested.

The march on would be exciting as each company would individually "march on" the field to greet the welcoming crowds. The marines would be in formation wearing their cammies, and then their commander would dismiss them to see their relatives. I thanked Karen, hung up the phone, turned out the light and tried to sleep. After all, I was 3 hours ahead and needed my energy for what was about to come.

Ring, ring, ring.

What was that noise! I was trying to sleep! I opened my eyes and realized that the horrible noise was my wake-up call. It was one in the morning. Holy shit! I had slept nearly 3 hours, and it felt like 10 minutes. I must have been exhausted because I never sleep when I'm excited. This was going to be the happiest day in my life. My love was on his way.

I hurriedly got out of bed and freshened up in the bathroom. What was I going to wear? I would make it simple. A sexy sweater with nice jeans would be perfect for the cool temperature outside, and I would let my hair flow down the length of my back. I barely trimmed it while Doug was away, and it was well below my bra strap. He would notice the length and any changes to my appearance. He wasn't the normal man; Doug paid attention to every detail and every inch of my body. He always complimented me and placed me high on top a pedestal. This man always made me feel good. Tonight, I couldn't wait to let him know how much I loved and missed him.

I arrived at the gate of Camp Pendleton and waited to get word from Karen. Around 2:15 A.M., she called to let me know 2/1 would be ready to march on in 30 minutes. I started the engine and drove through the hilly dark streets. Camp Pendleton was vast. I remembered driving on I-5 from Laguna Niguel to San Diego and the camp's length scanned almost the entire distance. Doug made a comment about how much the real estate would be worth if the United States ever decided to "give up" some of the land.

From most places within Pendleton, one could see views of the Pacific Ocean. There would be many places for oceanfront homes. However, this would probably never happen because our country couldn't do without the protection on the West Coast. The Marine Corps had its bases on both the East and West coasts which were both vital to the security of our nation.

Within the boundaries of the gates at Pendleton, the main road to the separate camp for each battalion was undulating, and I was very careful not to speed on the road. I just wanted to get to Horno. I could feel Doug's presence so close to me. We had a strong spiritual connection. I missed his physical touch, but I always felt him close within my heart. I was sure we would make it through anything together because of this spiritual relationship. We were soul mates, and everyone around us could sense it as well.

On many different social events, random people would come and ask us how long we had been married. Doug would grin at me and say, "We're not married yet."

They would respond, "Well, you guys make such a handsome couple, I would have thought you had been married for years. You just look like you belong together."

I loved when people would make such comments because it only reinforced our awareness of our special bond. It felt "right" being with Doug, and I needed him next to me physically once again.

The night air was cool and rainy, which was extremely odd for Southern California. The nights were cool, but it never rained there. I didn't even think to bring an umbrella, and I could only imagine what my hair and clothes would look like when Doug marched on the field. I tried to find a close parking spot as I entered Camp Horno, but was unsuccessful. There were many cars aligned on the street and in the parking spots. I was overwhelmed at the amount of family members who showed up to welcome their heroes home. It made my heart soft because there were others that cared as much as Doug and I cared. We lived in the best country in the entire world, partly because our soldiers and marines defended the freedom on which this country was based.

I finally found a parking space, and I pulled in carefully to avoid a collision. It was difficult getting out of the car because being by myself made me nervous, and it looked as if I was the only one by myself. After all, I was only a girlfriend and was treated completely different from the rest of the women who were wives. I didn't have anyone to walk with over to the field because the only person I knew well enough was Karen, and she was at home with her two children.

Slowly, I proceeded to the field and held my head up high. I would be a wife soon and would never feel this way again. As I walked, my anxiety diminished and I focused all of my energy on Doug. The rain was slowing into a fine mist, and I found an area that was close to the front where I could sit and wait. The battalion had chairs and refreshments set up for family members and an onlooker would've never thought it was almost three in the morning. The marines set up spotlights and were playing music to welcome their comrades back to the United States of America.

I was sure it felt good for the marines returning home to place their boots upon American soil. I began to take it all in because I wanted to tell our kids the story about when their daddy returned home from Iraq from his first tour. Doug had already been named "The Lion of Fallujah" in the *LA Times*. The *LA Times* wrote a special piece about Doug and Echo Company. The piece was called the "Unapologetic Warrior," and I was going to have it framed as a gift for him and his parents.

I was beginning to feel comfortable in my surroundings, and then I noticed a couple familiar faces. I looked to my left and saw some of the wives from Echo Company. I remembered their faces from the Marine Corps Ball in November of 2003. Doug and I attended the ball, and he introduced me to his lieutenants and their wives. I remembered one wife in particular.. How could I forget her and her husband? When Doug introduced me to this particular Lieutenant, I immediately had a sinking feeling. I could tell he felt uneasy around Doug. It was almost like he was scared or intimidated. Doug had a commanding presence but never disrespected anyone. Doug and I exchanged brief words with the two and moved on. I made a comment about the Lieutenant as he walked away from us.

"Honey, what is up with that guy? He seems like bad news to me. There is something about him that just doesn't seem right."

Doug whispered in my ear, "Babe, you nailed it on the head. He's the Marine that called in sick the other day. I have never in my entire career had a marine call in sick when under my command. He never owns up to his mistakes and has a difficult time following my orders. However, I can help him. I will make him stronger, and he will do fine."

I was sympathetic when I answered, "Honey, I know that most people do get better by being around you, but you can't fix everybody. He seems weak to me. What marine calls in sick? I hope you can help him."

I wasn't about to walk over and talk to her. Her husband was responsible for killing two marines by not following orders. They were killed by friendly fire because of his stupidity and arrogance. I had a bad feeling about that guy and was sad when I found out I was right. It killed me when I read Doug's letter about the tragedy because my man was hurting inside at the needless loss of his two marines. Doug loved his marines like his own family. How could she hang out with the rest of the wives knowing that her husband made this detrimental error? Or did she even know? Mistakes do occur in war, but not like this one. He ordered a mortar attack on his own men. It was out of complete stupidity, and it made me sick inside. I wasn't supposed to know what happened, but I did, and I was glad because I would never talk to that woman again. I avoided all the wives because of her and stayed in my own area waiting for Doug. Besides, I didn't want to disturb their huddle. They all looked extremely comfortable with one another, and I didn't feel like it was appropriate to walk over and introduce myself again. I felt abandoned by the wives of Echo Company during this deployment. I knew it was Marine Corps policy that only wives were privy to knowledge about the battalion, but I wish someone would've included me into the group somewhere. After all, Doug and I were getting married in April.

I waited and waited for what seemed like an eternity. Finally, I watched Weapons Company march on. Fox Company followed Weapons, and then Golf Company. Where the hell was Echo Company? The clock was ticking and ticking. I finally asked another marine, and he informed me they would be out within 15 minutes. At least I knew when.

The spotlights began to shine brightly as the indicator for Echo Company's march on. I stood up and moved to the front of the crowd. I could hear their boots hitting the concrete pavement. The marines were dressed in desert cammies with wide brimmed hats upon their heads. The lights were shining brightly upon Echo Company as the mist from the sky settled upon the ground. The mist seemed like fog blocking my vision. I had to refocus my sight as I stared urgently into the group to try to find Doug.

I noticed Ben Wagner and Ed Solis. Where was Doug? The marching continued as I continued my search for Doug . . . and then I finally saw him. The sight of him brought tears of joy to my eyes. He moved his arms and legs in unison with Echo Company, and I could see his side profile. He cammies were hanging loosely on his emaciated body. The outline of the back of his skull underneath his wide-brimmed hat was skin and bones. He had lost a great deal of weight; at least 20 pounds.

The marines stopped marching and came to a halt. Doug announced, "Marines, dismissed." Before Doug could finish saying his last syllable, I took off running to him. I ran through the crowds, and he saw me. He came barreling forward, and I jumped into his arms and kissed him over and over again. It felt like heaven being in his arms again, and we embraced each other like we were holding on for dear life. I wanted to run away with him to our room instantly, but we couldn't. He began introducing me to all his marines, and I was honored to meet the men who helped keep him alive the past seven months.

The car ride from Camp Pendleton to Dana Pointe wasn't what I expected. Doug wasn't himself, and I knew he needed my listening ear. Yes, we were holding hands and kissing passionately along the way, but something was bothering him. He was deep in thought about his experiences in Fallujah, even with me sitting by his side. I gently asked, "Honey, I know you just got home, but something is troubling you. Do you need to talk to me about it?"

He answered, "Babe, I'm sorry. It's not you. I just need some time to get readjusted. It feels so good to be with you and back on American soil. There are so many things I need to tell you about what happened over there. We can talk in the privacy of our room."

He leaned over and kissed me. I couldn't wait to get to the hotel to snuggle with him to feel his body and wipe away all of the tensions that were bottled up inside of him.

Driving up the road to the hotel, I could sense his worries were diminishing. He tried to focus his energy on us; at least for now. His gestures and facial expressions slowly turned back to the romantic Douglas. Even the color of his eyes was changing to the soft deep brown I recognized when we were together.

Doug's passion came through in his eyes. His eyes changed when his mood changed. Anger, excitement and tenacity changed his eyes to a dark, glowing brown. With romance, passion and calmness his eyes were soft and deep. I saw every change in his eyes, and it was a direct indicator of which mood I was getting ready to experience.

As I parked the car, I noticed I was about to embrace my romantic Doug. We hurriedly jumped out of the car, and I dragged him by the hand to the entranceway. We were trying to run to our room, but there were many people around us and everyone wanted to chat about his experiences in Iraq. I whispered in his ear, "Honey, can we just get to our room? I want you all to myself."

He whispered back, "I agree. Let's just get there."

Finally, we reached the door of our room and entered into our own little universe. We locked the door and began to discover each other once again. Our love had only intensified over the last seven months. It was a love that would last forever.

CHAPTER 31

ANNAPOLIS, MD, FRIDAY, MAY 18, 2007

"There is no way out, only a way forward."
Michael Hollings

Two days had passed since Doug was placed in the ground at Arlington, and I was barely surviving. I sat in misery and tried to focus on my daughter, but part of me had died with Doug. I didn't know what was coming next. My friends were still hanging around the house and tried desperately to help me move forward. I didn't want to move forward, I wanted to go back in time to warn Douglas. If only I could go back in time and tell him to stay with us and not go back to Iraq, but it was too late for "what-ifs." My life was over as I knew it.

What was I going to do next? My daughter was going to be my life, and my job would be second. Marathon training would be third. I could use the marathon training to help numb the pain of my loss. The training would be a good distraction, and maybe it would help deaden the anguish inside of me.

I decided to put on my running shoes and start on this day, May 18, 2007. I would begin the journey to finishing 26.2 miles in under 5 hours. My goal would beat my last time significantly, but I could do it. I kept reminding myself of what Doug used to say to help keep me focused. "Mind over matter. Marathon running is both physical and mental. Anything over 22 miles is purely mental." I was determined, and this run would honor my husband and the sacrifices he made for his country.

Kap was on his way over to help me "jump-start" my training. I was standing outside on Circle Drive as he drove up to me. He rolled down his window and showed me a copy of the *Washington Post*. There I was, plastered on the front cover as the mourning widow in what many Americans thought to be a needless war. My immediate reaction to the paper was anger. "I hate it, Kap. Why am I on the front cover? Why isn't there a picture of Doug as the war hero? He should be honored! Not my grief, for Christ's sake!" I screamed.

"Pam, I'm sure the *Washington Post* wasn't thinking about it that way. They probably wanted the people to know how upset you are at losing your husband."

I looked at the photo again. I appeared to be in complete misery as I clutched the flag of my dead husband. I looked as though I was searching for a piece of him somewhere within the folds. The photographer had captured my feelings perfectly and nothing had changed since then. I was still miserable and didn't know how to get away from it. Would I ever be happy again?

The run was difficult on my body. Kap and I traveled out of my neighborhood through the curvy roads and onto the 450 freeway which led to the Naval Academy Bridge. The view of the Naval Academy was spectacular as we descended down the hill onto the bridge. The grounds of the Naval Academy bordered the beautiful Chesapeake Bay, and the sun was shining brightly on the waters that mirrored the many buildings within the gates. It was a sacred place that housed many special memories for Douglas. I could think of nothing else but him as I ascended the steep incline of the bridge. When I finally made it to the top of the hill, I glanced over the side and stared into the waters. I thought, for a brief second, how much easier it would be to jump over the side and be with my husband. I would wash away the pain that was consuming was body, mind and soul. Instead, I shook my head and erased the thought of giving up. I would never leave my daughter alone in this world. Doug married me for many reasons, but most important, he trusted that I could raise our children if something ever happened to him. I would never let him down. My mind traced back to a letter he wrote to me for Mother's Day last year.

Dearest Pamela,

None of the Hallmark cards could possibly equal the letter I am writing to you. Besides, none of the Hallmark cards depicted two genuine 0331 marine machine gunners sighting in on the enemy so that mothers in America could enjoy this righteous occasion.

Sweetheart, I love you. I wrote you this letter and enclosed it in a special envelope because it is the same kind of envelope I sent you letters in when I fought in Iraq with the marines. It reminded me of you, of how the rare thought I allowed myself to think of you made me so warm inside. I remember how I looked at your picture before we attacked into Fallujah, so that I could see one truly beautiful sight before I crossed the line of departure. Pam, I came home for you. I knew you would make a great mother to my children soon after we met, and time has proven my assertion. You love Fallyn as only a mother could, and your love makes her grow strong! I look forward to raising our children from the little falcon chicks and lion cubs they are into women and men of character, into loving mothers and fierce warriors.

Pamela, thousands of years ago, in Greece, the birthplace of democracy, two million Persians (Persia stood where modern-day Iraq and Iran stand, so you can figure out what kind of people they were, of what kind of culture they had and how little they valued freedom) invaded Greece. Three hundred Spartans, the fiercest warriors known to man before the United States Marine Corps was created, were called upon to delay the Persians to allow the rest of Greece to evacuate the cities and prepare their defense. Though the 300 chosen knew they were a sacrifice, none backed away from their duty. In fact, they welcomed the opportunity to immortalize their comrades and themselves by their valor. And immortalize themselves they did. Historians estimate the 300 Spartans and 700 of their Greek allies killed upward of 15,000 Persians, and the rest of Greece successfully evacuated their cities and formed an alliance against the Persians.

Why do I tell you this? Most of the Spartan warriors had wives and children they left behind. How did they feel about their husbands going off to war? How did they feel, knowing they might not come back? Steven Pressfield writes of this in his book Gates of Fire, as one of the wives of the fallen Spartans is addressed by King Leonidas, the Spartan leader. "The city speculates and guesses as to why I elected those I did to the three hundred . . . I chose them not for their own valor, lady, but for that of their women . . . Greece now stands upon her most perilous hour. When the battle is over, when the three hundred have gone down to death, then all of Greece will look to the Spartans to see how they bear it. But who, lady, who will the Spartans look to? To you. To you and the other wives and mothers, sisters and daughters of the fallen. If they behold your hearts riven and broken with grief, they, too, will break. And Greece will break with them. But if you bear up, dry-eyed, not alone enduring your loss but seizing it with contempt for its agony and embracing it as the honor that it is in truth, then Sparta will stand and all Hellas will stand behind her! Why have I nominated you, lady, to bear up beneath this most terrible of trials . . . BECAUSE YOU CAN!"

Pamela, despite my sometimes frustration and impatience, I know, ultimately, that with or without me, you can raise our children into the type of citizens and warriors upon whose shoulders our great nation was built. I tell you this not as preparation for the possibility of me not coming home from my next deployment. I tell you this as the highest compliment I can give you. I love you.

Doug

That was it. I would stand high and make him proud. I would run this marathon to help get me through my anguish and grief. My tears would be nonexistent in public, and I would be the Spartan wife and mother that my husband described in his letter from one year ago. Doug would look down on me from Valhalla, and he would be proud because I would never let him down. I loved him too much. I kept running harder and harder, and I was beginning to feel better. Yes, training for a marathon would work. The more I pushed myself, the better I felt. Endorphins were flowing through my body like the vital blood that flowed through my veins. It was working like an antidepressant. For now, I would run to keep my sanity. Even though my life had turned for the worse, I felt like I had at least one goal that would keep me moving in a positive direction.

We finished the 6.6-mile run, and my body felt like I had been running for years. It didn't bother me at all. Over the past week, my body had been severely neglected. I hadn't eaten much, and I wasn't well hydrated. It was a blessing I made it over 6 miles in my physical condition. Grief was fueling my body throughout the run and would have to continue to do so for the next six months. I knew that would be the way. I would hold my grief tight during my normal day-to-day life and would let it loose when I ran. My plan was brilliant, and it would work. When I walked in my front door, I already felt like my grief was standing along Circle Drive. It would wait for me until I ran out the front door for my run the following day.

As dusk fell upon the waters of the Severn River, I sat at the Annapolis Yacht Club with many friends overlooking the beautiful sunset. I was among the company of good people, but I was alone without my husband. Everyone

199

was trying desperately to get my mind off of the loss of Doug, but nothing was working. Even being at one of the most beautiful places in Annapolis wasn't going to work because I had been there before with Doug. The place left another reminder of a time when my life was happy and full, but I kept my cool as the stoic Spartan wife, and my interactions with everyone were nothing but a show. I was becoming good at being an actress, and it became increasingly simple to hide my pain behind other people's conversations and lives. The wine was also going down easily; it was like water going down on a hot sweaty day. My thirst couldn't be satiated, and I lost track of how many glasses I had emptied.

The night continued to go on as the entire group agreed on traveling to the Severn Inn by boat. The Severn Inn was located at the base of the Naval Academy Bridge. It was a bright yellow building with huge bay windows that overlooked the Severn River and the Naval Academy. Doug and I frequented the restaurant for brunch on many occasions and even had Fallyn's christening party there. We loved the Severn Inn, and I was excited at the prospect of cruising in a beautiful yacht that would take us there. My senses were deadened from too much wine as I climbed on board the million-dollar boat. It was gorgeous, and the night was perfect for boating. A calming breeze fell over the river, and I could see the image of the boat as we passed by the lighted dock.

As we cruised, everyone began telling "Doug" stories, and I positioned myself on the side of boat and listened. Kap told the story of our ski trip, and I laughed for the sake of laughing. My mind became fixated on the overhanging wood bars that decorated the interior of the boat. The fixtures were located within five inches above my head and were perfect for hanging. I thought to myself, *I wonder if I could do a pull-up off that bar.* I didn't even think about it. I got up and instinctively grabbed the wood fixture and tried to pull my body upward. As my body lifted, the wood bar snapped and broke into three pieces on the floor of the boat. I looked down at the pieces and wondered why I tried to do something so stupid. How could wood support my body weight? The bar was a decorative piece without support. Of course it was going to break.

Everyone began to laugh, and Kap looked over at me and said, "I think Doug told you to do that. That right there was definitely a Zemmie move."

I began apologizing. I couldn't believe I had done such a stupid thing. "I am so sorry about the boat. I think Kap's right. I never do pull-ups. Why the hell would I try a pull-up on the frame of a million-dollar boat? Doug was working through me to get us all to laugh. I think."

When the boat docked at the Severn Inn, my body began to tremble as my mind became flooded with memories of Doug. Tom Ripley suggested we sit in the bar area because it was the only place Doug and I didn't sit together. I tried to relax and place myself in my stoic position, but I couldn't. I was too intoxicated and couldn't control my emotions. My body gave out, and I began to sob. It started slowly, and then I lost complete control.

My friends called a cab and took me home immediately. I could barely walk to the front door and as soon as I entered my house, I stumbled into the walk-in closet of my bedroom. The closet had everything I needed, and I grabbed all of Doug's worn shirts and placed them over my nose. I buried my face inside of his lumberjack shirt, and I could smell his scent. I looked around and discovered the flag from his coffin. I grabbed the flag, collapsed onto my bed and pressed the flag tightly to my chest. I screamed aloud for anyone to hear my anguish and sorrow. I didn't care anymore.

"Please, Doug, just let me see you in my dreams. You promised me you would never die, but you lied! I need to see one more time. One last time."

CHAPTER 32

ALEXANDRIA, VA, 2004

"There is only one success, to spend your life in your own way."
Christopher Morley

My five days with Douglas in Southern California flew by as we spent countless hours in complete bliss catching up on lost time. He shared many exciting stories about his battles in Iraq and the great victories he and his marines had won against the insurgency. Doug also spoke of the sadness that went along with losing his comrades.

It was difficult to admit to myself, but Doug was a changed man. Something inside of him was different. He was deeply saddened by the loss of his marines, as he loved them like he loved his own family. Doug was also angered by the actions of his commanders. He was a man who respected authority, and he had lost esteem for his leaders during the battle for Fallujah. His memories of Iraq would never go away, and I prayed for time to heal Doug's wounds. Whatever the reason for Doug's change, I was certain of one thing. My love for him was larger than life, and I was more than willing to help ease his pain in any way I could.

Coming home to Northern Virginia was a difficult journey, but I knew Doug would be coming back east in just one short week to spend an entire month with me. He wanted one week to travel home to New Mexico and visit with his family. I was willing to sacrifice one week for his parents. He needed to visit with them and talk with his father about the time he spent in Iraq. Doug and his dad were a great pair. They were tied at the hip whenever they were together, and I admired their friendship. Doug always seemed more at ease after he spent time with his dad. He was like a tame lion after meeting his prey.

I returned to work and was able to share my excitement with all of my teammates. Our wedding was six months away, and Doug and I had many tasks to complete before April 30. The first duty that had to be completed was the formal engagement. I had planned an exciting venue for our wedding. We were getting married at the Naval Academy Chapel, and our reception would be held at the Kent Manor Inn. I even planned a theme wedding that honored our nation. Our tables would be named after states that were special to us in some way. The head table would be named after our nation's capital, and we were having a martini bar with cocktails that would be named after a state theme.

I spent hours working on making our wedding the "perfect" party for our closest friends and family, but Doug hadn't officially proposed. I was disappointed when he didn't pop the question during my visit to California, but I understood he had just returned from seven months in Iraq. Where would he have gotten the time to buy a ring? He knew I didn't care about the ring and only wanted him. Doug always had numerous surprises up his sleeve, and getting engaged would probably be another one. He was coming back east soon, and I was certain he would propose then, but how and when were the big questions.

As I drove through the passenger pickup area at Reagan National Airport, I noticed Doug immediately. He was hard to miss: tall, dark and handsome with his Carhartt jacket and khaki pants. His face was smiling ear to ear, and I could sense his happiness from fifty feet away. Doug's presence filled you up with joy and excitement no matter how you truly felt inside. He had the power to lift a god up to another level and make him feel as though he was the only being who existed in the heavens. I never doubted why his marines loved and respected him above everyone else and were willing to follow him in battle. I was elated to finally have him in my arms again . . . but once again, disappointed about my proposal. It was difficult for me to concentrate on enjoying our time together because I was always second-guessing about whether this day would be *the* day.

We spent numerous dinners with friends and family and still nothing. Soon we would be running the Marine Corps Marathon, and I imagined he would propose at the finish line. Every event left my mind wondering as to when the engagement would occur. This began to spoil my time with Doug. He knew me well, almost too well, and my distraction was starting to alarm him. I couldn't tell him why I was so preoccupied because I was certain it would disappoint him. He gave me his word through voice and paper he was going to make me his wife when he returned from Iraq. A sudden doubt or question from me about this would only hurt and anger him.

I decided I would let it slide and move forward with our time together. A couple of weeks passed, and we enjoyed spending time planning the wedding and taking care of our first child, Vahli Zembiec. Vahli was enough to make anyone reconsider having children. Her energy levels were higher than Doug's and mine put together, and the only way she was ever satisfied was after a three-mile run with Doug. He would pace around a 6.5-minute mile, and Vahli kept right up with him. They were a team, and she was in love with Doug from the moment they met. We were one big happy family. The three of us ate together, ran together, and on occasion, slept together. Doug put his foot down when he woke up coughing from the yellow dog hairs that had managed to enter his nostrils while sleeping. And that was the end of our threesome in the bedroom.

Vahli B, as we called her because of her busybody nature, was forbidden on the bed. I was saddened and elated at the same time, but Doug was in charge of her, and I followed along with his wishes because deep down, I knew he was right. He was right the majority of the time, but I only agreed after I thoroughly thought through the process. This maddened and challenged Douglas, but he always respected and warranted my opinion.

The Marine Corps Marathon was upon us before I could blink an eye, and I was petrified. The idea of running 26.2 miles sent chills down my spine. The distance scared me, but the fact I hadn't trained nearly enough made it even worse. Doug convinced me I would be fine and told me again. "Babe, you're gonna make it. Anything past 22 miles is purely mental. Besides, I'll be there to support you in the cause."

Two weeks before the race, Doug and I finished a 12-mile run together, which was going to be my last run before the big race. It was my fault after all. I never ran a marathon and certainly didn't know how to train for one while Doug was in Iraq. I had moved from Virginia Beach to Northern Virginia and started a new job. In between those things, I also bought and tried, unsuccessfully, to train Vahli B, and was planning our wedding. No, I wasn't busy at all, but I lived by my own credo, "keep as many plates spinning as possible until one falls and breaks." For me, that was usually around five different life events at all times. I was, however, able to finish the Rock 'n' Roll Half Marathon, but I was sure that wouldn't be enough.

A week before the marathon, I kept my workouts to a minimum, ate a clean diet and kept my body well hydrated. Doug was supportive in my efforts, and he abstained from wine and beer as we both just hung out and loved each other. The impact of the marathon kept my engagement thoughts to a minimum, so we got along beautifully.

On Friday night, two days before the marathon, Doug scheduled a nice dinner with Mike and LuAnn. Mike was Doug's lt. commander at Camp Lejeune when Doug was a 2nd Force Recon platoon commander. I had met Mike and LuAnn on other occasions and loved spending time with them. We had many similar interests. Both Mike and Doug 2nd Force Recon Marines, LuAnn and I both worked in the medical industry, and all of us wanted to own our own companies one day. But most important, all of us loved wine. We loved nice red wine. Red wine we tasted during our winery trips, and red wine we swirled in our Riedel wine bowl glasses before it entered your mouth and made your taste buds dream.

Doug and I purposely saved our 1995 bottle of Opus One to share with Mike and LuAnn upon his safe return from Iraq. I swore to myself I would have one glass of wine during our dinner so I could taste our coveted bottle of Opus. Doug wasn't going to swear the same because he could drink much more than I without ever getting a hangover. I was extremely jealous of this quality. He had also run and finished many other marathons at a fast pace and wasn't concerned with running this one with me. I think he was looking at this marathon like taking a leisurely stroll through the monuments of Washington, D.C. The race would be something similar to sightseeing, but in his running shorts and bare chest.

We opened the bottle of Opus, and I had my first glass. The taste filled my mind with thoughts of oak and cherry as it slithered down my throat. The effect of the first few tastes was amazing as there were few things that surpassed your first glass of a nice bottle of wine. We drank wine, and our conversations went from work to home to the wedding to Iraq and one bottle led to two bottles, and my one glass was a memory from far, far away. Finally, after two bottles of wine, we gathered our things and went to Ruth's Chris.

Ruth's Chris was an incredible steak house located in Crystal City, Northern Virginia. It was known for fine steaks and amazing wines. Ruth's Chris was the perfect restaurant for Mike and LuAnn, and they were well-known in this particular establishment. They knew the manager and the majority of the wait staff. Every aspect of our meal was impeccable. Doug and I were completely spoiled by the company, food and service, and time was racing by like the speed of light.

It was difficult for me to remember just how many glasses of wine I consumed, but I felt very good. I was in a state of euphoria because of my friends, my future husband and my uncountable glasses of red wine. Before I could stop the process of drinking, it was too late and I wasn't about to spoil the fun for everyone else. For once in my life, I let go and forgot about my responsibilities. It felt lovely. I was living for the moment and not thinking about the eminent future. I was free, and I didn't want the night to end.

Little to my credit, the night was just beginning as Mike and LuAnn suggested we go to Freddie's pub in Crystal City. I wasn't familiar with Freddie's, but LuAnn helped me picture the place on our drive. "Pam, it's so much fun because no one cares about what anyone else is thinking. Guys don't hit on you because the majority of them are gay. Freddie's is a gay bar, and tonight is karaoke night. It will be a blast."

When we arrived at the entrance, I was completely at ease, and so was Doug. He whispered in my ear, "Babe, I think it will be fun, but make sure you don't leave my side for too long."

I said, "But of course, my love. If I were a gay guy, I would totally hit on you."

We both laughed in unison and walked in together hand in hand.

The bar was brightly lit. There was a nice young man singing a Celine Dion song as we found our way to a few empty stools at the bar. The walls were painted a bright green color, and every corner of the bar was colored in an array of bright pastels. Neon pinks, blues and yellows were everywhere. It reminded me of a place from South Beach, Florida, as white twinkling lights entwined a white wood frame that encased the top of the bar. There was a special place for all the bar glasses in this frame.

LuAnn and I took our seats as Mike and Doug ordered some more drinks. I didn't need anything else, but somehow a Red Bull and vodka found its way in front of my chair. As I drank my new drink, the guilt started to set in, and I began to think about my upcoming doom. Doug could see my hesitation and came over to help me.

He said, "Babeeeeee, you are going to be fine! You can sleep in tomorrow. Drink lots of water and you will make it! Besides, you already finished the Half and what's another Half? They say, if you can run 13.1, you can run 26.2."

I said, "Okay, honey, I trust you since you've done this before. I'll have some fun with you tonight, and I should be fine by Sunday."

As much as I wanted to believe what was coming out of my mouth, I knew it was going to hurt on Sunday. It didn't take a rocket scientist to know a person running a marathon in less than 48 hours should not be drinking alcohol in the amounts that were filtering through my veins and liver. However, it was too late, and I decided just to have fun for now and deal with the consequences later.

At that moment, Doug came rushing over with his vibrant, excited brown eyes and said, "Babe, you are going to sing karaoke with me. We're going to sing Madonna's 'Vogue.'"

I said, "What! Are you out of your mind?"

He answered, "Hell, no! You are going to be great. You know all of the words and have her hair, so why not? Come on, babe, you only live once."

I said, "Honey, do you realize we are running a marathon in less than 48 hours?"

Doug said, "Of course I do. But we can do it, and we will never forget this night. That's for sure."

I reluctantly answered, "Okay, ask the guy, and you better come on stage with me . . . or else!"

Doug left for a few minutes to find the karaoke guy, and I filled LuAnn and Mike in on what Doug had up his sleeve. They were all for it. I guess brilliant minds think alike as Mike began to laugh uncontrollably at the prospect of seeing Doug and me prance around on stage at Freddie's, pretending to be Madonna. Doug ran over to the bar and exclaimed, "Babe, get ready, you're on next!"

I was relaxed due to the alcohol in my system, but I was still nervous. Doug was doing it again: pushing me out of my comfort zone. At that moment, I heard the announcer say, "All right, let's give a warm welcome to Pam who will be singing Madonna's 'Vogue' without the words on the screen."

I looked at Doug angrily and mouthed the words, "What???"

Not only was I going to humiliate myself by singing, I was going to further embarrass myself by not seeing the words. Thanks, Doug Zembiec. I marched on the stage, grabbed his arm and said, "You're coming on stage with me!"

He said, "Of course, I am. I'm your backup dancer and singer."

I looked at him, and he had a bright pink feather boa wrapped around his neck. He looked like one of Madonna's backup dancers in the video. He was a sight for sore eyes, and I couldn't help but get excited at the thought of the upcoming music. This was going to be fun.

The music began . . . *"What are you looking at? Strike a pose . . . strike a pose . . . Vogue . . . vogue, vogue . . . vogue, vogue . . . look around, everywhere you turn is heartache, it's everywhere you go . . . I know a place where you can get away. It's called the dance floor and this is what it's for . . ."*

As I sang, Doug danced. He was receiving lots of claps and roars from the crowd of beautiful gay men surrounding the stage. He began to wrap the boa around my neck and body, and I couldn't control my laughter in the microphone. I tried to sing, *"Beauty's where you find it. Beauty's where you find it . . . Greta Garbo, and Monroe, Dietrich and DiMaggio. Marlon Brando, Jimmy Dean on the cover of a magazine. Grace Kelly, Harlow, Jean, picture of a beauty queen. Gene Kelly, Fred Astaire . . . Ginger Rogers, dance on air. They had style, they had grace, Rita Hayworth gave good face. Lauren, Katherine, Lana too Bette Davis, we love you. Ladies with an attitude, fellows that were in the mood. Don't just stand there, let's get to it. Strike a pose. There's nothing to it . . . VOGUE!"*

The room was spinning as I opened my eyes to the bright sun pushing its way through the blinds in my bedroom. My head was aching. It felt like my brain was trying to escape the recesses of my skull, to get away from the many drinks that had made their way through the blood-brain barrier. It was awful. I felt awful. *Someone save me,* I thought to myself. I wandered my hand aimlessly to my right to see if Doug was next to me. I felt the soft hairs of his left forearm and was relieved. I wondered if he felt like I did. I slowly moved closer so I could place my head in the safe barriers of his strong chest. Maybe the touch of his body would help me.

He leaned closer into me and asked, "How do you feel?"

I opened my mouth to speak, but realized the pain in my head had reached my lips and answered, "Like ass . . . complete total ass."

Doug slowly stroked my head and said, "I'll go get you some water and Gatorade."

I could barely answer. "Thanks, honey. How long do I have before we go to pick up our numbers?"

Doug answered, "Three hours."

I spent every last second in my bed until I was forced to get up and shower. Why did I do this to myself, knowing I was going to put my body through one of the most difficult, if not *the* most difficult, challenge ever? *Stupid idiot,* I thought to myself.

I slowly lifted my head from the soft recesses of my pillow, and I felt as though someone were using my head for a drum. "The pounding is relentless. Honey, please stop it!" I cried.

Doug answered in disappointment. "Babe, you better run the marathon. You gave me your word, and that means you can't back out. Now, get up and shower, and I'll grab you some Motrin."

I said wearily, "Okay. I'm running the marathon, but that's not until tomorrow. I'll be fine by then."

I maneuvered my body into the shower only after stumbling over several empty bottles of water and Gatorade. The cool and refreshing water from the showerhead hit my body with a vengeance. My body felt like it was getting washed for the first time in my life. I stood still and allowed the water to clear my senses and wash away the poisonous substances that were seeping out of my pores. I told myself, "I will be okay tomorrow. I'm gonna do it, and I will finish."

CHAPTER 33

ANNAPOLIS, MD, SATURDAY, MAY 19, 2007

"Every night in my dreams, I see you, I feel you. That is how I know you go on . . . near, far, wherever you are . . . I believe that the heart does go on . . ."
James Horner

I walked out my front door that morning. The air was clean, but a beautiful fog surrounded the black concrete pavement and lush green ivy that traced through my yard. The steep incline of my driveway was extremely difficult to climb this morning, and once I reached the top of the hill, I noticed Douglas standing in the distance with his back turned away from me. He was wearing his blue workout pants that glided down his long slender legs like a flowing stream. His lumberjack shirt was hanging loosely on his body, and he stood in the middle of Circle Drive, very still. I could sense something was wrong.

Standing next to me was his friend Ken, and I looked at Ken and asked, "Does Doug know he is dead?"

Ken answered, "No, but I'm going to tell him now."

Ken walked over to Doug and placed his arm around his back as they strolled around the circle ever so slowly. I noticed a halt in their pace, and Douglas quickly turned around in his quick fashion. I could see his shirt was open, and his beautiful barreling chest was exposed. His face was very sullen, and his left eye was covered with a beige bandage. I could only see his right eye. He walked over to me and grabbed my arms ever so gently. As I stared into his right lifeless eye, my mind knew what was happening. He was saying good-bye. I looked into his serene face and said, "I just want to be with you."

He responded, "Not now, but in time. But you need to know something. Amy is pregnant, and she is going to be worried about Ken getting killed in Iraq. You need to tell her that he's going to be okay."

I opened my eyes, and at first, I didn't know where I was. *Damn!* I thought to myself. I'm in my room, alone, and my dream was just a dream. What did Doug mean by "Not now, but in time"? How much time would it take? I waited my entire life for him, and now I would have to wait again. The anger and pain rose in the pit of my stomach, and I punched the flag that was wrapped in my arms. This damn flag was all I had left of him until when? I yelled, "Our lives are over as we knew it because you went and got shot. I hate you right now!"

Doug was dead. He was six feet under the ground. His body was cold and lifeless, lying in the casket carefully placed under Section 60. I stared at the perfectly folded American flag. It was in the shape of a triangle, only allowing the eye to see the blue background with white stars. I blinked my eyes heavily and tried to hold back the hot tears burning my eyes. I was back to reality and knew exactly where I was and what had happened. Yes, my friends thought drinking would help sooth my pain, but it only deepened the wound and allowed me to express my true self. I was miserable and nothing was going to help.

Soon, the alcohol was long gone from my veins and I was once again back to stoicism. I would move through life like a robot and get on with it. What else was I to do? I rose from my bed and immediately began packing for our trip to Albuquerque. At least I could run away for a long week and hide from all the media and uproar. I was beginning to realize just how important Doug's service was to our country. He was in every paper from the *Washington Post* to the *Baltimore Sun* and was all over the Internet. I needed to be away from my home for a little while to get some alone time. Fallyn loved visiting Albuquerque, and I wanted a nice place to feel closer to Doug.

The flight to Albuquerque was a unique experience, considering all four adults were in a dreadful state. Doug's parents, brother, Fallyn and myself were treated like celebrities as we boarded our first-class seats on American Airlines. We were all dressed nicely with our purple heart and American flag pins plastered closely to our hearts. We were still in disbelief. Fallyn was sleeping in my arms, and I cradled her with every ounce of love I could give. She needed everything right now. I looked at her soft and angelic face as she slept. She was so innocent and at peace. I wished I could crawl beside her and enter into her mind for just one moment. To be able to experience her peace would give me some hope. I tried to smile as I focused my gaze on her, but I felt as though my face might crack. In fact, I had forgotten how to smile. The moment I heard the words, "Doug was killed in action last night . . ." made me forever forget the happiness which was once mine.

When our plane landed in New Mexico, we were informed by the flight attendant a police escort would be close by to take us to our baggage. Walking through the Albuquerque airport, I stared blankly at all the reminders of my previous trips here with Doug. I noticed the deli where I bought a latte and a banana on our last trip and the McDonald's where Doug got his three filet of fish sandwiches and his Cookies and Cream McFlurry. I wondered if these memories would ever stop and how I could live with remembering every single piece of our lives together.

My mind and body were exhausted by all the memories flooding me like water rushing through the newly opened gates of a dam. By the time we exited baggage claim, I could barely move. I looked forward through the gates and noticed a large number of uniformed police officers waiting to escort us to our vehicles. As we exited the entrance of the passenger pickup area, my eyes were blinded by exploding red and blue lights. Countless police vehicles were in position and ready to escort our cars straight to the top of Sandia Heights. This was the place where Douglas grew up and became a man; the memories there would shake every bone in my body.

I took my seat next to FJ and placed my head on her sleeping shoulder. I couldn't bear to look around. All I wanted was to fall fast asleep on my husband's chest.

CHAPTER 34

ARLINGTON, VA, 2004

"Running a marathon is one of the hardest things you will ever do physically in life. Anything beyond 22 miles is purely mental."
D. A. Zembiec

"BEEP, BEEP, BEEP."

What was that sound? Oh my God, it was Doug's alarm going off so soon. I felt as though I had just climbed into bed. I opened my eyes and looked at the clock. It was 5:30 A.M.

"Okay, babe, get up and let's get moving! Time to run the Marine Corps Marathon! I'm so excited," Doug exclaimed.

How the hell could he be so chipper this early in the morning? That was Doug for you. He was excited about life and never let anything get in his way. Every day, every hour, every minute and every second of his life was treated like the most important adventure. He lived life that way, and I was prepared to live mine in the same fashion. It was good Karma, and he was good Karma.

I felt much better than yesterday, but, boy, oh boy, I wasn't up to running 26.2 miles! I lazily removed my body from our warm and comfortable bed and tried so desperately to make myself want to run this race. I knew how important it was to me to do this. That was before I decided to get completely wasted less than 48 hours ago.

"Can I do this?" I asked myself. Before I could answer, Doug came barreling in the bathroom door with water, body glide and a bagel.

"You look great this morning. You look like you are going to run a marathon!"

213

"Thanks, baby," I simply replied. I was going to run this race for me, for my man and for our country. Many lives had been given in keeping our nation at the top of the world, and I was going to place myself in the most sacred marathon in our country: the Marine Corps Marathon.

The subway was filled with thousands of runners. The excitement flowed through the narrow passageways down to the dark recesses of the train station. We all waited there at the stop that would take us to the Rosslyn exit. I could hear the screeching brakes of the train in the distance, and my stomach began to fill with the anticipation of getting on board. I was going to get on this train, and I was going to run this race.

Doug's face was smiling. His eyes were deep brown, and his pupils glittered like black pearls. He was filled with pride as he stared into my fear-filled eyes, and I knew he could feel my apprehension. He looked at me with inspiration and said, "Honey, you are going to make it! Don't worry, I will stay with you the entire race. I will feed you power gels, and I will make sure you drink water. I will take care of you because you are going to be the mother of my children." Those words took much of the anxiety away, and I knew in my heart I wanted to make it . . . but still wasn't convinced even with his complete devotion to my cause.

The train flew by us with a burst of cold wind that sent shivers down my spine. As it came to a halt, the doors briskly opened and the crowds hurried into the small entryways that barely fit the loads of runners. Doug pushed us through just in time as the closing door lightly touched the edge of his red shorts. We were on our way to the race. The two of us stood in each other's arms as we held the cold steel pole for support. I nestled my head in his chest, closed my eyes and prayed to God.

The train stopped at Rosslyn in what seemed like a few seconds. The doors opened briskly, and Doug jumped out, grabbed my hand and headed up the escalator. We walked briskly to the start of the race at Arlington National Cemetery. Doug thought it was an unusual start as the race usually began and ended at the Iwo Jima Monument. Whatever the reason, we were starting at the sacred burial place of our nation's warriors. Doug was proud and glowing as we strolled past the pristine white headstones that went on for miles and miles. How many had gone before us? The answer to that question would remain a mystery in my mind. The headstones were glorious and sad at the same time. I focused my mind on the reason for being here and the reasons why we live our lives: for a bigger cause. I realized the price of the cause when Doug was gone from me for seven straight months. I questioned myself about how many others knew what price these men and women had paid and would pay for our nation's freedom. Some Americans would never understand, but I was proud to know and proud to be running this marathon with my marine who was part of the bigger plan.

Doug held on to my hand with the intensity only two lovers knew. He hurried me through the crowds of runners to place us in our starting spot. My goal was to finish in 5 hours, which would be around an 11-minute mile. I was shooting for the stars, considering I had only run 13 miles before this event. We placed ourselves behind the 11-minute mile pacer, and I stood there taking in all the other runners. I wondered if they felt like I. My stomach was sick. I could feel my entire breakfast begin to slowly resurface from the depths of my intestinal cavity, back up through my esophagus, soaked with hydrochloric acid.

The whistle blew and the race began, but my group wasn't moving. Doug looked at me and could sense my bewilderment.

"Babe, we're not moving because there are thousands of others that must go through the gates before us."

I didn't say anything. I just stood there wanting to move and wanting to get this journey started.

The crowd before me moved ever so slowly. They looked like a row of dominos beginning to slowly creep forward with a means to an end. Suddenly, Doug and I began to move. At first, it was a walk, and then a shuffle, and then a slow jog. My slow jog remained stagnant for a couple of miles, and then it hit me. The adrenaline began to fill my veins. I could no longer contain myself and had to find a path away from the crowds. In and around, back and forth, I traveled until I could move without hitting someone with my elbows. The adrenaline was in full swing as the announcer's voice was in the distant past with the loud music pumping from behind. The music was fading, but I was running, and it felt great! How could this be? My body was poisoned, but now I was going to make it!

Doug and I ran through Georgetown, past the Lincoln Memorial and through the streets of downtown Washington, D.C. It was a glorious day. We ran the marathon in honor of the Marine Corps as we viewed the capitol of our nation that the Marine Corps defended. I was filled with vigor and pride because the man next to me was a national hero, and I was going to be his wife.

Doug was an excellent coach as he fed me every 45 minutes with power gels and made sure I was drinking plenty of fluids. He was also my biggest cheerleader when I started to slow down. At one point, I heard the crowd yell, "Go Pam!" I wondered how they knew my name and then I heard them say, "And go Pam's helper!" I turned around and there was Doug, smiling ear to ear, holding a large sign with my name on it.

The miles began to wear on my body as we approached Hains Point. Hains Point is a 3.2-mile stretch of flat road that sits along the Potomac River. Doug warned me about Hains Point and told me that this place was the "wake-up call" in the marathon. As I entered this long 3.2 mile stretch, I understood why. It was very quiet and peaceful, which was not what I needed at this point in the marathon. I was headed into mile 17, and I needed the support of the crowd. Where were the people cheering?

Doug was behind me, but I was beginning to get sick of him. He was on his cell phone talking to all of his friends as he strolled behind me with zero signs of fatigue and pain. I couldn't see an ounce of sweat on his body. How could this be? Doug wasn't normal. He was superhuman, and it was beginning to bother me. I was struggling to make my next move, and he was laughing on his cell phone. My legs felt like logs, and I could barely shuffle.

Then it happened. My calves froze in midstride. The pain moved up my leg like a hot needle being inserted in my muscle. It was mile 17. What was I going to do? I had to stop because the pain was unbearable. Doug grabbed my arm and sat me curbside. He placed an ice bag on my calves and comforted me the best way he could. My eyes said it all. I was filled with rage and disappointment. It was my fault, and I overestimated my mental ability. How could I possibly think about finishing a marathon without training for it?

Doug knew I was enraged and tried to calm me. I was waiting for him to tell me it was my own fault for not being prepared, and I was ready to scream at him. Instead, he looked at me with his deep dark brown eyes and said, "Babe, you can quit if you want, but you've already gone 17 miles. You only have 9 more left."

At first, I didn't say a word. I wanted to think about it. Could I make it 9 more miles? Somehow I could do it, but it would be a mental test. My body was finished, but I knew my mind could take me there. He was right. I had already gone 17 miles. There was no way I was going home without my finisher's medal. I was going to make it and didn't care if it took me the rest of the day and night.

Slowly I moved each leg, the right, then the left, and I suddenly realized I could do this. I was going to finish this thing. The running turned into a quick walk as I tried to ignore the paralyzing pain jolting up the back of my Achilles tendon, into the lining of the soleus muscle and finally ripping the belly of my gastrocnemius muscle. I ignored the pain and kept going.

I finished Hains Point and moved onto the 395 freeway, and I could hear Doug in the background talking on his cell phone. How could someone not be affected by running over 20 miles? I could hear what he was saying on the phone and wished I hadn't.

"Kap, man, you don't want to be back here with the slow group. It's like a battlefield. People passed out on the ground. Ambulances taking them away and the bus, dude, the bus is right behind us picking up all the people who aren't going to make it over the bridge."

I turned around and yelled, "What bus? What do you mean they are picking up the people that aren't going to make it over the bridge? What's going on? I'M NOT GETTING ON THAT BUS!"

Doug quickly got off the phone. "Babe, you have to be over the bridge by two o'clock or the bus will have to pick you up."

I looked at my watch. It was 1:45. "I'm getting over that bridge." I picked up my pace and once again ignored all the old pains in my body and pretended like new ones weren't starting. "Give me more Tylenol." I took the pain pills and kept going.

At approximately 2:45 P.M. I walked over the finish line of the 2004 Marine Corps Marathon. The race took me 6 hours and 23 minutes, but I finished and went home with my finisher's medal. That night, Doug answered every doorbell for every trick-or-treater as I lay on the couch with ice covering my body. He made several phone calls to all of his family and friends and was gleaming with pride for the woman he loved, and I was happy for him.

CHAPTER 35

ALBUQUERQUE, NM, MAY 20, 2007

*"The best thing about dreams is that fleeting moment, when
you are between asleep and awake, when you don't know the
difference between reality and fantasy, when, for just that one
moment, you feel with your entire soul that the dream is reality,
and it really happened."*
Anonymous

He held my hand, and we were drifting on the Milky Way. I could see the
most vivid, bright stars as we flew briskly through the air. The wind was
whipping through my hair as a cool breeze moved along my flowing gown. I
could see the outline of his strong jawline and the deep brown of his eyes as we
sailed together on the most exhilarating ride I had ever been on. It was like being
on a roller coaster, but without the fear or butterflies of going down the steep
descent. I was safe with him and was home. It was Doug, and he was smiling at
me and I asked, "What is it like here?"

Doug replied, "Everyone is just hanging out not doing much of anything."
Then he showed me our dog Vahli, and she was bleeding. I could see the stitches
on her belly where she had just been spayed.

Fallyn was asleep in her pack and play next to my bed as I awoke from another
dream about her father. I felt so close to him in the dreams, but they were torture.
Waking up to the reality of my new life wasn't good. I was in Albuquerque in
his parents' home and sleeping in the bed where we slept together during visits.
I wasn't going to be able to run away from my life.

I remained in bed thinking about my dream until Fallyn woke up. Her eyes were beaming when she saw me next to her. The innocence and beauty of her look tore me away from my fleeting thoughts for just a split second. She stood against the edge of the soft canvas cage motioning with her arms for me to pick her up. "Mommy," she said. My heart filled with joy every time I heard her call me mommy. Yes, I was finally a mother, but not in my happy home.

My dream from the night before kept me alive for the day. The dream made me feel as though Doug was still with me. I could feel his presence, but maybe it was because I was in the house where he grew up, sleeping in his bed and looking at his pictures. I wasn't sure of the reason, but when the phone rang, the news from the other end brought back a premonition from the night before.

"I have to take Vahli back to the hospital," my friend sadly said. "She is bleeding from her stitches, and I can't seem to make it stop." For a moment I couldn't breathe. I knew it. I knew that if anyone could transcend into my dreams, it would be Doug. He was trying to help me, even in his death.

Could he still communicate with me even from the grave? I wasn't sure of the answer, but my dreams seemed so real. I had to find out more about the afterlife. Where was Doug? What is he doing? Is there life after death? All these questions swirled through my mind like the clouds cascading over the planet Jupiter. I would have to get to the bottom of this, and the only way would be through reading about the afterlife. I was raised as a strict Catholic and always believed in God and heaven. Doug, on the other hand, was the skeptic. He certainly believed in a Higher Power, but never lived his life on the principles of the Catholic religion. He did believe in something bigger than himself and lived his life doing the right thing every day. Doug was the most morally righteous man I had ever met in my life, but was never baptized in any religion. He made me question the teachings of the Catholic faith, but in a way that made me a better person. Therefore, I knew Doug was somewhere with his Higher Power. I wasn't sure where that place was, but I was going to research and read so I could find this place and feel closer to him in any way I could.

CHAPTER 36

ANNAPOLIS, MD, NOVEMBER 7, 2004

"Love is like an eternal flame, once it is lit, it will continue to burn for all time."
Kamila

Here we were. It was already the last day before Doug's departure back to Laguna Niguel. He was scheduled to return back to his duty at 2/1 and transfer his company over to Captain Ray Mendoza. I wasn't thrilled to be away from Doug for another month, but this was our situation, and I knew it would be over in just five short months. However, I thought for sure I would have my "official" proposal and ring before he left.

"Today we are going to Annapolis. I want to look around the area for a waterfront house we are going to buy after we get married." Doug stated these words as though we had a million dollars to purchase a house. He was living on a captain's pay, and even with both of our salaries combined and the basic housing allowance, we couldn't afford a waterfront home in Annapolis. I kept this thought to myself because Doug would have some type of answer like "if you think it and say it out loud it will be so." Instead, I just looked at him with a smile and said, "Okay."

"And afterward, I want to stop by the colonel's house and have a good talk with him about leadership and get some pointers for my next position in the Marine Corps."

Colonel Ripley was Doug's mentor and was infamous for his gallantry and leadership abilities. Most of all, Colonel Ripley was the most humble man I had ever met, and I loved being in the company of him and his wife Molene.

November 7th was a beautiful sunny day, but the temperature was only around 35 degrees and windy. We drove around areas such as South River, Winchester on the Severn and Chesapeake Beach. Doug was on a mission to find the house of his dreams. As we approached potential homes for sale, I would jump out and grab the flyers on each one. Every home listing was well out of our price range, but he kept at the search.

"Babe, mark my words, after we get married, we will find a waterfront home in Annapolis. I'm not going to settle for anything less," Doug retorted with utter confidence. Once again, I just sat there and agreed with him. I knew my thoughts would be considered negative thinking, and my future husband firmly believed in the "power of positive thinking."

Finally, Doug had had his fill of viewing many overpriced waterfront homes, and we decided to take a drive along the Naval Academy grounds. Once inside the yard, we parked and took a leisurely stroll heading toward the sailing center.

"Honey, you seem uptight about the waterfront house thing," Doug said.

I answered, "I am. I don't want to get into something over our heads. You will be busy traveling back and forth to D.C. the majority of the next three years if you get the job you want, and I will be in charge of everything. I can see me now—new house, new job, new marriage and new baby. Sounds like fun, right?"

Doug replied, "Why do you think I chose you? You are strong. If I didn't think you could handle being a Marine Corps wife, I wouldn't be marrying you." He always had a way to make things better, no matter what the situation.

We continued our stroll along the grounds and decided to take a break by the docking area. The view of the Severn was tremendous as the wind whipped briskly upon the water, causing whitecaps to rise and fall. It was a beautiful sunny day, but it was extremely chilly for early November. Next to the pier was a photographer taking photos of a beautiful young girl. She was in her early teens, and it was fun watching her pose amid the beautiful views of the Academy and the Severn.

Doug and I decided to sit on a small marble bench where we cuddled each other tightly. He kept me warm with just his smile sometimes, but this day, I needed the warmth of his jacket and body. We sat there in silence and took in the enormous views that followed your eye whichever way it decided to go. From the front, I gazed at the blue November sky with white sails held firmly in place by the strong winds whipping. On my right was the beautiful young model, and on my left, my handsome soon-to-be husband.

"Honey, do you remember the time when we jumped into the Chesapeake Bay during the middle of January. We did the polar plunge, remember?" Doug asked.

"Honey, of course I remember. My body was pink for 2 hours. Why do you ask?" I answered.

"Well, I thought since we were in Annapolis, it would be fun to do it again. But this time it can be here at the Naval Academy."

I looked at him with big scared eyes. He retorted, "Come on, babe, it will be fun. We can jump in the water, and then climb back out. I will be with you the entire time, and you will be just fine. Let's live life to the fullest. Come on, honey, let's do it!"

I exclaimed, "Absolutely not!! You are crazy, Doug Zembiec." As I cried out all the reasons why I wasn't going to jump in the Severn River with him, I knew somehow, and in some way, he was going to get me in that water. I was terrified beyond belief. The temperature outside was only 35 degrees, and I couldn't imagine what the water would feel like. Besides, the whitecaps on the waves would be enough to scare even the smartest swimmer away.

Doug was relentless and unwilling to take my no for an answer. "Honey, I promise you if you jump in the water with me, it will be very good for you and me both."

What did he mean by that? How could jumping into freezing cold water with all of our clothes on be good for both of us? He was beginning to approach me, and I knew I had to come up with something quickly.

"Okay," I said. "I will take my boots off and put my feet in the water with you."

"Okay," he said. The model and photographer around us were beginning to get a bit anxious at my screams, and I could tell Doug was going to make a quick move before they called security.

As soon as my boots hit the surface, Doug's large frame came toward me. His words came with his steps. "Pamela, will you walk through the fire of life with me? Will you be the mother of my three children?"

Before I could answer, he picked me up, and we both went barreling into the Severn River. We hit the water with a huge splash, and I lost Doug's grip on my body. My heart was pounding with both adrenaline and fear as I started to sink in the cold waters of the Severn. My sweater and jeans were weighing my body down, and I struggled to swim to the top. Doug reached down and grabbed me and pulled me to the surface. We were both gasping for air as the waves bobbed our bodies up and down. I felt as though I was stuck inside of a whirlpool being sucked up and down through the continuous motion of the treacherous waters.

At that moment, he finally spoke the words I longed to hear. "Pamela, will you be my wife?"

I didn't know whether to kiss him or hit him. Who asks someone to marry them like this? I slightly hesitated to answer the question. For just a moment, the tumultuous waters seemed to stand still for both of us, and I finally answered, "Of course I will."

In an instant Doug said with excitement, "Wait, I have a ring. Which hand does it go on?"

"The left one!" I yelled while trying to stay afloat. Only Doug would ask that question and only Doug would risk possibly dropping my ring, the one I waited for for four years, in the deep waters of the Severn.

As he struggled to put the ring on my left hand, I noticed the Naval Academy security surrounded the area. There were boaters throwing life preservers and police lights on the surrounding shore. Doug hurriedly helped me climb up the side of the dock where rough barnacles scraped through my jeans. I could feel them cut the skin on my legs like a sharp razor cut that continues to bleed.

A large crowd had gathered around the commotion. The photographer taking pictures of the model had decided our pictures were much more important. Doug approached the crowd and simply said, "Everything's okay, we just got engaged."

The crowd clapped and said congratulations, the police officers retreated and the boaters moved away. I stood there not sure whether to laugh or cry. My clothes were dripping and weighing me down. Doug grabbed my hand and swept me away from all the commotion. We walked briskly over to the colonel's home to share the news with him and his lovely wife.

As we walked through the Academy grounds soaking wet with drippings of the Severn River, I didn't care who saw me or what they thought. All I knew was I was going to be Mrs. Douglas A. Zembiec, which was all I ever needed, and everything I had ever wanted.

CHAPTER 37

ANNAPOLIS, MD, SUMMER OF 2007

"I believe that imagination is stronger than knowledge, that myth is more potent than history. I believe that dreams are more powerful than facts—that hope always triumphs over experience—that laughter is the only cure for grief. And I believe that love is stronger than death."
—From the movie The Crow

Where was Doug? Was he in heaven with my Catholic God, or was he in Valhalla with Odin? Was Doug in my Catholic hell because he was never baptized Catholic? I knew the latter would never happen. Doug was too good, too wonderful and a war hero. He saved many lives during his 34 years of living on our earth, so there was absolutely no way he could be in my Catholic hell. The Catholic doctrine would have to make an exception for Douglas Alexander Zembiec. If anyone was in hell, it was me living in hell on earth dealing with the loss of Doug.

My obsession with the afterlife began the moment I stepped off the plane in Baltimore after our return from Albuquerque in June. I couldn't stand it. I needed to find out where Doug was, because I knew his spirit was somewhere. I wasn't sure where, but I was going to explore the many possibilities of where his spirit could be. The dreams were too vivid for me to just dismiss. There was meaning behind them. He was trying to protect his friends and me even in his death.

Between my training runs for the Marine Corps Marathon, work and raising

Fallyn, I kept my evenings free to read about the afterlife through several different authors. I explored the possibilities online and discovered that Sylvia Browne, Jonathan Edwards and James Van Praagh had written novels about dreams and communications from the afterlife.

Sylvia Browne was my first choice because I watched her several appearances on *The Montel Williams Show.* Her premonitions and psychic abilities were astounding, and Montel was a trusted, retired marine. I began reading her book on dreams and realized that Doug was contacting me from "The Other Side." I read Sylvia's book *Life on the Other Side,* and she explained a spirit's journey as having three different paths.

> *When a spirit leaves the body that's provided it with temporary housing for another visit to earth, there are basically three different places it might go. And make no mistake about it, which of those three places the spirit travels to is our decision, not God's. He never stops loving us, never turns away from us, and would never condemn any of us to an eternity of banishment from His presence. It's only when we stop loving Him and turn away from Him that we take such foolish chances with the health and well-being of our souls.*

> *The vast majority of us, who love God by whatever name we call Him and try our best to honor His love while we're here, immediately transcend to The Other Side, that sacred, exquisite, perfect world we came from, where we live joyfully among the Angels, the messiahs, our Spirit Guides, our soul mates and loved ones from an eternity of lifetimes both on earth and at Home. Residents of The Other Side are called spirits, and their appearances in our midst on earth are called visitations.*

> *A much smaller percentage of humankind, those dark, remorseless souls who choose evil over God, travel to an unspeakable unholy void called the Left Door, from which they horseshoe right back into an earthly womb, to be reborn into another Godless incarnation. The Dark Side, as we call those travelers through the Left Door, don't communicate with us or appear among us while they're in vitro.*

> *And then there are those poor trapped souls who, for their own often confused reasons, refuse to acknowledge the very real tunnel leading to the Other Side, illuminated by God's brilliant white light, and remain earthbound. Earthbound souls are called ghosts, and their appearances in our midst are called hauntings.*

Sylvia's explanation about the paths of a spirit comforted me beyond belief. I knew after reading her book that Doug was on the Other Side and was able to visit me in my dreams. I was terrified he would stop his visitations. Each night I would cry out loud, "Doug, please let me dream about you tonight. I miss you." But, night after night, there was nothing. My dreams were empty and black as night.

As each day passed by, I lived my life like nothing had happened. I was living in denial as I kept to my usual schedule. It felt like Doug was on deployment, but without the constant phone calls. I found a way to hear his voice every day by calling his cell phone and listening to his voice mail message. Doug's voice was so strong, deep and masculine. Just hearing the words "This is Zembiec, leave a message" was enough for me to get by each day.

The 11th of June came and went. I had made it thirty days. One month as the widow of Doug Zembiec. I had to say the words out loud because I couldn't believe them. I didn't feel like a widow, and besides, I could feel Doug's presence surrounding me. I felt as though someone was watching over my shoulder, and it was a warm, fuzzy feeling. Fallyn was also staying up in her crib to play "peek-a-boo" with someone who wasn't there. She would play with her imaginary friend as mysterious white lights ran across the infrared screen of the baby monitor. I would continuously watch the screen and as soon as Fallyn fell asleep, the white lights would end as quickly as they began.

My thoughts brought me back to the books I was reading about spiritual visitations, and I knew, without a doubt, it was Doug. I discovered through some research the white lights I saw on Fallyn's monitor were called "orbs." Shows such as *Ghost Hunters* illustrated orbs by using their infrared cameras to record them. The white lights on Fallyn's monitor looked exactly like the ones I had seen on the show. I wanted another witness to see the orbs on Fallyn's monitor; someone who wasn't as close to Doug. I needed validation for my own selfish reasons, and it would make it even more believable. I would also be more certain that Doug's spirit was living on, which gave me great comfort.

The next week, my sister Denise and my friend Kim came over to spend the night. My family and friends were alternating their visits to help me cope with the loss of Doug. I specifically wanted Denise and Kim to witness the baby monitor with me. Both were very interested in the afterlife, and they both had had experiences with spiritual encounters.

My grandmother visited my sister Denise shortly after her death. My father's mother died when my sister Denise was three years old. Shortly after her death, my family was at our shore house, and Denise was playing too close to the water's edge. My mom looked up and saw Denise running toward her telling my mother, "Mommy, Grandma just told me to stay away from the edge of the water."

My mother said, "Denise, your grandma is in heaven right now."

Denise said, "Mommy, she was floating in her nightgown right above the water, I saw her."

Kim's experiences stemmed from the death of her father, who tragically killed himself when she was thirteen. Throughout our entire friendship during high school, I would have sleepovers at her house, and you could feel the presence of her father. However, the feeling in Kim's house was definitely not the warm and cozy feeling I had in my house. I was actually a bit frightened at times when I spent the night with Kim. She had several spiritual encounters with her father through the years until she moved out of her parents' home.

I made both Kim and Denise sit by the monitor as soon as I put Fallyn in her crib. On that evening, the white lights were overwhelming. My sister and Kim couldn't believe what they were seeing. Denise spoke out loud, "Pammy, those lights are orbs, and they look exactly like the ones I've seen on *Ghost Hunters*. You know it's Doug. Only someone like Doug, who was larger than life, would be able to get back to earth to see his baby girl." I just sat and stared at the monitor. Doug was still with us.

CHAPTER 38

ANNAPOLIS, MD, APRIL 30, 2005

"I knew from the moment I met you that you would be my wife.
I was too afraid to admit it."
D. A. Zembiec

For what seemed like an eternity had finally arrived, our wedding day. It was 2:00 A.M. on April 30, 2005. Today, I would be Mrs. Douglas Alexander Zembiec. I should have been elated during the early-morning hours of my wedding day, but for some reason, I tossed and turned in my bed the entire night. *Why can't I sleep?* I thought to myself. It was probably the rain pelting the roof of the Kent Manor Inn. The sound was so intense it made me feel as though I was about to get drenched through the walls of the building.

The simple fact that my wedding reception was going to be outside on the muddy grass might have been the sole reason for my insomnia. "It's going to be okay," I said to myself out loud. "I'll call the tent company and make sure they put something on the ground to keep my guests safe and dry. My aunt will take care of everything."

My aunt Rose, my mother's sister, was my mistress of ceremonies, and she had all the details of the wedding forged in stone. She met with the manager of the inn, and they were ready for anything that would occur. However, my controlling nature was getting the best of me. I was having a difficult time letting go of the plans. How could someone else put the final product together? After all, it took me a year to get everything in order.

My wedding theme was centered on the United States of America, the land of the free and the home of the brave. Each table would represent a state in our country that had meaning in my life or Doug's life. Most important, the states being represented had meanings of our past, present or future; just as Doug chose my engagement ring with the three stones.

I searched many Internet sites and had table items shipped from states such as Idaho, California, North Carolina, Florida and New Mexico. Each state table had favors and decorations that represented "the taste of each state." I found things such as tiny Florida oranges and pink flamingos, to crab mugs and Baltimore Ravens' bobble heads. I went as far as having the tables organized in the room according to where they were geographically situated on the map. Of course, the head table was our nation's capitol. The tables had a large tabletop centerpiece with long stemmed red roses that stood high on each table, but yet the guests sitting across the table would still be able to see one another.

The state theme also made its way into the bar area. We had a specialty martini bar which featured martinis named after the states. Martinis such as the Snake River Splash, the Baltimore Raven and the Annapolis Appletini were among some of the favorites. In fact, the entire bar was going to be an endless selection of beverages for our guests. My fiancé decided on one of our visits with the wedding coordinator that the bar must be the "Super Premium Bar" with extra Jack Daniels for all of his fellow military friends. Running out of Jack Daniels wasn't an option.

The food was cultivated to represent the seafood of Annapolis and included the authentic "Maryland" crab cakes. Many of our guests would be traveling from different parts of the country, and we knew how much these crab cakes were coveted. Doug also requested salmon because he believed it was "God's fish." Of course, there were vegetarian, beef and chicken options for those who didn't prefer seafood.

Our wedding cake was simply elegant with four tiered squares encased within white fondant. The wedding cake was decorated with the most beautiful red roses, and each square had either a chocolate chip or raspberry cream center. We also had a separate station with additional desserts that included chocolate-covered strawberries and miniature cheesecakes.

The ceremony was much less complicated due to the strict Naval Academy wedding policies. I was going to walk down the aisle at precisely 3:00 P.M., and we would walk out of the chapel at precisely 3:30 P.M. as husband and wife. Flowers were not allowed, and the readings were extremely short. Chaplain

Radetski was going to marry us, along with a certified Catholic priest standing there to assist. My eight bridesmaids were wearing Marine Corps red, and the flower girl and junior bridesmaid were wearing white with red sashes.

I made sure every aspect of our wedding was planned to absolute perfection. However, I was still anxious. Would everything turn out according to my 150-page plan? I tried to convince myself that everything would be okay, but it wasn't working. My mind kept going and going like a Ferris wheel spinning incessantly . . . never once stopping for new passengers. As long as I could remember, my mind worked this way. It never stopped thinking, especially before any major life changes.

As I glanced over at the clock, I noticed it was already 4:00 A.M. I rolled over on my side and sleep was finally allowed to enter my room, my body and then finally, my mind.

Knock, knock, knock, knock!

The knocking on the door was so intense I felt as though someone was banging on my head. "Okay, okay," I said. I looked over at the clock. "Oh no, it's nine o'clock!" I exclaimed. I quickly got out of bed and opened the door. It was the entire bridesmaid crew ready to report for the day. Everyone was so perky.

"Can someone please get me some coffee?" I asked. My friend Kim quickly responded by calling room service for us. Today would be my day to be treated like the princess bride.

CHAPTER 39

ANNAPOLIS, MD, SUMMER OF 2007

*"Time goes by, life goes on, and all I can think of
is why you're gone."*
Patrick Swayze

I couldn't wait for July 11th to pass, and then I would be sixty days into my journey. The news media about Doug was beginning to ease up slightly, and I was able to be in Annapolis without having people stop by my home at all times. My family and friends were still taking turns spending the night with us, but after becoming overly obsessed with watching Fallyn's baby monitor, I decided to turn it off for good and keep her in bed with me. Having Fallyn next to me gave me comfort and security that allowed me to stay in my house alone. I knew that if my daughter was next to me there was no way anyone could wake me up in the middle of the night and tell me she was dead.

I followed through each hazy and hot humid day of July with my schedule of getting up early to run and train for the Marine Corps Marathon. Each morning, I set my alarm to 5:45 A.M. and got up to run before the sun sank into the black asphalt, consuming the heat of the long summer day. Dealing with the humidity in the early-morning hours was doable, so I forced myself out of bed bright and early to avoid the combination of both heat and humidity.

My runs were very focused as I played songs on my iPod that centered around my past. Most of my songs were very sad, so I listened, ran and cried on almost every run. It was very therapeutic to hear the songs that reminded me of Doug and my incredible life with him. The hill climbs didn't bother me, and the length of my runs didn't bother me. The only thing that bothered me was when my runs ended because the pain in my heart would return. The pain in my heart was so deep it felt like someone had reached into my chest and grabbed my heart, leaving a huge vacant hole that was black and empty. The wound seemed as though it would never heal, and it didn't matter how much I pushed the rest of my body because the pain was nothing in comparison. Training was my drug, and it temporarily helped mask the hole in my chest. I was going to finish the marathon and finish strong by shaving 2 hours off the time of my first.

I ran each day through the month of July, dreading what was about to come at the end of the month. The Marine Corps had scheduled the Silver Star Ceremony for Doug's heroism during the night he was killed. They told me he saved at least twenty-five lives that night and was going to be honored with the Silver Star. What did that mean to me and Fallyn? For now, it meant absolutely nothing. I didn't want some award for heroism; I wanted my husband home alive. Why did he sacrifice his life, knowing he would leave his family alone for the rest of their lives? I couldn't stomach the thought of having to go to an award ceremony for something I didn't want. I wanted to give it back and get Doug back. However, that was not an option. I would go to the ceremony, accept the award and not shed a tear. Doug would want me to be the stoic wife. He wouldn't have had it any other way. As angry as I was at Doug for getting killed, I knew he did what he was trained to do. He led from the front, and it didn't matter that he had a family at home. The men he led when he was fighting were his Marine Corps family, and Doug died for his brothers.

The entire country knew of Doug's heroism as soon as the secretary of defense, Robert Gates, gave his speech at a Marine Corps dinner and he spoke of the loss of Doug Zembiec. As he spoke, he shed tears about how Doug's death was a great loss to our nation's warriors. At first, I didn't know about the speech, but as soon as my phone rang and the voice on the other end was Andrea Mitchell from the NBC Nightly News, I knew something of great magnitude had occurred.

"Hi, may I please speak to Pam Zembiec?" the voice said on the phone line.

I answered, "This is Pam Zembiec."

"Hello, Mrs. Zembiec, this is Andrea Mitchell from the NBC Nightly News, and I wanted to see if I could speak with you for a few moments."

"Yes," I said.

"Well, Secretary of Defense Robert Gates was at a Marine Corps dinner last night, and he spoke very highly of your husband and got extremely emotional about him. I was wondering if I could come by and interview you for a few moments today, if you had the time."

I sat there silent for just a few seconds. My stomach began to get the too familiar sick sinking feeling. There was something about my gut that I had to follow. I answered, "I'm sorry, Ms. Mitchell, I'm really not in the right place at this point to get interviewed by the media."

"Mrs. Zembiec," she replied, "I completely understand and sympathize with your decision. Is there someone else local that we could contact for an interview? It can be another family member or a close friend."

I didn't have to think long about this one. I immediately answered, "You can contact either Tom Ripley or Eric Kapitulik."

She answered, "Thank you, Mrs. Zembiec. Would you mind if I had an NBC official come by and gather some personal photos of you with Doug and Fallyn? It would really give the public an idea of Doug as the husband and father."

I said, "Of course. I will gather some appropriate photos and give them to your representative."

"Mrs. Zembiec, thank you for your sacrifice to our country, and I'm so sorry for your loss. I will have Tamara Jones call you before she comes by."

"Okay," I replied.

I couldn't believe what just happened. The secretary of defense was crying over Doug's death? Doug was an extraordinary person, but there were many men who had sacrificed their lives for our country. Why Doug? I didn't want this type of attention. All I wanted right now was to pretend this didn't happen, but I couldn't with all these reminders slapping me in the face. Doug was dead, and he was never coming back.

The sick feeling in my stomach returned, and I desperately needed to call Kap. He would know what to do. I picked up my cell phone and quickly dialed his number. Kap immediately picked up the phone. "Beautiful, what's going on?" he said.

"Kap, Andrea Mitchell from the NBC Nightly News just called, and she wants to interview me because Secretary of Defense Bob Gates spoke of Doug at a Marine Corps dinner and got very emotional about him."

"Pam, that is great. When are they coming over?" he asked.

"Kap, I told her no. I don't think I'm up for it right now. It's too soon. I can't!" I said as I started to cry.

Kap said, "Pam, you're going to be okay. But you need to let her interview you. When will you ever get this opportunity again? The public needs to know about Zemmie and the great man that he was. You need to let them interview you. Please tell me you will."

I was taken aback by his response. How can I do this? "I'll think about it. They're coming by to pick up photos of Doug, and I'll make my decision then. I just don't know. I just don't know," I said.

"You do what you feel is right, but this is a good thing. Not many times in U.S. history has the secretary of defense cried over a fallen warrior. That tells just how special Zemmie was."

I paced back and forth around my living room and waited for the phone call telling me they were coming to get the photos. I thought about my conversation with Kap. He had a point. Not many war heroes were mentioned on the NBC Nightly News. It would be an honorable way for the American people to get a complete picture of the man who was my husband and the father of my daughter.

"Mrs. Zembiec?" she asked.

"Yes," I replied.

"This is Tamara Jones of the NBC Nightly News, and I was wondering what would be a good time for me to stop by and get some photos of your husband?"

"Tamara, there has been a slight change of plans. I've decided to let you come and interview me," I replied.

"Oh my goodness, that is wonderful news!" she exclaimed. "I'll let Andrea know you have changed your mind. She's going to be very excited. Thank you, Mrs. Zembiec. If it's okay with you, we need to come over in an hour so we can edit and have the final video available for tonight's broadcast."

I said, "That would be fine."

I was about to be interviewed by the NBC Nightly News for thousands, maybe millions, of Americans to see, but I didn't care. Before I received the phone call, I was getting ready to go for a training run, and was dressed in my running gear. I was about to get dressed for the interview, but decided against it. It wasn't a happy interview. This interview was about being a stoic wife of an American war hero, and I would represent my husband and my family honorably. Wearing my training gear for the Marine Corps Marathon was exactly how I wanted to represent my family.

The crew showed up right on time, and I decided that they should set up their gear outside on my deck. It was a very humid day in July, but the deck had an amazing view of the beautiful green trees overlooking Chase Creek. It was Doug's favorite place to be when he was home. He loved hanging out on the deck, listening to the wind through the leaves of the trees and looking for the crazy geese as they fluttered on the water. We loved sitting on the deck together, dreaming about our future and writing down our goals. The deck was the best place for an interview to take place about a man who loved his country, his family and his life.

I wasn't nervous as the crew began to roll the camera. I thought it would be easy to talk about someone I loved so dearly.

"Mrs. Zembiec, can you describe your husband to me?" Tamara asked.

I stood there for a few moments and was speechless. I tried to talk, but I couldn't get words out. I took a deep breath and began, "Doug was the most amazing man I had ever met in my life." I paused as I tried to swallow, but the knots in my throat were so large, I couldn't. It felt like someone had stuffed mothballs at the back of my mouth. My eyes became hot and inflamed, and the tears were beginning to flow. "No," I said to myself. "Not now. You need to suck it up and finish this interview. You made your decision, so stick with it."

I took a deep breath and began to speak again. "Doug loved his country and his family. When he walked into a room, the entire place would light up. He was larger than life." I stopped.

"Mrs. Zembiec, what did you think about Secretary of Defense Gates's emotional response when speaking about your husband?" Tamara asked.

"Actually, I wasn't surprised. Doug was just that type of warrior. He had that effect on people. My family is also very grateful he responded in that way, and we thank him for speaking so highly of Doug."

Tamara said, "Thank you for letting me ask you a couple of questions. I know this has been difficult for you. We would like to get some footage of you running around your neighborhood to show how you're training to run the Marine Corps Marathon. It's great you're running to honor your husband."

As the crew filmed me running around Circle Drive, I felt inspired and knew if other widows saw it, they might be motivated to do the same. The training was helping me make it through my initial days of dealing with the loss of my husband, and if I could help just one other person, the pain of going through the interview was worth every second.

Chapter 40

Annapolis, MD, April 30, 2005

"It seems like I waited for you for an eternity."
Pamela Zembiec

It had been four long years of waiting to marry the man of my dreams. Finally, I stood at the back of the United States Naval Academy Chapel without an ounce of nervousness. My beautiful dress, hair and makeup also increased my level of confidence. I felt so incredible and elated. I had never been surer about anything in my life. In other relationships, I had always felt like there was something missing. Fortunately, those relationships ended before I took the final vow, and I didn't have a doubt in my mind about becoming Mrs. Douglas Zembiec.

As the "Wedding March" began, with my arm enveloped in my father's elbow, I proudly walked down the vast and spectacular aisle of the chapel. The room was full of beautiful sculptures and exquisite detailing, but those didn't matter to me on this day. My eyes were focused on Doug, standing tall and wearing his finest of uniforms. I would've run to him, just as I did when he returned home from Iraq in 2004, but that would've been unacceptable. My heart always skipped when I saw him, and it didn't matter if he was waking up from a nap or returning home from a long deployment. On this day, my heart skipped twice, knowing at the end of this journey we would be man and wife.

The aisle length was enormous as I walked with my father to greet Douglas. He was standing at the end of the walkway with his men standing to his right. His brother was the closest to him and was the only one not in uniform, but striking all the same. My focus went back to my future husband who stood broad shouldered in his finest uniform of Marine Corps Blues with white bottoms. His chest looked like a shadowbox filled with many gold-plated medals. All were awarded for his acts of valor during battle.

I flowed down the passageway and was entranced by the scenery surrounding me. I felt like I was in a dream. Doug and I had finally made it! My dad and I worked our way to the end of the aisle that ended with Doug. At that point, Chaplain Radetski asked, "Who gives this woman to be married to this man?" My dad turned and looked at both Doug and the chaplain and said, "I do." At that point, my dad handed me over to the most-deserving man, gave me a kiss and shook Doug's hand.

Doug reached for my hands. I willingly grabbed them and immediately looked into his eyes. The eyes of my future were a dark and captivating brown color housed underneath long flowing eyelashes. His stare was intense as he looked at me and whispered, "Babe, you are the most gorgeous woman I have ever seen." I simply smiled up at him, and we walked to the chaplain to say our wedding vows.

Chaplain Radetski served with Doug in Fallujah and was with all Doug's men who perished during the months they spent battling the insurgents. He was cherished in Doug's eyes. Doug wasn't going to let anyone else marry us. Therefore, in order for us to get married in the Catholic religion, a Catholic priest was assisting in the ceremony.

Doug and I both looked at the chaplain and expected him to start the service. Instead, he yelled out loud, "Douglas and Pamela, look at each other! This isn't about me! This is about the two of you! Don't look at me again and don't take your eyes off of each other!" We both looked at each other and laughed out loud, along with the entire congregation. The chaplain began again, "Okay. That's better. We can begin.

"Today is a remarkable day as we have all joined together to witness the marriage of two special people. Doug, I served with you in Iraq and have witnessed your bravery in battle, and now, I am witness to your bravery in marriage. Marriage is a most precious union of a man and woman, and you have chosen wisely. Throughout our deployment, I was able to listen to you talk about your 'Princess from Valhalla' and how you were going to marry her upon your safe return home. On this day of April 30, 2005, I am honored to be witness to you marrying her. Let me charge you both to remember that your future happiness is to be found in mutual consideration, patience, kindness and affection. Douglas, it is your duty to love Pamela as yourself, provide tender leadership and protect her from danger. Pamela, it is your duty to treat Douglas with respect, support him and create a healthy, happy home. It is the duty of each of you to find the greatest joy in the company of the other; to remember that in both interest and affection, you are to be one and undivided."

Doug and I stood hand in hand while listening carefully to the chaplain's strong words. He was very outspoken, and his voice resonated through the vastness of the chapel. When the readers took their places on the podium, their voices seemed so soft in comparison to his. Even through the echoes of the immense place of worship, the readers' voices were like soft chirping birds on a spring day.

While I waited for everyone to finish their words, my patience was getting slimmer by each second. It was difficult to concentrate on everyone else when all I wanted to do was hear our vows echoing through the church. Finally, the chaplain looked at both of us and nodded his head in agreement. He whispered, "Are you ready?" Doug and I both nodded our heads in agreement. Chaplain Radetski began, "Douglas, will you have Pamela to be your wife, to live together as friend and mate? Will you love her as a person, respect her as an equal, sharing joy as well as sorrow, triumph as well as defeat and keep her beside you as long as you both shall live?"

Doug answered, "I will."

The chaplain went on, "Pamela, will you have Douglas to be your husband, to live together as friend and mate?"

During his words, I was nodding my head up and down saying yes with my body motions while the chaplain was speaking. The entire crowd laughed aloud, and it made me realize I might have been a little too overzealous with my body language. I calmed down and with a smile on his face, the chaplain continued.

"Will you love him as a person, respect him as an equal, sharing joy as well as sorrow, triumph as well as defeat and keep him beside you as long as you both shall live?"

I shouted, "Yes, I will!"

The chaplain replied heartily, "Okay, looks like Pamela is very excited for this day. I guess we should move on to the wedding vows quickly." We all laughed.

The chaplain whispered the words in Doug's ear, and as Doug repeated his vows, the words echoed through the church and into my soul. "I, Douglas, take you, Pamela, to be my wedded wife, to have and to hold from this day forward, for better for worse, for richer for poorer, in sickness and in health, to love and to cherish, 'til death do us part: according to God's holy ordinance, and thereto I pledge you my love and faithfulness."

My eyes remained focused on his, and I noticed tears streaming down his cheeks. After all, he was the hopeless romantic, and saying your wedding vows to the woman of your dreams obviously triggered the highest of emotions. I was deeply moved because I knew this man would be mine forever, and very soon it would be official; not only in the eyes of us, but in the eyes of God and the law.

When it was my turn, I stared into Doug's tearstained eyes and realized just how much this man loved me. I didn't want to say my vows, I wanted to just grab him and love him. Instead, I held tightly onto his beautiful and strong hands. My grip was so tight I could feel the circulation of blood pulsating in his veins. I began.

"I, Pamela, take you, Douglas, to be my wedded husband, to have and to hold from this day forward, for better for worse, for richer for poorer, in sickness and in health, to love and to cherish, 'til death do us part: according to God's holy ordinance, and thereto I pledge you my love and faithfulness."

The chaplain turned to us and began. "The wedding ring is a symbol of eternity. It is an outward sign of an inward and spiritual bond that unites two hearts in endless love. And now, as a token of your love and of your deep desire to be forever united in heart and soul, you, Douglas, may place a ring on the finger of your bride."

Doug looked over at his brother John as he handed Doug the rings. As always, he patted John's back and said, "Thanks, bro."

Doug began, "Pamela, I give you this ring as a symbol of my love and faithfulness to you." He looked at me, and I immediately held up my left hand to him. I didn't want him to make another mistake with the ring thing. He knew what I was doing and simply smiled. He gently placed the beautiful wedding band on my finger. I secretly wondered what was engraved inside my ring. We wanted to surprise each other, and I was curious about his choice of words.

The chaplain looked at me and said, "Okay, Pamela, now it's your turn."

I began, "Douglas, I give you this ring as a symbol of my love and faithfulness to you."

Doug gave me his left hand, and I quickly put the ring on his finger. I waited for four long years to see this man wear a wedding ring. Finally, the ring was on his finger and it looked strange. I was sure it would look "normal" to me in time. Maybe Doug never needed a ring to show his love in the first place. I didn't care. Our hearts, bodies and souls were connected from the moment we met.

We quickly moved to gather the candles our parents lit at the beginning of the wedding procession. Together, hand in hand, we approached the unity candle and ignited the wick, symbolizing the end of our separate lives. Doug and I both turned back toward the chaplain and waited impatiently for his closing remarks. We were both eager to have all the formalities conclude and share our excitement with our friends and family during the reception.

The chaplain began his closing remarks. "Because Douglas and Pamela have desired each other in marriage and have witnessed this before God and our gathering, affirming their acceptance of the responsibilities of such a union, and have pledged their love and faith to each other, sealing their vows in the giving and receiving of rings, I do proclaim that they are husband and wife in the sight of God and man. Let all people here and everywhere recognize and respect this holy union, now and forever."

He then looked at Doug and smiled. "Doug, go ahead and kiss your bride."

Doug grabbed my face with both hands and while he ardently kissed my lips, he tilted my body as though we were ending a passionate dance routine. The crowd cheered and laughed in unison. Chaplain Radetski proudly announced, "Please give a warm welcome to Captain and Mrs. Douglas A. Zembiec."

CHAPTER 41

ANNAPOLIS, MD, SUMMER OF 2007

"Larger than life, that is what you are."
Pamela Zembiec

The training for my marathon was cruel, but necessary. It kept my body worn and tired, which helped me sleep at night. The intensity didn't give me the option to think about or feel reality. Between Fallyn, work and training, my thoughts about Doug dwindled to every other second. However, his constant presence throughout my home never left me alone. I could sense him everywhere and knew he was feeling my sadness all the way through whatever dimension or spirit world he was sent to. He was staying with me in order to help me throughout my days and nights. It was comforting and beneficial, but my life was a fantasy world. My body was being challenged, but my mind was still with Doug. By feeling his presence, I pretended he was still alive, and it enabled me to move by each day, not accepting the truth.

After the incident with my sister and friend Kim, I couldn't look at Fallyn's baby monitor screen without feeling alone and protective. My feelings were difficult to explain. In one sense, I was comforted by Doug's visits with Fallyn, and in another sense, I was petrified. Would God take Fallyn away from me too? I solved this problem already by taking Fallyn out of her crib and letting her sleep in my bed every night. Doug would have to visit both of us at the same time. He was completely against having our children in bed with us, and so was I . . . until he left me.

My parenting was changing, my life was crazy and I was out of control. I knew the second I put Fallyn in my bed, it was the wrong thing to do for her. It was selfish, but I didn't care. She was my precious love. I rationalized, confessed and was comforted by Fallyn's presence there. My mom was the only one who supported my cause. She wanted Fallyn with me. She didn't like Fallyn's room being on the lower level and not right next to me. My mom, just like me, was worried about losing Fallyn and was calmed knowing she was safe in my bed. It was good she agreed with my "family bed," considering she spent almost every day with us and tucked us both in bed many nights.

Another part of my mom's job was being witness to Doug's presence in the house. This made her uneasy, simply due to her strict Catholic upbringing. She believed Doug was in heaven with God, but had a difficult time agreeing to his spiritual presence remaining on earth. The orbs on Fallyn's baby monitor scared her. She simply avoided staring at the screen, and when the baby monitor went away, it helped ease her anxiety.

I think Doug was trying to test my mom for the purpose of making her comfortable with his presence. He loved her dearly, and one evening, she, Fallyn and I came home from shopping and I noticed the blinking red light on my home phone. Most people called me on my cell, so I was curious about the message. All three of us walked downstairs and into my office, which housed the answering machine. Fiorella, was sitting at the computer so I reached over her shoulder and pressed the PLAY button on the recorder.

At first, the sound of the recorder was silent, and then I heard it . . . the most exquisite music filling the room. The recording was beautiful, but encased within static. It sounded like music coming through a radio from the 1940s. You could hear it, but it wasn't crystal clear, like listening to a CD or iPod. The music was something "not of this world." I jumped back from the recorder, and my eyes searched the room.

My mom looked at me and said, "Who would call you and leave a message like that?" Fiorella turned around and just stared at me. She couldn't say a word.

I pressed PLAY over and over again. Where was the music from? I knew the sound. It was familiar to me, but I couldn't place it. I asked, "Fiorella, have you been home all night?"

She answered, "Yes, Pam. I've been home all night, but I didn't hear the phone ring once."

I said, "Well, maybe you were in the shower or something when it rang."

She said, "No, Pam, I didn't take a shower, and I had the phone with me. I was waiting for a call from my mom."

I picked up the hand piece to the phone and frantically pressed the previous calls button. She was right. There were no calls for the evening or the entire day. The last received call was two days prior. I pressed PLAY again. "This is Doug," I said.

My mom looked at me with belief in her eyes and said, "I think you're right. If it were any other person, I wouldn't believe it, but that had to be Doug."

After everyone was fast asleep, I was drawn back to my office so I could hear the music again. As the music played, chills ran down my spine, and then it finally came to me. The heavenly sound coming from my phone recorder was the music that played when Doug and I were on the beach at Louie's Backyard! Only he would know about the music. Together, we searched everywhere for the music, but never found it! I guess Doug was in a place where all "unknowns" were found. My eyes were filled with tears of both pain and joy. I was joyful knowing Doug's spirit was still with me, but saddened because I knew I would never feel the warmth of his embrace ever again.

CHAPTER 42

VIRGINIA BEACH, VA, LABOR DAY WEEKEND, 2007

*"No marathon is easy. The halfway point only marks the end of
the beginning."*
Joe Henderson

From my perspective, the best thing that happened during the month of August 2007 was the completion of the summer, which meant the end of another season without Doug. Time was moving, and I prayed to God I would heal with the passage of time. Fortunately, my schedule was still filled with taking care of Fallyn, handling work assignments and training for the marathon. My body and mind were weary, and each night before bed I continued to beg and plead with God to let me dream of my husband. "Please God, I know Doug's with you right now. Let him come to me in my dreams. I miss him so much. I miss his touch, his warmth, his voice." Most nights, my prayers were left unanswered, and I woke up angry. Maybe being angry was a good thing because it made me train harder during my runs.

My training led me on a short trip for Labor Day weekend. I was running in the Virginia Beach Rock 'n' Roll Half Marathon. Running 13.1 miles two months out from the full marathon was a great way to fill in my time and also train my body. I ran this race once before, and I didn't train at all. It was in 2004, just before Doug returned home from Fallujah. He wanted me to run the race to help prepare me for the Marine Corps Marathon. I signed up, but never trained. Therefore, my time was horrible, and my body felt like shit when I finished. I think it took me 2 hours and 43 minutes to complete and I wasn't surprised when I finished the Marine Corps Marathon the same year in 6 hours 23 minutes. I made a promise to my husband to run in the Marine Corps Marathon when he returned from Iraq, and I would never back down on a promise.

When Doug returned home from Iraq in 2004, he visited back east for thirty straight days. During those days, we were supposed to do some additional training for the marathon. Unfortunately, training was the last thing on our minds after being apart from each other for almost eight months. We managed to get one run in during the month of October about two weeks before the marathon. I remembered what Doug said to me, "Babe, we only need to run around 12 miles today. If you finish 12, you can finish 26.2. It's amazing what your body can do when you have mental toughness." I didn't doubt his words for a second and went along with him. After all, Doug was an honest broker and would never steer me in the wrong direction. I trusted him with my life.

The second time around was different. I wanted to make my husband proud. He was fulfilled the first time I finished, but I always wondered what time I could get if I actually trained. In my heart, I knew Doug was probably thinking the same thing. Besides, Doug's friends from the Naval Academy were running the Half with me. Their continual support over the past three months was a big reason why I was making it through each day. When I was around Doug's friends, I felt closer to him.

Jon, Joe and Bridget were part of the Rock 'n' Roll group. Jon played a big role in supporting me the past three months. Jon, otherwise known as Doug's spiritual Jedi Master and was now mine, was willing to give me much-needed help, and I soaked up every ounce of encouragement he dished out. I think we were both helping each other. We spent several hours a week talking on the phone. Jon was a true friend, as well as an incredible athlete and role model.

Joe was back in Virginia Beach after being sent overseas for work. I remembered when he called me on the phone the day after Doug's death. He was stricken with grief. I will never forget our conversation. He cried, "Pam, Pam, I'm so sorry I can't be there with you right now. I promised Doug I would take care of you if anything ever happened to him. I'm not there, and I want to be there for you. I'm so sorry."

I cried back, "Joe, you will be there for me when you get back to the States. Don't worry, the rest of the guys are here now. You can help later." I think my words might have calmed him momentarily, but he was hurting. Doug's death was affecting thousands. Joe kept his word, and when he arrived back to the States, he, along with his wife Liz, immediately came to my rescue. I graciously gave Joe the faded, but still beautiful America flag, that hung in the front window of Doug and Joe's house in Virginia Beach. It was for no one else but Mighty Joe.

My friend Bridget was there for me every step of the way during my training. She would visit Annapolis on a regular basis and help me through my preparation. She was an inspirational wife of a Navy SEAL and an incredible mother. Bridget served in the navy after graduation and decided to retire when she started having children. Her husband Coleman was another one of Doug's best friends. He wrestled with Doug and the two of them were very similar in character. Out of all Doug's friends, Coleman reminded me of Doug the most. Doug always thought he was most similar to Bo, but I wasn't convinced. The bottom line was this . . . All of Doug's friends were incredible people and were very supportive during this horrible time. Everyone grieves in their own way. Some isolate themselves from others, and some need to be in the core of the "mess."

One of my blessings during this time was my friends. The morning of the race, we all gathered at station 12. Being the slowest runner of the group, I was setting the pace. Jon, Joe and Bridget were fast runners, and I knew they were running the race for me and Doug.

I looked around at the large crowd gathered for the run and wondered if all these people could see the hurt inside of me. My heart was broken into bits, and the feeling was so strong, it felt as though others could see it through my clothes. Everyone had their own reasons for participating in various races. The first time I ran the Half, I was oblivious to the hundreds of charities who had runners representing their causes. Today, I knew exactly why those people were running. They were running for satisfaction, hope and strength in a world left so darkened by the loss of their loved ones. For these reasons, I was running too.

My race clothes were the colors of red, white and blue to honor our country; the country my husband loved enough to die for. I was saddened at the possibility of him loving his country more than he loved me and Fallyn, but deep down, I knew he didn't. By defending our nation, he loved us more because he defended our right for freedom and safety. He wanted to keep terrorism locked far away from the United States and his family.

Joe was dressed in a white shirt, green shorts and military boots. I didn't question his reasoning. I knew why. It made the race more difficult for him, and he was sacrificing comfort; something Doug would have loved. In the distance, we heard the crowd cheer as the front runners made their way over the start line. We waited patiently for our group to move, and once we moved through the crowded street, I took off. Bridget's voice was loud and clear as she said, "Pam, slow down, you don't want to peter out at the end. We start off slow and finish strong. You'll see." I didn't question Bridget's advice and slowed my stride. After all, her words were the Bible for me.

When we reached mile 1 after 11 minutes I freaked out. "Bridget, our pace is too slow!"

She said calmly, "Pam, trust me. We will finish strong."

I answered, "Okay, okay." I had to finish in 2 hours. My goal for the marathon was 4:20. If I didn't finish the Half in at least 2 hours, I would never reach my goal for the full.

Kap warned me, "Beautiful, you finished your first marathon in 6:23. Having a goal of 4:20 is pretty steep. That means you'll have to shave 2 hours off your last time, which is unheard of."

I thought to myself, *Don't challenge me, Kapitulik.* I knew I could finish stronger this time if I trained.

The miles were moving, and each marker brought me closer to my goal. My team was rocking and rolling through Virginia Beach as we talked about Doug's antics. Each person shared a different "happy" Doug story which made time fly. By mile marker 8, I was beginning to feel a little tired. I asked Bridget, "What's our time?"

She answered, "We are flying right now. Our last mile was 8:25 pace."

I was going too fast. She knew by my look something was bothering me. "Pam, we should slow down. I want you to finish strong." Bridget was the best coach. I felt an overwhelming sense of gratitude for her. She remained completely focused and calm. Her motivation was genuine, and it made me work harder.

As we headed into mile 9, I noticed someone wearing a shirt honoring Doug. I quickened my pace to catch up, but my coach started yelling, "Pam, slow down!"

I yelled back, "Okay, Brid. I need to catch up to the guy with the Doug shirt."

247

We both raced up and recognized him immediately. It was John. He was another one of Doug's Naval Academy buddies and old roommate when Doug lived in Virginia Beach. All four of us ran up to John and stayed with him for just a few moments. His pace was definitely faster than ours. I tapped John on the back. "Hey, thanks for running in honor of Doug."

He nodded his head with a smile and took off for a few paces with Joe. Bridget, Jon and I were running our race pace when we passed over mile marker number 9. Jon said, "Only 4.1 more to go, Pam Pam. You are a rock star!" He sounded like Doug for just a split second. Oh, how empowering it was to be around Doug's friends! They made me stronger and faster. My tempo was definitely faster. I'm sure it was the combination of their strength and my adrenaline.

Silence was beginning to set in on us when we passed over mile marker 11. I wasn't able to talk any longer. It was all I could do to just finish the race. Bridget knew I was beginning to "bonk." She quickly motioned for me to get some Gatorade from the stand. I walked over, grabbed two cups full and drank quickly. Hopefully, the sugar rush would get me to the finish line. We turned the corner on Ocean Drive and made a right onto the boardwalk. "Thank God," I said to myself. The last 2 miles were running along the ocean. The sun was beginning to beat down on my face and skin, and I could feel the salt crusting around my lips. The sweat on my body whittled away and cold chills were forming on my arms and legs. I knew this had to be a bad sign, but I ignored it. "Pain is weakness leaving the body. You are weak without mental toughness." I said these things to myself over and over again.

Finally, I saw it: the end of the race. I heard the band playing and saw the banner swaying. With every ounce of energy left in my body, I picked up my pace. Bridget and Jon were right by my side.

"Yeah, Pam, you're almost there. Keep going. One-tenth of a mile left!" Jon and Bridget both cheered.

When we crossed the finished line, I could barely make it to pick up my medal. *Thank God it's over,* I thought to myself. I looked to my right and saw Jon, Bridget and Joe all smiling ear to ear. They seemed unfazed by the race. I was sure all three of them could've finished 20 minutes ago. However, I knew our time was probably pretty good because they pushed me hard.

I looked at Bridget and asked, "What was our time?"

She looked at me with a satisfied smile and said, "Pam, you rocked it! We finished in 1 hour and 56 minutes."

For the first time in almost four months, I felt a glimmer of hope. My life would be harder without Doug physically, but he would always be there for me spiritually. I couldn't believe I finished the race 46 minutes faster than my last one. There was only one answer: Doug was with me.

CHAPTER 43

ANNAPOLIS, MD, FALL OF 2007

"Better never to have met you in my dream than to wake and reach for hands that are not there."
Ōtomo no Yakamochi

Virginia Beach always made me feel safe and happy. It was the place where my life with Doug began, and visiting it made me feel closer to him. I cried during my drive back to Annapolis, knowing I would have to return to my new realty. As I passed over the Chesapeake Bay Bridge, thoughts of jumping into the bay began to creep into my mind like the movement of low tide waves along the shoreline, slowly oozing into the sandy earth. *Would it be easier if I simply ended it now?* I thought to myself. "No!" I shouted aloud. I wasn't going to give up. I made it this far, and I would keep going. *After all, your beautiful daughter, oblivious to the loss of her father, would be parentless.* These thoughts were scary but were part of my new life now. I prayed they would only be temporary.

When I arrived home, I was able to spend quality time with my little girl. She was the one person who brightened my soul in the sea of darkness. I couldn't wait to snuggle in bed with her, kiss her and hold her tight. I missed her during my race weekend. One day, she would be able to understand the importance of mental toughness by finishing anything you start. A shiver went down my spine thinking about my horrible thoughts of "leaving this world." Hopefully, one day, these thoughts would go away. For now, I was going to take each day step by step and cuddle with my baby.

After such a tiresome weekend, I wasn't surprised when my body submitted to sleep the moment my head hit the pillow. I don't know how long I was sleeping when a gentle touch woke me up. I looked to my right, and I saw him. My eyes were cloudy, but I could make out his face—it was Doug. He wasn't in full body form and looked as if he was floating next to me. His figure was an iridescent white form that reminded me of the rematerialization process a person went through in a *Star Trek* transporter machine. I was in complete shock. He wasn't saying anything, just staring at me. The sight of him was so comforting, I felt as if he had never left me.

When he didn't say anything, I reached out and tried to touch him, but my hand couldn't feel anything. I whispered, "Douglas, is that you?"

His facial expression seemed troubled. He looked like he was trying to figure something out and answered, "Babe, it's not fair! It's not fair I got taken away from you and Fallyn so soon. I've been talking to Him, and He's going to try to get me back to you. I don't know how or when, but I'm gonna do it. I will talk to Him and see what He can do!"

I couldn't believe what was happening. He was making me so happy. I was overjoyed with his words, but not sure how he was going to come back to us.

I whispered back to him, "Douglas, how are you going to come back to life?" He looked at me with a blank expression and said again, "I'm going to talk to Him and see what He can do to get me back to you! I've been visiting my friends and their families this week and it's just not fair! I didn't get to keep my promise to you! I'm gonna talk to Him and see what He can do!"

In a moment, he came over, and we began to passionately kiss each other. It was like our first kiss in Virginia Beach. I was with my love once again. Everything felt so real, I even felt worried about waking up Fallyn, so I told him, "We're going to wake up the baby. Let's move on the floor."

I awoke with Fallyn sleeping next to me and realized everything from last night was only a dream . . . or was it? Was Doug in my room last night, and was he coming back to life? I couldn't shake it off. My dream was too unfeigned.

As soon as I got in my work vehicle, I began to bawl uncontrollably. There was no way I could call on doctors today. I was in a fog and convinced Doug was coming back to life. Who could I reach out to for help? Who would understand and not think I had completely lost it? First, I tried Kathy, but she didn't answer. Jon. I would call Jon. He's been dealing with my craziness for the past few months and would understand. I quickly dialed his number. The phone rang once, twice.

"Hey, Pam Pam!" Jon answered.

"Jon," I said through painful sobs, "I can't work today. I had this dream about Doug, and it was so real. He told me it wasn't fair he was taken away from me and Fallyn. He said he was going to talk to Him and see what He could do to get him back to us. Jon, is Doug coming back?"

He answered emphatically, "Pam, you had a vivid dream about Doug. I'm sure it felt real, but no, Doug is dead. There is no way he can come back to life."

I cried hysterically. "Jon, it was so real. It felt like we were together. I woke up this morning completely exhausted like I was up with him all night. How can you explain those things?"

Jon sat silent for a moment. He was trying to calm me down. "Pam, please. I know losing Doug has been difficult on you, and I can't begin to understand how you're feeling. I only know what it feels like to lose one of my best friends. I miss him like hell. I'm sure your body was dreaming about how it used to feel when you were together. Where are you?"

"I'm sitting in front of the house. I wasn't feeling up to driving yet," I answered.

He said, "Okay, do me a favor. Take a deep breath, dry your eyes and think about Fallyn. She needs you to pull it together. Go get a cup of coffee, and then go see a few doctors. Do what you can do today. Your company knows you're gonna have some rough days. For Christ's sake, you lost your husband."

Jon was right. I needed to pull it together for my daughter and myself. I answered, "Okay, thanks, Jon. I'll take it easy today." I started the ignition and moved around the circle driving toward Starbucks. I would feel better after a cup of coffee.

On my way to Baltimore, I couldn't stop thinking about my dream. It was so real. Doug was such a powerful man on earth, I was sure he had some influence in the heavens above. My books about the afterlife mentioned spiritual visits through dreams, and I knew from my readings there was the possibility of seeing Doug in that way.

While I sat and ate my lunch, I thought about calling more friends to get their take on my dream, but I decided to just be with myself for a bit and look at the positive side. I did feel like I was with Doug and was able to spend "dreamtime" with him. However, when I received a phone call from two of Doug's friends, Ken and Dan, I couldn't help but believe in the reality of my dream. Ken and Dan both called to tell me about their Doug dreams. Ken said his dream was so real; he felt like he was hanging out with Doug. He also confirmed Doug's prediction about Amy. She was three months pregnant and was having nightmares about him getting killed in action. I assured Ken he was going to be fine because of his guardian angel friend in Valhalla. Dan said he hadn't dreamt about Doug at all since his death. Dan was pissed at Doug for not visiting him in his dreams, and then, just last week, he had a dream about Doug. Dan said Doug was sitting in a chair with a big grin on his face. Dan tried to talk to him, but he didn't say anything, he just kept smiling and that was the end of the dream. Both Ken and Dan had their dreams during the prior week. I remembered what Doug said to me, "I've been visiting my friends with their families over the past week . . ." Was my dream a reality? In my heart I was sure Doug was coming back, but my head was beginning to come out of the fog.

CHAPTER 44

STEVENSVILLE, MD, APRIL 30, 2005

"All I want is a big party for our family and best friends. I want the best of everything for everyone. After all, we're only going to do this once."
D. A. Zembiec

As Doug and I drove down the long and winding road to the Kent Manor Inn, we sat in full of anticipation for our reception. The guest list consisted of our closest family members and best friends. Who knew the list would add up to 200 people? It didn't matter; we spared no expense on our wedding because we both knew it would be our only one. Divorce would never be an option for us. "'Til death do us part" it would be for Mr. and Mrs. Douglas Zembiec.

Before we arrived at the manor, I silently took off my wedding ring. I couldn't wait to see the inscription. We wanted to surprise each other with our words. Doug saw me and immediately grabbed my hand. He said, "Curious about what I wrote, are you?"

I smiled back at him and said, "Your words amaze me, but I'm a little concerned with the space. It's so tiny."

Doug had a shit-eating grin on his face. He chuckled while saying, "Don't ever doubt me, Princess. Wait, let me take my ring off and we'll read them together, but you go first."

I quickly looked inside the tiny band and put it toward the light of the window. I could barely see the words; they were so teeny inside of the thin band. I read aloud, "Eternal love, April 30, 2005." I smiled deeply. The words were minimal, but stated the truth.

It was Doug's turn. He read aloud, "'You are my love, my life, my dream.' Honey, you're being the romantic now. You do have it in you. I'm so proud of you." He kissed me deeply, and we toasted with our fine champagne as the limo traveled over the Chesapeake Bay Bridge. For a moment, I glanced outside the darkened windows and viewed the gorgeous scenery. There were sailboats, motorboats and fishing boats scattered throughout the deep recesses of the glorious bay. The sun was casting its light over the water, which revealed the tiny whitecaps forming in the glaze. How happy I was by knowing my future with Doug was as bright as the scenic waterways of the Chesapeake Bay.

When we arrived at the manor, several of our guests were waiting on us. Fortunately, we hired an incredible photographer, but his expertise took up lots of time that we wanted to spend with our friends. He was considered a "photojournalist." Photojournalists were known for using photography to tell the story of a wedding day and not dictate it for you. Whatever he was, he was certainly expensive.

As soon as we hopped out of the limo, our photographer was all over us. He took pictures in every possible direction. Finally, we both had enough and hurriedly entered the inn to greet our guests in the Bridal Suite. All of my bridesmaids were hanging in the room, which was exquisitely decorated using ornate flower wallpaper and antique furniture. I would never decorate my house in this fashion, but it fit the mold for the inn.

My sister Kimmy came over first with a "Snake River Splash Martini" in hand. She said, "Pammy, I don't know what's in this drink, but it's good. I better be careful. What do you want? I'll go get it for you."

Before I could answer, my friend Kim came over holding an "Annapolis Appletini." She asked, "Do you want one of these?"

I nodded my head yes, but I knew my drinks would be minimal. Doug and I made a promise to ourselves that we wouldn't get intoxicated so we would remember every detail of our wedding to share with our children one day. Kim hurriedly left for the bar, and Kimmy sat next to me on the antique couch. I could tell she was already feeling at least "her cheerios."

My sister Kimmy was the second born daughter in our family of four girls. She was the only sister born with brown hair, while the rest of us were all towheads. From the beginning, Kimmy stood out with her competitive nature and tomboy qualities. She was an extremely talented, competitive tennis player when she was a teenager and kept a good workout schedule into her adulthood.

While growing up, my sisters and I would come up with inside jokes that only we would understand. One good example was how my dad would explain his personality changes after having a couple of beers. He would always joke with us by saying such things as, "I'm feeling my cheerios." My sisters and I would kid about "feeling your cheerios," and I simply added "Frosted Flakes" and "Captain Crunch" to the mix. The different cereals explained the levels of intoxication. "Cheerios" would be the first level, followed by "Frosted Flakes," and then finally "Captain Crunch." A person "feeling their Captain Crunch" was probably a very drunk person.

Tammy, my youngest sibling, sat next to me as well, but brought with her some mini crab cakes for me to savor. My little sister Tammy was the "baby" in our family. I think my sisters and I were always jealous of her because she was given "special" privileges during certain times. Things changed when we were old enough to understand the reasoning behind my mom's favoritism. My mom experienced an extremely difficult delivery with my sister Tammy and almost lost her. By coming into the world weighing over 10 pounds, there was no questioning why it was tough for my mom.

Being in the Bridal Suite gave me the opportunity to catch up with all my bridesmaids. Everyone looked elegant in their floor-length red gowns. I picked a gown that complimented everyone's figure. Most of my girls seemed overjoyed as we chatted about the ceremony and the fun things to come throughout the reception except for one person: my sister Denise.

Denise, who was my eldest sister, seemed "out of sorts." She looked tired and distraught, and I could tell something was bothering her. "Denise," I asked, "are you okay?"

She said, "I'll be okay, my throat is a little sore."

I knew something was wrong with her because, out of all four girls, Denise was the most resilient. She never let anything get to her, and if she did, you would never know. Denise kept most things inside and was in some ways "hard-hearted." By being the eldest of four girls, she was expected to act a certain way and set the example. Therefore, she was an excellent role model for all of us and was one of my closest friends because I respected her completely.

Our little bridesmaid party got interrupted when the wedding coordinator gathered everyone for the wedding party introductions. The entire group of both groomsmen and bridesmaids congregated in the Garden Room and were paired with their coordinating escorts. My head instantly lifted, and I beamed when I heard Doug call, "Where's my wife?" Immediately, I walked over to the sound of his words, which filled my heart with both love and pride. I grabbed him by the arm, and we walked over to join the rest of the wedding party. In total, there were eight groomsmen, eight bridesmaids, two flower girls, one junior bridesmaid and one ring bearer.

The music began to play, and one by one, each pair was introduced to the guests. After everyone from the wedding party took their places, there was a brief moment of silence, and then the DJ announced our entrance. "For the first time, as husband and wife, let us give a warm welcome to Captain Douglas Zembiec and Mrs. Douglas Zembiec."

In an instant, the music began to play, but this time it was way too noisy— almost deafening. I could hear it resonating from my ears, to my head and finally, to the rest of my body. I knew what song Doug picked for our entrance, but I wasn't prepared to hear it being played so loudly. The instruments of Metallica, "For Whom the Bell Tolls," echoed through the entire tent. It sounded like a heavy metal concert at Merriweather Post Pavilion.

As I walked into the tent, I noticed my feet were sinking into the green tarp. I kept going forward, but almost tripped from the wetness of the ground. *Of course, the tent flooring was soaked through the green carpeting!* I angrily thought to myself. I knew it was going to rain, and I asked the wedding coordinator to get the tent up last night, not this morning. I was furious.

The floor only got worse as we approached the dance area where the DJ was stationed. There were water and mud puddles forming from the edges to the middle of the brown solid dance floor. How would my guests be able to dance without getting wet and muddy? I looked up at Doug to try to complain, but he wasn't paying attention to the small details. I could tell by his contagious smile he was completely ecstatic about seeing all his friends sitting around the room. He moved unreservedly through the muddy floor with his free hand pumping the air to the rhythm of the music, which made him look like a groupie at a rock concert. His carefree and fun-loving attitude inspired me to let the "little things" go, so I took a deep breath and focused on the bigger picture.

The room around me was magnificent with each table standing amid gold-backed chairs, shimmering candles and gold-plated centerpieces. Inside the centerpieces, an eruption of perfect long stemmed red roses with green shining foliage filled a large perimeter of the tables' centers. There were smiles on all the faces of our guests.

When we finally made it to our Washington, D.C., table, my anger dissipated as I focused on the beauty around me, filled with many familiar, loving faces. Our groomsmen and bridesmaids were all standing, ready to welcome us to our places. Doug, along with his men, sat to the left of the center, and I, with my girls, sat to the right. The excitement was overwhelming. My wedding day was happening, but I still felt like I was in a dream.

After all the welcoming was over, the DJ asked everyone to stand so the best man, John, Doug's brother, could give the toast. John was Doug's older and only brother. He was very similar to Doug in looks, but their personalities were completely opposite. John was more intellectual and introverted, while Doug was athletic and extroverted. Both were raised the same way, by the same parents, but chose two completely different paths in life. When Doug was trying to choose a best man, he didn't have to ponder over the decision because he had too many great friends and his brother was his blood. Besides, the two were very close, being raised in a two-sibling family.

The DJ walked over to John and handed him the microphone. John pulled a small piece of white paper out of his pocket and slowly began his speech.

"Good evening, ladies and gentlemen. It is my honor to be here today at the wedding of my brother. As most of you know, I'm the older of the two of us. We both grew up side by side and shared many great moments as brothers. I couldn't be happier for both him and Pam today. Pam, welcome to the family. Congratulations." John raised his glass, and everyone toasted to our new marriage. I could hear all the glasses clanking in unison. Doug and I looked at each other and were astonished because we thought his speech would be different, but we both understood John's introverted personality and continued on with our toast to each other.

There were so many of our best friends at the wedding. Everywhere I looked in the room, I saw someone I loved, and they were all in high spirits. My dad, who wasn't a social person, was even having a good time. It was a fantasy day because I had all of my favorite people gathered into one place.

The music continued to play while I decided to roam around the reception area to meet and greet everyone, as well as make an assessment of the area. My first stop was the Garden Room, which housed the bar along with an extra area for the special Martini Bar. The Kent Manor Inn utilized the Garden Room exclusively for weddings under one hundred guests. It was a beautiful room that was the first stop for my guests during cocktail hour.

While evaluating the area, I noticed there was a dance floor in the vicinity of where the bar was located with several cocktail tables scattered throughout the rest of room. My mind was still racing for a solution to my muddy dance floor in the tent, and I immediately moved toward the main house to find our wedding coordinator. I couldn't let it rest and had to find a solution to keep me and my guests happy. I was sure Doug and the other marines, Navy SEALs, Army Rangers and navy pilots were just fine with the mud-spattered dance floor, but it wasn't okay with me.

When I found the wedding coordinator, we decided together to move the DJ and dance party into the Garden Room. However, the flooring would have to make it through the first dance and dinner. She resolved my anger by offering an additional hour of super premium bar to make up for their mistake of not getting the tent ready the previous evening. The decision made me happy, but I was a little worried about what my guests would be like after 6 full hours of endless drinking.

As I strolled into the tent to give Doug the good news, I couldn't help but stare in awe at the sight. The entire room was filled with countless men of valor who could've crushed Al-Qaeda if they attempted to step one toe anywhere near the manor. For our guests, it was the safest place on earth . . . and also the craziest. I could tell everyone was having a great time, and when the DJ announced our first dance, it seemed like either no one really cared or they were having too much fun among themselves to pay attention to anything else going on around them.

Doug and I strolled hand in hand to the wet and muddy floor to have our first dance together as man and wife. He carefully placed his left hand around my rhinestone-laden waist with both our hands entwined together. We started moving slowly as the music commenced. When the words of the song began, Doug and I mimicked the words, *"Last night I had a crazy dream. A wish was granted just for me, it could be for anything. I didn't ask for money or a mansion in Malibu, I simply wished for one more day with you. One more day, one more time, one more sunset maybe I'd be satisfied. But then again, I know what it would do. Leave me wishing still for one more day with you."*

The song was appropriate for our relationship. We spent many nights apart from each other during his deployment and would continue to do so until he parted ways with the Marine Corps. Every time Doug had to leave me to go somewhere, we would listen to the song on our last night together and "wish for one more day, one more time." The unfortunate part of the song was the true meaning behind it: the song was written about the deceased wife of the lead singer for Diamond Rio when she died of cancer.

We danced together as if no one was watching, and it felt like we were the only people in the room; we were completely focused on each other. Doug did his usual dance moves by twirling me around the dance floor and picking me up in the air. My dress was long, so I wasn't worried about everyone seeing my panties. At the end of song, he dipped me low to the floor, without hitting the mud, and gave me a sweet kiss on the lips.

As soon as our first dance ended, the DJ packed up his equipment and headed over to the Garden Room. They were going to set up while our guests were enjoying their meals of salmon, crab cakes and beef tenderloin. Doug and I walked over to the food stations and grabbed a few items, but I was too excited to eat. Instead, I enjoyed conversations with my friends and watched happily as Doug bonded with his best friends. He was truly a sight for sore eyes with a freshly shaven face and sparkling brown eyes. It almost seemed like his medals were shining from the brightness of his face. I loved seeing him like this because he was entirely full of life.

The crowd began to mingle again, and I decided to spend some time talking with all my favorite people. Doug and I made the smart decision not to visit with all the tables because it would waste too much time. We also didn't perform most of the regular traditions because we weren't sure when we would have the opportunity to spend time with everyone we loved again. Therefore, we sliced the four-tiered cake with the ceremonial sword cutting, and started the party.

Most of the older, tired adults decided to leave after dessert, and we were left with the crazy party group. I was completely sober, so it was interesting to see all the drunken behavior surrounding me. In one corner, Andre was flipping Steph upside down during the swing dance. In another corner, I watched one of Doug's uninvited acquaintances, who brought two additional uninvited guests, grabbing my sister Kimmy's behind as my mother angrily pushed him away. I looked over at the martini bar, and the line was wrapped around the corner. Everyone left at the wedding reception was completely "feeling their Captain Crunch."

My friend Susan came over, grabbed me by the arm and took me to the DJ stand. She said to the DJ, "Please play Madonna's 'Vogue.' The bride wants to sing to the crowd." I angrily smiled at her, but was more than happy to take the challenge due to my experience at Freddie's. The DJ announced my karaoke performance, and then handed over the microphone. I was, once again, performing Madonna's "Vogue," but this time, for my wedding crowd. On the other side of the reception tent, Doug's boisterous Navy SEAL friends were stripping off their uniforms and diving into Thompson's Creek.

My new husband caught wind of the action and quickly ran out to join his friends. As I finished my song, I noticed the head bartender running out to find the guys. I asked Steph, "What's going on? He looks mad about something."

Steph answered, "I think he's pissed at Joe for stealing an entire bottle of Jack. Joe took it to the water's edge so everyone could drink shots before stripping."

At that moment, I was forced to run outside to see the craziness for myself. When I arrived at the creek's edge, I immediately noticed Joe, shirtless, leaning against the tree while he sipped on the bottle of Jack. I guessed the bartender gave up his search because he wasn't anywhere near this all-star crowd of men. In a distance, I saw Bridget, who was seven months pregnant, snapping pictures as she waddled close to the water's edge. And then I heard the guys, laughing as they splashed away in Thompson's Creek. There was a small light on the end of dock, which allowed me to slightly see their naked bodies in the black waters of the Creek. As the guys began to emerge from the water, it looked like something from a movie; ripped six-pack abs, bulging biceps and sculpted shoulders. Every guy was ripped to the maximum. Before their privates erupted from the black waters, I quickly turned away and headed back to the manor.

I thought the madness would end when I got back to the manor, but as soon as I entered the house, I noticed my sisters going crazy. Kimmy was profusely vomiting in her room, while Denise was screaming something about her husband running around the manor stark-naked with Doug's friend Andre. That was it for me. I needed to relax in my room.

As I headed back to my Bridal Suite, I realized my husband was in the dirty waters of Thompson Creek, and I didn't know when he would be back. I felt a little angry, but knew he deserved this time with his war-fighting friends. If it were anyone else, I would be fuming. I therefore looked out my door and grabbed my two junior bridesmaids. Instead of my new husband undressing me on my wedding night, I was in the care of two nine-year-old little girls.

CHAPTER 45

ALEXANDRIA, VA, SUMMER OF 2005

"Our marriage started out a little rough, but it grows stronger every day. I am so proud to be married to you. There is no other woman with whom I'd rather ride the river."
D. A. Zembiec

Alexandria, Virginia, was a beautiful place to begin our new lives together, especially after a long ten days spent in Italy for our honeymoon. Who would have known my honeymoon, with the most wonderful man I had ever met, was going to be a complete disaster. The idea of going to Italy seemed incredible, but the idea ended up failing miserably.

Doug was in charge of planning our honeymoon, which was usually the mission for most grooms. However, being in Iraq for seven months limited his scheduling abilities, and he decided to give the operation to his mom. Jo Ann did an incredible job at setting up our hotel in Venice, our B&B in Siena and our wine tours in Tuscany. Unfortunately, Doug was convinced he could "wing" the rest of the trip. He said, "We can figure it out when we get there." Since I trusted him completely, I never thought it would be such a disaster.

It was miserable from the start when we drove to Dover, Delaware, the Monday after our wedding, and hopped on a military flight to Germany. Instead of getting on a plane with regular seating, we were forced to take a plane, the C-17, which had pull-out bright orange racks for seating. The "cushions" for the racks consisted of bright orange and braided netting that had spaces large enough for my butt checks to pass through to the other side. I was able to adjust the seats by using my jacket as an extra cushion, but when we achieved our cruising altitude, I began to shiver uncontrollably. I asked Doug if the pilot was going to turn up the heat, and he looked at me, smiled and said, "Babe, this is a cargo plane. It's not getting any warmer. Here, take my jacket."

I sadly looked at him and said, "No, you need your jacket. We can stay warm together." We spent the entire 8 hours to Germany trying to sleep while cuddled in each other's arms. Doug seemed perfectly fine with the situation, and I figured maybe this was why he always referred to sleep as "hitting the rack."

When we finally arrived in Germany the next morning, I was exhausted, hungry and jet-lagged. The only thing I wanted to do was get to a hotel and relax for the remainder of the day. Instead, we had to go through customs and find a map because Doug wasn't sure about our plan. In fact, he didn't have a clue about anything. I kept trying to give him the benefit of the doubt, since I knew he wasn't sitting at home twiddling his thumbs over the last year; he was fighting for our freedom. I think this was the first time as being a Marine Corps wife that I realized our family was secondary to Doug's duty to country.

The remainder of our honeymoon ended up being just as tumultuous as our first year of dating. Of course, we had fun sightseeing, wine tasting and meeting the locals, but our bond was weaker. For the first time in my life with Doug, I wasn't connected to him. Even during our breakups, I still felt him in some way. This was different because we were together and weren't enjoying each other . . . in any way. We spent more time fighting than loving each other.

My idea of a honeymoon was making love with my new husband in a beautiful suite while meals were being sent to our room. Instead, we hardly spent any time in a room as we were forced to drive all over Europe in order to get to our next destination. I could tell Doug was preoccupied, and I wasn't sure if he was feeling guilty for not doing his part or if he was having "second guesses" about our marriage. My persistence was the main reason we got married before he turned thirty-five, and I knew why he made the decision to move up his time line; I was thirty-five and my window for having children was getting smaller. Since we both wanted three children, we had to get started as soon as possible.

When we arrived back home from Italy, his preoccupation continued and our life wasn't happily ever after. We fought about money, houses and jobs. He was trying to control every move I made, and nothing I did was ever good enough. Doug was unhappy about something, and he was taking it out on me. He was back in the real world, not surrounded by his marines, and I knew that had to be his problem. When he told me he was being stationed at the Pentagon for a different job, away from his marines, I knew it would never be good enough for him.

Throughout our entire relationship I always understood his need of being "part of something bigger than himself," but it was difficult for me to try to understand why "just being with me" wasn't good enough. *Why did he always need his marines too?* I had to make a move to push us in a positive direction and the only way would be to give him something bigger in his life. The thought of having him home without long deployments was appealing for me, but not for Doug. After our terrible honeymoon, I wanted to work on getting back to us, but for some reason, my intuition told me this wasn't about us or me; this was about Doug.

While I searched for an answer to try to help my lost husband, I kept the peace by allowing him to make many of our decisions. Of course, he would consult me, but I let him take the lead because in some way, I felt this might give him more satisfaction. I was going crazy inside due to my controlling nature and wasn't sure my tactics were working at all. Doug would never be at ease with just living a "normal" life.

A couple of weeks into the summer of 2005, Doug came home from work and asked if we could talk. At first, I was uneasy and felt nervous, considering our relationship hadn't been easy during the last few weeks. When he began the conversation, he seemed excited, and, therefore, I was more relaxed when he began.

"Honey, I've been told I'm deploying to Afghanistan for an important mission. I was so excited I wanted to call you on my way home from work, but I thought it best to tell you in person. I know you were looking forward to spending some time with me, but I know this is what I got to do to keep you and our country safer."

For the first time since our wedding day, the life in his brown eyes was back and I didn't need a second to think about my answer. "Doug, I would never hold you back from something like this. In fact, I think it's exactly what you need right now. I'm sad because you'll be gone, but being a warrior is what you're made of. Honestly, you haven't been yourself since you left 2/1. The excitement of the wedding kept you going, but I don't know where my Doug went."

He just sat there with his head bowed down, and then looked me in the eyes and told me, "Babe, you're right. I haven't been the same. I love you more than anyone else in the world, but I love the Marine Corps and my country too, and it's my duty to defend our nation. Not being able to be on the battlefield is like a death sentence for a marine."

I understood him completely and knew he would always be a warrior, in sickness and in health, until he retired one day. I slowly spoke to him, "Go to Afghanistan and keep making a difference."

CHAPTER 46

ALEXANDRIA, VA, SUMMER OF 2005

"If you think it, you will become it. Trust me. We are going to buy a house on the water in Annapolis."
D. A. Zembiec

Things were changing in the Zembiec household, and they were changing for the better. Doug's news transformed his entire outlook within our family. It seemed as though he was given another purpose after he heard the news about getting deployed to Afghanistan. I wasn't overjoyed at the fact that he was leaving, but I certainly enjoyed my husband's newfound happiness. Even though he wouldn't be with his marines of 2/1, he was still going to defend our country and he seemed like himself once again, while our relationship started to move in a positive direction.

As we started discussing our next steps as a married couple, Doug would always bring a notepad and pen so we could write out our daily goals, weekly goals, monthly goals and yearly goals. He was consumed with getting everything written on paper because he said, "There is nothing stronger than the written word."

On one night, Doug came over to me with his notepad and asked if I could read something he had written. I looked at his very distinct handwriting and carefully reviewed his words. Doug's handwriting was very difficult to read, so I had to squint and figure out what it said. I began slowly, "Monthly goals: Sign a contract for a house in Annapolis on the water. Get Pam pregnant before I leave. Be able to do fifty dead-hang pull-ups. Okay, honey. The pregnancy thing will be easy, you doing fifty pull-ups even easier, but the house in Annapolis . . . I'm a little worried about that one."

He quickly responded with his usual, assured stance, "Babe, why are you being negative? It's about positive reinforcement, babe, and we will get our house in Annapolis. Remember, one of the main reasons I married you was, and is, because of your positive attitude, your confidence and energy and maybe your rock-star body had something to do with it too! Speaking of that, let's start this baby-making thing now. I already told my friends I was going to get you pregnant tonight, and you know I'm a man of my word."

The next weekend we were on our way to Annapolis and had several showings set up by a real estate agent who was referred to us by Tom Ripley. Her name was Laverne. Doug described her as being an older, classy lady, and she was also a military widow. He said she was "the rock-star real estate agent," and Tom Ripley told him she knew every good house for sale in the area. She represented both the colonel and Tom when they bought their houses in Annapolis, and we, therefore, completely trusted Laverne.

When Doug and I showed up at the Coldwell Banker Real Estate Agency on Church Circle in Annapolis, Maryland, it was one of the hottest days of the year. We met Laverne at her office and drove with her to all the home sites. My first impression of Laverne was exactly how Doug described her. She was an older woman, probably in her early sixties, with short white hair. She was extremely stylish and was definitely a classy woman. I knew immediately that Laverne was going to find us a house. I wasn't so sure about waterfront, but she would find us something.

We were in a seller's market and house prices were at their highest in years. I knew this because my town house in Virginia Beach was selling for $80,000 more than my purchase price only two years prior. Doug explained to Laverne what he wanted, and she tenderly explained to him, "Doug, I'm not sure we're going to find a house on the water in your price range. There are a few for sale, but the prices are well over a million dollars. Let me show you some great homes with water access first and see how you like them." Doug listened to Laverne and was smart not to give her his positive-thinking speech. After all, she was an expert in her field, and he was willing to let her take the lead.

Laverne took us to several water-access homes located in places such as Edgewater, Round Bay and Spa Creek. All the homes were beautiful, but not waterfront. Doug wasn't going to settle. I liked one of the houses, but it was

$780,000 and needed work. Finally, Laverne decided to give us some advice. She said, "I know what you guys are looking for in a home. However, it's going to be almost impossible to find a 'nice' house on the water that's within your price range. There is one house for sale in Winchester on the Severn. It's waterfront, but I need to be 100 percent honest with you about the property; it needs a lot of work and there's a contingent contract on the home. But, if you like it, I'm sure we could figure something out."

Doug seemed to jump as he answered, "Let's do it!"

I silently sat in the backseat of the car as we traveled over the Naval Academy Bridge, past the World War II Monument and down the 450 freeway. We made a left onto a road called "Boulters Way" and moved along until we hit the beginning of the B&A Trail. I started to get hopeful as we passed beautifully wooded neighborhoods along Winchester Drive and noticed homes on my left were sitting along the Severn River. I could tell Doug was very excited when he said, "Babe, this is the neighborhood where the Samples live! Remember when I took you here a couple of years ago and we rode their elevator to the dock?"

I answered, "Yes, their house was really nice."

Laverne interrupted quickly by saying, "Don't get your hopes up. This house is nothing like the Samples'."

We made a left onto Circle Drive, instead of continuing straight on Winchester Road, which was where the Samples lived. I kept looking around the neighborhood and was pleased with the houses, so I didn't understand Laverne's comments until we drove around the circle and stopped in front of the ugliest house I had ever seen. I gasped inside as she stopped the car and said, "Well, guys, here it is." Doug couldn't get out of the car fast enough and almost ran to the side of the house. I slowly stepped out of the car to take everything in.

The house was deep red in color and sat at the bottom of a driveway so steep, I almost fell from the incline. If there wasn't a house at the bottom, the hill could've been a skate boarder's dream. There was a small front yard covered in ivy instead of grass, with two large trees cascading over the entire area. The foliage from the trees completely covered the view of the home. In fact, there were so many plants, bushes, flowers and weeds, I could barely see anything. As we turned to the left of the front driveway, I had to watch my step due to the broken brick pathway. There were spiderwebs hanging from every corner as though the house had been abandoned months before. We made another right and walked up uneven steps as I held tightly to a small black iron banister. I noticed Doug take a turn down the steps when he noticed the only thing he wanted in a house: the waterfront.

He yelled back to me, "Come on, babe, let's walk down to the water! Laverne, we'll be right back, unless you want to join us."

Laverne didn't hesitate to go as we both descended the stairs and tried to follow Doug, but struggled on rocks and stones while we moved webbing from our faces. Doug was well ahead of us as he easily glided down the old and crumbling concrete stairs to the water. We followed slowly behind him as sweat poured down our faces and mosquitoes feverously bit our skin. I was miserable and didn't say a word because I could tell Doug was in heaven. He stared at the water and the view with admiration, and I knew this was it. He wanted this house even without seeing the inside.

When I joined him, he said, "Babe, isn't this view amazing . . . Think of it, our friends hanging on the dock and our dog learning to retrieve in the water. I can see Jonnie, Coleman and me swimming in the water right now. This house rocks!"

I wasn't happy and even his contagious smile wasn't going to bring me to the light. I simply stared at him and said, "Can we at least look at the inside?"

He smiled and said, "Sure, we can."

As we climbed back to the house, I was out of breath and sweating, but tried to be optimistic about seeing the inside. Laverne cautiously opened the front door and said, "Prepare yourselves; it's not a pretty sight."

When I walked into the mudroom, I could smell mildew and noticed the dirty white linoleum floors. The kitchen wasn't as bad because the cabinets were oak and in decent condition, but the appliances would have to be replaced, and the hideous, white, blue and bright yellow wallpaper would have to be removed. As we walked down the hallway, I noticed two entranceways; one was to the master bedroom and one to the master bath. It was scary for me to uncover what was going on behind those doors. Doug jumped out in front of me and opened the door to the master bedroom. I slowly followed him and noticed it was small with old wood floors and a tiny closet that had a hanging string to turn on its light. I kept moving on without saying much, but Doug was elated while he searched each room. He kept saying over and over again, "Babe, this place is great. We can put a little paint on the walls, and it will be just fine!"

This house needed much more than paint; it needed an entire face-lift.

I was pleasantly surprised by the original wood floors and the brick fireplace, but when Laverne showed me the lower level, I almost passed out. We walked down the steps, which were surrounded by dark brown paneling, and I became aware of my reflection in an iridescent koala bear mirror. I didn't think it could get any worse . . . until I observed black tile flooring that ran down the hallway into a "den" area. To top it off, there was a masking taped vanity in the second bathroom and an old rug thrown on concrete flooring in a second bedroom. The house was dreadful!

Laverne could sense my apprehension after we finished the tour, but she knew Doug wanted the house. He didn't care about the cosmetic issues; he wanted waterfront within our price range, and the house at 1501 Circle Drive was both of those.

To ease my pain, Laverne talked Doug into looking at another property in Epping Forest. She said to him, "It's not waterfront, but it has water access and has a community beach." She smiled at me while saying, "And it's been completely renovated." I hoped this new house would change Doug's mind in some way because I didn't want to fight with him. He was hell-bent on 1501 Circle Drive. Doug could live anywhere. He was used to sleeping in harsh conditions.

The house in Epping Forest was gorgeous, and Laverne was right, it was completely redone, but it only caused a fight between me and Doug. He tried to console me and tell me we could "eventually" fix the other one up, but I didn't want a fixer-upper for the simple reason that *I* would be the one taking care of everything while he was gone.

It didn't matter what I said; my argument would never sway his mind. Doug's persistence was too great, and in the end, he won the battle. On July 23, 2005, while secretly crying inside, I reluctantly signed the closing papers, and we became the proud owners of 1501 Circle Drive.

CHAPTER 47

ANNAPOLIS, MD, FALL OF 2005

*"I can't imagine going through life without ever having the
experience of giving birth to a child. Being a mother is the most
important job a woman will ever have."*
Pamela Zembiec

We started moving into Circle Drive during the first week in August, which gave us time to go back and forth from the rented condominium. Our lease didn't expire until September 1st, and we were able to slowly move our belongings during the month of August while I painted the rooms that weren't on the renovation list. In the end, Doug and I agreed to reconstruct the master bedroom, both bathrooms, as well as put hardwood floors throughout the lower level. We also budgeted for the removal of the koala bear mirror and paneling, which were being replaced with dry wall and paint.

There was so much to be done before Doug left for his deployment, and I was also worrying about my missed period. It was already two weeks late, and after several negative pregnancy tests, I was convinced something was wrong and decided to see my doctor. However, Doug wasn't worried about me. He knew my family was the "fertile zone." All three of my sisters were pregnant within the first year of marriage, and Doug was convinced I would continue the tradition. I guessed all of my stresses were causing my irregular cycle; we were moving, I was interviewing for a new job and my husband was leaving me. I explained all of these things to my doctor, but she still wanted to do an ultrasound as well as give me another pregnancy test. Her tech performed the ultrasound and everything looked good, but from what she could see, I wasn't pregnant. It was liberating knowing my body was healthy, but I wanted to be pregnant so desperately the good news didn't matter to me. So, I decided to ignore the tech and wait patiently for my blood test results.

Each weekend, Doug and I went to Annapolis and worked on the house. He moved our belongings, while I painted and organized. I started painting in the den, and was working my way through the downstairs bedrooms so they would be done before the flooring was installed. The kitchen was getting painted and our handyman was already working diligently on reconstructing the master bedroom and bathroom.

Things were moving quickly with the house, and I was getting used to the idea of owning a "shack" on the water. In time, I knew this house would be transformed into something beautiful and safe for our future family. Doug began to realize the safety issues with an old house, especially when I received a phone call from my doctor's office telling me I was six weeks pregnant. We both had a strong feeling I was pregnant, even though the pregnancy tests kept coming back negative. My emotions were out of control, I was beginning to gain weight and I was exhausted all of the time. When we found out we were having a baby, it was just confirmation for what we already knew deep inside our hearts.

Everything was beginning to fall into place. We bought our house, I was pregnant and also landed a new job closer to Annapolis. My fears of losing the baby were slowly creeping away as well when my pregnancy was reaffirmed with a continual nausea that began only three short weeks after we moved into our new home. My husband had this horrible habit of telling the world all of our news prematurely and almost everyone we knew found out I was pregnant the minute I received the phone call from my physician. In fact, the day after we initially tried for a baby, he called the majority of his best friends and told them I was pregnant. I even had a friend call me and ask me when I was due. Therefore, a "safe" waiting period never existed for Doug, which kept me anxious about my initial first weeks. I welcomed the nausea with open arms, knowing the cause was from increasing hormone levels in my body and a growing embryo.

My body wouldn't permit me to go without food for more than an hour, and if I did allow more time to elapse I was doomed. The nausea just wouldn't go away unless I ate junk food; it felt like I had a continual hangover and McDonald's cheeseburgers were the only thing that helped me. I guessed it was because of the protein, but I wasn't sure. This was extremely difficult for me because I was a junk food hater, but my husband, on the other hand, was a junk food junkie. He loved McDonald's cheeseburgers, and we were both convinced "his" baby was making me eat them.

I went from a size six to a size ten in only four weeks, but Doug was happy about my newfound love of McDonald's. He didn't care about my weight; he wanted me to eat the junk with him and feed his son. My mom would come to visit, and Doug would say as he laughed, "Mom, you should see all the empty bags from Burger King and McDonald's in her car. That's the first time I've ever seen her eat fast food. I love it! My son is making her eat the stuff because she needs the calories."

Doug didn't understand how difficult it was to lose weight because he tried desperately to keep weight on his body. I wasn't about to gain 60 pounds during my pregnancy and was getting tired of eating junk so decided I would make my own "healthier" cheeseburgers at home. My husband was kind enough to run to the grocery store for the beef and also cook the dinner, but he couldn't do it fast enough and I ended up getting sick before I took a single bite. I got angry with him when he forgot the ketchup, and he simply looked up at me with sad eyes and said, "Babe, how am I supposed to know what you like on your cheeseburger? I've known you for almost five years and never saw you eat a burger!"

I sadly responded while trying to control my vomit, "You're right. I'm sorry." At that point, I realized I couldn't control my raging hormones and discovered the true meaning of fast food. I gave into it in order to avoid the immediate consequences; the long-term effects would have to be worked off.

From the moment we conceived our child, Doug was certain we were having a boy, and I let him keep his opinion without saying too much. There was a fifty/fifty chance, but he came from a long line of males and thought because of his "alpha male" status he would, of course, have all boys. He had the names picked out for two of the three sons we would have together. Our first son would be named "James Storm" after Jim McGee. Doug liked the name "James" because it was a strong one-syllable name and he also looked up to Jim as a man and father. The middle name "Storm" was something he thought sounded great with "James." Our second son would be named "Bo Donald" because of his love and admiration for his friend Bo and his dad. I let Doug keep his wishes about the names of our "sons" because I didn't care about the sex; my only wish was for a healthy child.

Time was ticking away as Labor Day approached and Doug got ready to leave for his deployment. He tried to have our master bedroom completed before he left, but it wouldn't be done until Christmastime. I was given the option to sleep in one of the two additional bedrooms downstairs, but I wasn't about to sleep down there alone. The basement made me feel uneasy, so I decided to camp out on our new living-room sofa instead. My husband wasn't happy with my decision, but since I was the one home, I was going to sleep where I felt the safest and Vahli B would be able to lie on the carpet next to me for comfort.

Doug's trip would be a short one. He was scheduled to be home right before Christmas, but then he would have to go back shortly after the holidays. I was happy about being able to cut down our first Christmas tree and maybe spend time with him without being sick. I couldn't even kiss him because I could smell everything he ate during the day housed inside the beard he was growing for his deployment. My girlfriends, who were already mothers, gave me their word I would one day, after twelve weeks gestation, wake up feeling like a million dollars.

I wasn't so sure after week twelve came and I was still sick, but during week fourteen, I woke up, and my body felt incredible. My energy was back, I wasn't nauseated and I could work out. The best thing was I actually looked pregnant and not just fat. It was great feeling like "myself" again, and it was just in time. I was starting my new job, handling all the construction in my new house and keeping my lab from jumping in the Severn—all without my husband.

Life continued with Doug being away, and I, once again, quickly adjusted as being "head of the household." It was a little different this time due to his frequent phone calls and e-mails, but I was still ultimately responsible for making quick-witted decisions about our house and our life. It also helped that my friend Christine from Virginia Beach was pregnant, and we were able to share all the stages of our pregnancies with each other. She was due on March 10th, and I was due on April 12th. Doug was adamant about having an "Aries" child, just like him, and his wish, along with many others, was coming true.

When it came time for me to go to birthing classes, I recruited my sister Denise and my sister Kimmy to take notes. And when it came time for me to go to Chicago for training, I recruited my neighbor to take care of Vahli. I went to weddings, birthday parties and all family functions alone.

This was the life of a military wife. There were times when people would question whether I even had a husband, but I didn't care. This was my life, and I was honored to be a Marine Corps wife. I always knew, from the moment I met Doug, this was my destiny, and I would do everything in my power to make it work because my husband wasn't meant to do anything else in life. He said he was going to retire after twenty years, but I wasn't so sure. I still had my sights set at living in the "Big White House" on the 8th and I, Marine Corps Barracks.

When it came time for me to get my amnio test, I elected my mom and sister Kimmy to be by my side. In fact, Kimmy was going to be the godmother of our first baby, but Doug wanted to go away and think about our choice for the godfather. I didn't want to do the test alone because there was a slight possibility it might cause damage to the fetus. Doug and I weighed the pros and cons before he left, and we agreed it was the right decision for us. When it came time for the test, Kimmy went into the room with me while my mom stayed in the waiting room due to her nervous behavior. She was known for being a "worrywart," but it was only because she cared too much.

During the test, I was extremely at ease due to the wonderful specialist who was performing the procedure. He had an excellent bedside manner, and his reputation was solid. While he carefully executed the amnio, I looked at my sister, and she was smiling. I wasn't exactly sure why, but I think it was because the doctor was smiling.

Kimmy asked, "So, can you tell what the sex of the baby is?"

The doctor was careful, but positive when he answered, "Well, I can't be 100 percent sure until we get the test results, but I'm pretty sure this little baby is a girl."

Kimmy nearly jumped out of her seat and said in an excited tone, "I told you, Pammy, I had a feeling the baby was a girl. All your symptoms were similar to mine when I was pregnant with my girls."

The doctor calmly finished the test and said, "Okay, Mrs. Zembiec, I'm finished here. You should get your results within two weeks, and I'm pretty sure the news will be good."

I was relieved with his words and elated about my baby girl.

A girl!

My thoughts were filled with joy . . . until Doug's voice began to echo inside of my head. *I'm going to have a son! Besides, I wouldn't know what to do with a girl.* My happiness became overshadowed with worry over how Doug was going to react to our news. I thought to myself, *Who can I call for advice?* The answer came to me both quickly and clearly: Don and Jo Ann.

When I called, they were both overjoyed. Jo Ann always wanted a little girl, and now she would have a granddaughter to spoil. Don was happy as well, but gave me a warning for his son. "Pam, I know Douglas was certain he was going to have a son, so I'm not so sure how he's going to react positively to the news. If he gives you any problems, let me know, and I will have a talk with him." My father-in-law understood his son very well.

When my phone rang that evening, I was prepared for the worst. Doug began the conversation with his usual upbeat tone by asking, "How's the most beautiful woman in the world?"

I answered, "I'm great!"

Before I could say anything else he quickly added, "Or, more important, how's my healthy son doing?"

It took me a few moments to answer, and my hesitation alarmed him. He questioned, "Babe, are you okay? What's wrong? I can tell by your voice something is bothering you."

I quickly responded, "Honey, I'm good. No, actually, I'm great! But I have to tell you about my amnio test today."

He excitedly said, "Oh, that's right, that's right. How did it go, babe? I want to hear all about it."

I answered, "The test went very, very well. Kimmy and my mom went with me, and the doctor who performed the test was fantastic. In fact, he said he could tell what the sex of baby was from looking at the screen."

He quickly interrupted. "Okay, then, what's the sex?"

I immediately replied, "It's a little girl."

He remained silent for a few moments and finally said, "Are they sure?"

I replied, "The doctor said we will get the results within the next two weeks in order to be 100 percent positive, but he's pretty certain it's a girl."

Doug retorted, "Well, there you have it! It could still be a boy. Don't start buying pink until we get those results. Babe, you almost sound happy it might be a girl. Are you?"

I responded calmly, "Honey, like I said before, my one wish is for a healthy baby, but I have to say, the idea of a little girl warms my soul. She'll be daddy's little girl."

He answered back, "You're right, I want a healthy baby too, but I want a son.

Babe, I wouldn't know what to do with a girl. Of course, I could always call Jim and see what he's done all these years with his girls. They're pretty awesome."

The following week, Doug was forced to give up all hopes for a son when the test results came back telling him he was going to be the proud daddy of a healthy Portuguese Princess.

CHAPTER 48

ANNAPOLIS, MD, FALL OF 2005

"I joined the Marine Corps to serve beside men like your father. There is no other marine I'd rather have protecting my flank in combat than your dad. Even now, as I write this letter in Iraq, I will honor him on the field of battle by slaying as many of our enemies as possible, and fight until our mission is accomplished."
D. A. Zembiec

As the fall trees in Maryland began to produce their beautiful yellow, orange and red leaves, I was off to Chicago for continued sales training. Fortunately, our new neighbors proved to be extremely helpful by knowing Doug was traveling for work. Winchester on the Severn was full of great people who looked after one another all the time. I, therefore, was getting better at accepting our choice of a new home and left for training with confidence that Valhi and my house were safe.

While Doug was doing great things on his deployment, he was also getting used to the idea of having a little girl. However, when he remembered he told me I would be able to choose the name for our girls, I think he was under the impression we weren't going to have any. He sweetly asked during one of our conversations, "Babe, I know I told you, you could pick the name of our girls, but I meant the first name. I get to pick the middle name."

Since I wasn't too concerned, I agreed with him, and we decided to do it together during Christmas. Doug also contemplated his choice for our daughter's godfather. In the end, he decided Kap would be the best choice for his baby girl.

Kap was best suited for the position because he had a very strong mother and grew up with two sisters. I agreed with Doug's decision because I found it easy to talk to Kap about certain things, especially after he realized I was going to be his best friend's wife. Once he gave into the idea I would be around for Doug's lifetime, our relationship finally became real.

During my flight to Chicago, I worried about my stamina because of the high stressors involved with pharmaceutical training: there were meetings all day, and then study groups at night. I was witness to other trainings, and they were always filled with constant challenges. Doug tried to counsel me before I left, and he slightly helped ease my worries. Like he said time and time again, "Babe, we are part of the top 10 percent of this nation that leads the other 90 percent. Just remember that and you will make it!" He had a way to always boost my self-esteem.

My training was scheduled for three weeks, which brought me home in time for the Thanksgiving holidays with my parents and sisters. Each night after a grueling nine-hour day, we would gather into small groups and have dinner at various restaurants throughout the city of Chicago. Of course, we had a spending limit, so many of our nights were spent in the hotel restaurant or a different "chain" restaurant.

On one particular evening, a friend and I decided to have our meal at P. F. Chang's, which was located only a few blocks from our hotel. The moment I entered the restaurant, my cell phone rang. I didn't recognize the number, but noticed it was a California area code. Normally, I would ignore numbers I didn't know, but for some reason I was compelled to pick up the phone.

"Hello," I answered. When the voice on the other end began to speak, I instantly became nervous.

"Pam, it's Justin. I have some really bad news. Are you in a place where you can talk?"

My heart pounded so heavily, I could almost see it through my shirt. I anxiously answered, "Yes, J. D. Tell me what's going on."

He continued, "I just found out Ray Mendoza was killed in Iraq."

I began to scream and cry, "Oh no! Oh my God! J. D., this can't be true. No, no, not Ray! He has a wife and two small kids! Why? How?" I leaned on the counter for support, and my body bent over in pain.

J. D. tried to console me over the phone, but it was impossible. He calmly began to speak again. "Pam, it was an IED. He was patrolling with Echo

Company when he stepped on an IED. Each of his men walked over it, and the thing never went off. Ray was such a big guy, his weight set it off."

I was crying uncontrollably when I heard J. D. say, "Pam, I need you to tell Doug. We haven't been able to contact him."

I tried to calm myself down when I realized that I was carrying my child and knew how stress could affect the baby and answered, "OK, OK, J. D., I'll tell Doug as soon as I hear from him."

He answered, "Thanks, Pam. I'll be in touch to let you know all the funeral arrangements."

While I waited for Doug's call, I couldn't help but selfishly think how thankful I was when J. D. said it was Ray Mendoza. For just one scary moment, I thought the call was about Doug. I was five months pregnant, and I couldn't imagine being without the father of my daughter. Our life was just beginning, and I thought how awful it would be for Doug to never experience fatherhood. He was meant to be a husband and father as well as a marine. At least Ray was able to spend some time with his wife and two children. However, our lives would never be the same without Ray. He was like Doug, "a man of all men," and irreplaceable. My thoughts wavered from sadness to relief. The idea of Karen, Keana and Alec without Ray made my heart break, but then I was relieved knowing Doug was still alive. Was I being selfish?

When I broke the news to Doug, he took it like a man, but I knew he was silently suffering for the loss of his good friend. He calmly said to me, "Babe, I know you're upset, but our country is at war, and with war there is death. Unfortunately, Ray was our friend and a great marine. I'll call Karen when I get home, and then I'm going to write a letter to the Keana and Alec so they will be able to understand their father's sacrifice."

I answered, "Honey, I know you will do what's right, but I have to tell you how scared I was when J. D. called. I thought it was you. I don't mean to be selfish, but I hope you don't get hurt or killed. I don't want anyone else to be killed, and I certainly don't want it to be you."

He was silent for a moment, and then said, "Babe, that is the most meaningful thing you have ever said. It shows me you get it, that we are part of something bigger than ourselves. You understand why I fight—for freedom, for justice, for principle, for my comrades, family and country. I love you and our little baby girl inside your belly."

I didn't know what to say because I wasn't sure I got it. I didn't want him to die for our country. I wanted him to fight and lead an honorable life, but never die; not until we were at least grandparents. So, I just responded, "Thanks, baby, I love you too."

I returned home from training, knowing I would see Doug soon, and knowing I was going to love him like never before. The loss of Ray put a cut in my heart, which made me almost too aware of the reality of war. I thought Ray was like Doug; he was "too trained" and "too tough" to ever get killed. But I was wrong. Ray's death scared the living hell out of me, and I tried to accept it but knew this wound would only heal into a lasting scar.

When Doug returned home from his deployment, he was determined to write a letter to Keana and Alec. He wrote many drafts, and we discussed them together, but finally, over one year later, December 19, 2006, his final draft was ready to be mailed. The letter to Keana and Alec began:

Dear Keana and Alec,

Ray and I had a conversation late May 2004 while we were deployed in Iraq. He spoke of why he fought. He fought to give the people of Iraq a chance. He fought to crush those who would terrorize and enslave others. He fought to protect his fellow marines.

The last thing he told me that day was, "I don't want any of these people (terrorists) telling my kids how to act or how to dress. I don't want to worry about the safety of my children." Keana and Alec, your father fought for many things, but always remember, he fought for you.

As you fight this battle we call life, you will find your challenges greater, your adversity larger, your enemies more numerous. The beautiful thing is, you will grow stronger, smarter, faster, and you will overcome the obstacles in your way. No one could've prepared you than your father. In the month and a half your family stayed with me in Laguna Niguel, California, while waiting for base housing to open up, I saw how, with the help of your incredible mother, he instilled in you the essentials for life:

LIVE WITH INTEGRITY, for without integrity, we deceive ourselves; we live in a house of cards. FIGHT FOR WHAT YOU BELIEVE, for without valor, we lose our freedom. BE WILLING TO SACRIFICE, for anything worthy in life requires sacrifice. BE DISCIPLINED, for it is discipline that builds the foundation of your success.

You will encounter misguided people in your life who may question America's attempt to help the people of Iraq and the Middle East. These pathetic windbags, who have nothing so sacred in their lives that they would be willing to fight for it, will argue and debate endlessly on what we should've done. While they criticize, they forget the truth, or conveniently overlook the fact that **it takes men and women of action, willing to make a sacrifice, to free the enslaved, to advance in the cause of freedom.**

Our great nation was built on the shoulders of men like your father. While the naysayers and cowards hid in the shadows, sniveling that nothing was worth dying for, men like your dad carved our liberty away from the English, freed the slaves and kept the Union together, saved Europe from the Germans, twice, rescued the Pacific away from the Japanese, defeated communism, and right now, fight terrorism and plant the seeds of democracy in the Middle East.

Your father was a warrior, but being a warrior is not always about fighting. He was patient with those he led, and he understood people make mistakes. He cared about the men he led as if they were his own family. To him, they were. His work ethic was tremendous, but he made time for his family, to enjoy life. He was balanced, at equilibrium. He was an inspiration. He was my friend.

In your future, when you are pushed against a wall, in a tight spot, outnumbered and seemingly overwhelmed, it may be tempting to give up, or even use the absence of your father as a crutch, as an excuse for failure. Don't. Your father's passing, while tragic, serves as an endless source of your empowerment. Your father would not want you to wallow in self-pity. I know you will honor him by living your life in the positive example he set. Respect and remember him. Drive on with your lives. Serve something greater than yourself. Enjoy all the good things that life has to offer. That is what he would want.

Keana! I have never met a more capable young lady in my life. You are the most well-read, articulate, disciplined young person who I know. Often I tell people of the arm-bar you demonstrated on me in your parents' garage. When you become a worldwide Judo champion, I will say with great pride, "That woman nearly torque my shoulder out when she was eleven years old!" If my daughter grows up with a quarter of the strength of your principles, determination and intelligence, she will be an incredible human being. Like your mother, you are a beautiful woman, a fact of which you should be proud.

Alec! You are blessed with your father's strength of character and his unbreakable will and his broad shoulders. Your mother gave you her determination and unwavering mental toughness. Your mother told me the story of you hanging up the sign, "Be a leader, not a follower." My eyes well up every time that I think of you doing that. My eyes fill not with tears of sadness, but of pride, to know you grasped the mind-set your father passed on to you. This mind-set will allow you to be a leader and protector, like your father, and one day, to raise an upright, solid-as-a-rock family of your own. When I look in your eyes, I see your father. Courageous, determined and resolute, your father embodied all that is virtuous in a warrior. Even now, you strive to embody his character. Remember, there will never be any pressure for you to be exactly like your father. Be your own man, but build your character in his image.

Many people may be concerned about your future because of the early passing of your father. I don't worry at all. Your Dad gave you all you ever need to become a great woman and a great man. Don't wait for someone to rise up and lead you to victory, to your goals. If you do, you might wait for a very long time.

Ray died a warrior, sword in hand, in service of his country, his comrades, and you, his loved ones. His spirit and example gives us all hope, reaffirms our faith. Your father reminds us there are men willing to fight for people that they don't even know so that all may live in peace.

I joined the Corps to serve beside men like your father. There is no other marine I'd rather have protecting my flank in combat than your dad. Even now, as I write this letter, I will honor him on the field of battle by slaying as many of our enemies as possible and fight until our mission is accomplished.

You will always be in our lives. Please stay in touch. We will always be in your corner for assistance, advice or conversation. Pam and I plan to retire in Idaho and would love for you to visit us so we can take you whitewater rafting and mountain climbing.

Very Respectfully,

Doug

CHAPTER 49

ANNAPOLIS, MD, THE HOLIDAYS, 2005

"You being home, is the only Christmas present I want."
Pamela Zembiec

Ray's death put a solemn blanket of clouds over the holiday season. Neither one of us wanted to believe Ray was gone. Doug was selfless trying to console me, but I knew he was hurting deeply inside. We tried to lighten things up by celebrating our first Christmas together as a married couple. We picked out a fresh Christmas tree and made sure we woke up on Christmas morning to the songs of the holiday season. Doug and I were spending most of the day by ourselves, and then we were scheduled to head to my parents for dinner. We didn't want to squander too much of our time with others because Doug was headed back to the Middle East soon after the New Year.

Our Christmas gifts to each other were supposed to be the renovations on our home because we had some unexpected costs come up at the last minute. Doug and I didn't need material items to express our love to each other, and our gift was having him home during the "good" months of my pregnancy. However, Doug had a difficult time keeping up with our deal and showed up two days before Christmas with a little black box. I immediately told him to take it back, but when he refused, I was forced to wear the beautiful stainless steel, diamond-faced TAG Heuer watch. This watch was meaningful because it was something I admired nearly three years prior, and my husband didn't forget; he simply stored it in his mind to surprise me one day. This man never ceased to amaze me with his romanticism.

We spent our short time together going to the movies, listening to music and eating great meals. Doug brought home DVDs called *Rome,* and we both became addicted to the series. Vahli was also in seventh heaven with her master at home. She worshipped him like no other, and Doug was the only one who could tame the wild she-beast. However, our most important focus was finding a name for our daughter.

As we listened to our baby's heartbeat together, Doug and I both knew it was time to name her. The quest began by searching baby name books and exploring online, but it was a difficult task due to our differences in opinion. I liked Elle and he liked Liberty, Justice or Integrity. I knew he would never be satisfied with Elle, and I wasn't giving in to his constant requests to let him have the first name. We, therefore, kept searching to find something for both of us. There were hundreds of names, but nothing felt right until we came across the name Fallyn. It sounded like her and when we discovered the Irish meaning behind the name our search was over; the name Fallyn meant "in charge." Her full name would be Fallyn Justice Zembiec.

Fallyn Justice Zembiec was already pulling all the punches. She would sleep in my belly all day, and then kick me in my stomach and ribs all night. I guessed she already felt "in charge" of her life and was going to do what she wanted, no matter how exhausted it made her mommy. Doug would lie next to me at night and feel her kicks. He would say, "Babe, how the hell do you get any sleep with that craziness going on in there? What is she doing? Doesn't she know it's bedtime?" He would touch my belly and say, "Fallyn Justice Zembiec, I hope you know you will be on a sleeping schedule when you come out of there. Daddy needs his rest or how's he going to beat the bad guys?" It didn't matter what Doug said to my belly, she didn't care. I eventually got used to her kicking and was asleep in no time, especially with Doug by my side.

Unfortunately, my sleep ended abruptly when I was startled awake by a horrific dream. I grasped onto Doug to make sure he was still there because in my dream, I was alone in my bed. My daughter was in her crib, but for some reason, I knew Doug was gone, and I was raising Fallyn on my own. Doug asked me, "What's wrong, honey?"

I sobbed when I answered, "I had a bad dream, and I was without you, raising our daughter by myself."

He laughed and said, "Awe, babeeeee, it was only a bad dream. You and your crazy dreams! Sometimes, I hear you talking in your sleep, and I try to listen to what you're saying, but it never makes any sense. Don't you know you dream about your fears? I have a risky job, and I'm sure it worries you; besides, I'm going to die an old and wrinkled man salmon fishing on the Snake River. Now, go back to sleep, Princess."

Doug left only a few days later and I quickly dismissed my bad dream to welcome our new baby into the world. There were many things I needed to complete before she arrived, like working on her nursery and finding an au pair. My dog also kept me busy with her "missing in action" antics, where she would escape from the front door and play in Chase Creek for hours.

My sister Kimmy was also helpful by going to Babies 'R' Us with me to choose my registry items. I didn't know what I needed for a baby, and she was more than experienced in this department. She also planned and executed an exquisite baby shower, with my relatives and friends purchasing many things I needed for my little girl. It was a great feeling knowing I would have the tools necessary for the beginnings of motherhood. I guess I could say I had the "material" tools for motherhood, but I wasn't sure I was truly prepared. Even the thought of the "actual" delivery was intimidating since I was going to try the "natural" birthing method. Most of my friends were given the epidural, but the thought of a large needle being inserted into my lumbar spine with the possibility of paralysis was unnerving. Doug was in agreement that we should try the natural method for as long as I could take it. At first, he wasn't okay with the epidural at all, but after several fights and talks with me and his friends he came to his senses. He would say, "Babe, women have given birth to children for centuries without the aid of modern medicine. You were born to breed children; it's in your blood. You don't need meds, you're a Spartan wife!"

Even with all Doug's "positive-thoughts" talks, I was still petrified with the idea of a baby's head traveling through the tiny birth canal. I knew it was a natural process, but the suggestion sent chills down my spine. Of course, I would "man up" for the process and stay "au naturel" for as long as possible. I would also have some words of wisdom from my friend Christine, who was going to deliver a month earlier.

CHAPTER 50

ANNAPOLIS, MD, MARCH 2006

"I'm looking forward to a little me and you running around."
Pamela Zembiec

My pregnancy was progressing at a lovely pace with Fallyn's scheduled birth date for April 12th being right on track. Doug was due home on April 2nd, which gave us ten days for our final preparations. Historically, first children were "overdue," and this was the case in my family as well. My sisters' first babies were all born a few days after their initial due dates, which gave me extra insurance Fallyn would arrive when her daddy was home. I couldn't imagine giving birth to my first child without my husband; however, like all marines, we had a backup plan . . . just in case. Since Kimmy attended the birthing classes with me and was Fallyn's godmother, she would assist in the delivery in the event of Doug's absence. After Doug and I discussed our alternative plan, we filed it away in a locked box because it was something we were sure wasn't going to happen to us.

During my last trimester, Doug tried to call every day and check in because I was getting very tired from working on my feet, taking care of the house and chasing after our ninety-pound lab. I was also not getting much sleep. Between Fallyn kicking me and Doug being gone, I was a walking zombie and could barely function. For the first time in my life, I settled for mediocrity in my career because I was completely exhausted. I also hired a dog walker to help me with Vahli.

By the beginning of March, I was 30 pounds heavier with four weeks left.

Christine was 40 pounds heavier, but she was too skinny when she got pregnant in the first place, so she needed a few extra pounds. My fellow pregnant friend and I conversed every day on the phone and "bitched" about our aching backs, our swollen ankles and tender breasts. Christine was still working in pharmaceuticals as well, so we had all the same complaints. We both discussed our thoughts on the delivery process, and she was getting the epidural as soon as possible. It was her choice, and I respected her decision.

On March 13, 2006, Christine gave birth to a healthy eight-pound little boy named Nicholas. I couldn't wait to talk to her and give my congratulations. When I dialed her number, I was shocked when she answered. Her voice sounded weak, but she said, "Pam, oh my God! I'm not going to lie to you, that hurt like hell, and I'm glad it's over. After being in labor all day, the doctor had to deliver him by C-section. Nicholas was just too big. Oh, Pam! He is so beautiful! He has peach fuzz blond hair and blue eyes. My mom and dad think he looks like me, but I think he looks like my dad. I love him so much."

I answered, "Christine, I'm so happy for you! I wish I could come to Virginia Beach and see him! So, as soon as we can travel with the babies, we will get together. I promise. Now, get some rest and call me if you need anything. Love you."

She answered, "Thanks, Pam. Love you too!"

Over the next couple of days, I waited patiently to hear back from Christine and see how this whole "mother thing" was going. I didn't want to call and interrupt her sleeping schedule because other moms warned me about the difficulties of getting a new baby on a schedule. Finally, I received a phone call from her late one evening. When I picked up the phone, her words were impossible to hear or believe. She whimpered through the phone, "Pam, Nicholas is in intensive care. They're not sure he's going to make it." I didn't understand what she was saying because I just talked to her a few days ago and she was beaming with pride over her son and motherhood.

I frantically responded, "Christine, what happened? You just gave birth to a healthy baby boy. I don't understand."

She cried out in a defeated and whispered tone, "Pam, they don't know what happened. I was breast-feeding him one minute and he was fine. Then I looked down while he was on my breast and noticed he wasn't breathing. I quickly called for the nurse; they grabbed him and took him away. Now he's in intensive care fighting for his little life."

She began to cry with what seemed like her last tear, and I tried to ease her pain by saying, "Christine, he's going to be fine. He's a strong baby because you're his mother! He *will* make it! Keep thinking positively! I wish I could drive to Virginia Beach right now, but I'm not allowed. Who's there with you?"

She slowly responded, "My parents are here. Don't worry, I understand. I know you would be here if you could."

I quickly responded, "Please, please, call me and let me know what's going on. I will say a prayer for Nicholas."

On March 20, 2006, Nicholas was taken off life support. By the time the nurse resuscitated his little body, it was too late; his brain went without oxygen for an excessive amount of time and he would never recover. Christine and her family made the decision, one week after his birthday of March 13th, 2006, to take him off life support. I wasn't allowed to travel to Virginia Beach for his funeral and burial, which killed me. Christine was one of my best friends, and we shared our pregnancies together. Our kids were supposed to grow up together. Those dreams were now lost, and I was devastated.

Again, my selfish thoughts came back to haunt me as I thought about my baby. I asked God to keep my daughter from harm. I was troubled by the death of Nicholas and by not being able to help Christine; the thoughts never left my mind. My mom decided to stay with me in Annapolis because she knew how Nicholas's death was affecting my behavior, and she was very worried. Even though she felt horribly for Christine, she wanted to make sure someone was taking care of me.

When Doug called, he already knew by my voice, that something was terribly wrong and asked, "Babe, what's going on? You sound like you've been crying?"

My voice came out in a squeak. I could hardly answer, "Honey, something happened to Nicholas. He died."

Doug was taken aback and said, "What! What happened? Just a few days ago you told me he was in intensive care, but I didn't realize it was that serious." I was crying so hard my words could barely form, but said, "The doctors don't really know. They think it was SIDS. He stopped breathing and was resuscitated, but not in time. His brain lost too much oxygen. Christine was forced to take him off life support. Honey, I couldn't make the funeral and feel horrible I can't be there for her."

Doug was calm when he answered, "Babe, sometimes this stuff happens. I feel bad for Christine, but you're getting ready to have our baby, and I'm glad you didn't go to the funeral. You would've stressed out Fallyn Justice. Do me a favor, calm down and please listen to my words: **We can always make another Fallyn, but we can never make another you or me.**"

His words were true, but easy for him to say since our baby wasn't growing inside his body. I already had a strong connection with my daughter and couldn't imagine being in Christine's place. I wanted so badly to get in my car and make the four-hour drive, but it was impossible. My daughter was more important and one day, Christine would understand.

Over the next few weeks, I tried to focus on work and get my nursery completed, but Nicholas never left my mind. I thought about him and Christine every day, and when she was ready, we would be able to talk. I knew, for now, I would continue on with my pregnancy without my friend because it was too hard for her. She was grieving the loss of her child, and I was getting ready to give birth to mine.

The days after Nicholas's death were difficult for everyone; even Fallyn Justice Zembiec. When I woke up on March 29th, I felt completely exhausted, but dismissed it and went about my day. I wasn't due for two more weeks, and my husband wasn't expected home until April 2; there was no way she would arrive before then. My dog Vahli was giving me another wild adventure on this morning by going for a long swim in Chase Creek, and before I left for work, I was climbing down the rocky steps to the creek in order to retrieve my pup from the water. It seemed like she was especially difficult to maintain on this day, and I wasn't sure if it was her or my exhaustion which had gotten the best of me, but I was ready to go back to bed before getting into my car for work.

All day long, nurses in my pediatric offices were commenting on how "I looked like I was in labor." I simply dismissed their thoughts and said, "No way, I'm not due until April 12th, and I need my husband for this. He's not coming home until April 2nd!" They told me they would pray for me, but were sure I would have my baby before the 12th.

I was relieved when I had to leave work early for my checkup. During my exam, my doctor said, "Pam, it looks like you're one centimeter dilated."

I asked, "What does that mean?"

She said, "Well, some people remain a centimeter dilated for at least a week before they deliver. My guess is you probably won't have this baby for at least another week." I was relieved to hear that, knowing my husband wasn't due home until the 2nd. We needed only three more days.

As soon as I left the doctor's office, my phone rang like clockwork; it was my husband calling to see how my appointment went. He excitedly asked, "How's the most beautiful woman in the world?"

I laughed at his voice and said, "I'm good, honey."

He hurriedly asked, "How was your appointment?"

I responded, "Well, the baby is good, but I'm one centimeter dilated."

He nearly jumped through the phone and said, "What! You're not due for another two weeks!"

I tried to calm him down and said, "I know, honey. The doctor said some people stay one centimeter dilated for at least a week, and you'll be home by then."

He thought for a second and said, "Hold the phone to your belly. I want to talk to my baby girl."

I placed the phone to my belly and heard him say, "Fallyn Justice Zembiec, you better wait for your daddy. Don't come out before I get home."

I was laughing when I heard his words. Doug didn't understand that his child was going to come when she was ready. Fortunately, he was smart enough not to trust Mother Nature and boarded the next flight home.

My mom, being the ultimate caregiver, decided she was going to stay at my house until my husband came home. It would take about 24 hours for him to get back to Annapolis, and I was relieved knowing Doug was on his way home and my mom was with me. I looked forward to a restful sleep, but unfortunately, I tossed and turned all night and was being tortured with an aching pain in my low back.

I woke up the next morning feeling as though I never slept a wink. My mom was already dressed for the day, but took one look and me and said, "I was going to go home for some fresh clothes, but you don't look good. I think I better stay and help with Vahli."

Normally, I would make her leave, but I wasn't physically able to say anything and just nodded in agreement. I rested my body on the couch, but was immediately startled with a sudden urge to urinate. When I went to the restroom and sat on the seat, there was an instant gush of water in the toilet basin. Instantly I knew this wasn't normal. I screamed, "Mom, I think my water just broke!" My mother came running into the restroom ready for action. She looked at me along with the surroundings and said, "I think we need to call the doctor. You're in labor!"

We arrived at the hospital around 7:00 A.M., and I was admitted as soon as the nurse confirmed my water broke, but when my physician did the initial examination, I was only two centimeters dilated with eight more to go. Kimmy was the first to arrive and help in the delivery process while my mom answered my calls, hoping one might be from Doug.

By noon, my labor wasn't progressing as planned, and my doctor began to worry about the timing. Since my water broke at 6:30 A.M., she would have only 24 hours to safely deliver Fallyn. She was trying to wait as long as possible before she gave me the medication, which would help expedite the delivery process, because she knew Doug was on his way home. However, after careful consideration for the safety of Fallyn, she decided to give me potocin, otherwise known as "the devil juice." I was warned about potocin and how it impacted the intensity and timing of labor pains. Immediately, I noticed a huge difference in my pains. I probably could have dealt with them, if I had time to recover, but they kept coming at me in full force, like a machine gun shooting off rounds. I felt defeated and knew it was time for the epidural.

When Denise arrived around 5 P.M., I was seven centimeters dilated and wasn't sure when Doug would get to the hospital. When my mom finally spoke to him, he said his plane would be landing in Northern Virginia around 7 P.M. and he was hoping to be in Annapolis by 9 P.M., but my doctor was still hanging on in order for him to make it to the delivery. I was worried if Doug was going to be disappointed I "caved in" to the drugs, but the epidural was definitely not overrated. It allowed me to relax and let my body do what it needed to do in order for Fallyn to make it into this world. I wasn't sure why my baby was coming two weeks early, but I suspected the stress of Nicholas dying and Doug being gone was the culprit.

Around 6 P.M., my uterus was dilated to ten centimeters. At that point, I could tell by the look on my nurse's face I was ready for delivery, but I didn't want to do this without Doug. My doctor's examination only confirmed what I already knew. Fallyn was ready to come into the world. I was crying, not because of fear or pain, but for the reason Fallyn would be born without her father. I was crying because of the pain my husband was going to feel by missing the birth of his first child. I was crying because I didn't have my mentor, my love and my best friend by my side. And finally, I was crying because I realized this was the life of a military wife, and I would, therefore, accept it and move forward.

Even with pushing over 2 hours with my two strong sisters holding my legs back, our attempts at delivering my daughter failed miserably. Fallyn was, therefore, delivered by emergency C-section at 8:20 P.M. at a healthy 7 pounds, 2 ounces, and 21 inches long. Her umbilical cord was wrapped around her body and she kept going back into the birth canal after every push. She was also "sunny-side up" which told me she really wasn't ready to be born, but the stress in my life, especially dealing with the loss of both Ray Mendoza and Nicholas, had caused her to come early. I felt so bad for Denise because she was the one who broke the bad news to Doug while I was in surgery; he was only 20 minutes away. She told me, "Pam, he was so disappointed; I didn't know what to say to him."

As the nurses wheeled me into the recovery room, I noticed Doug barreling down the hallway. The look on his face was heartbreaking, and I could feel the frustration reaping from his pores. He didn't have to say a word. My mom and sisters instantly parted from my bedside and quietly left the room. He came to me, grabbed my hand and asked, "How are you?" His voice was cold and unwelcoming; I could tell he was troubled.

I weakly answered, "I'm doing okay, just tired."

He nodded and said, "I'm going to see my daughter." He quickly turned away from me and left me there, with a heavy heart.

The next two weeks were disastrous as we tried to make the adjustment into parenthood. I was recovering from major surgery and Doug didn't seem to understand the complexities in having a cesarean section. He wasn't present for the surgery and also wasn't accustomed to the fragile side of Pam; I was rarely sick and always took care of everything. He tried to compare my wound with the injuries he saw on the battlefield which wasn't fair. However, he did step up with Fallyn by changing her diapers, rocking her to sleep and burping her after feedings. It was fun watching his big hands change her tiny diapers as I sat in my rocking chair trying to pump between feedings. Doug looked massive standing over Fallyn's little body.

One thing was certain, my husband loved his little girl, and his thoughts for a son dwindled away like winter into spring. He began to play songs for her and sleep with her lying on his chest. Every morning we would both wake up to the sounds of Fallyn's morning cries and go downstairs together, hand in hand, because he wanted her to see his face with mine as much as possible. In a sense, he was making up for his absence during deployments.

From the beginning of Fallyn's life, Doug was adamant about instilling his

293

zest for life in his daughter by using one of his favorite methods, music. The moment he heard the words of "I Hope You Dance" by Lee Ann Womack, he began to play this song over and over to Fallyn. He would turn the song on each morning before he left for work, cradling Fallyn in his arms while swaying back and forth to the lyrics:

"I hope you never lose your sense of wonder, you get your fill to eat, but always keep that hunger, may you never take one single breath for granted, God forbid love ever leave you empty handed, I hope you still feel small when you stand beside the ocean, whenever one door closes, I hope one more opens, promise me that you'll give faith a fighting chance and when you get the choice to sit it out or dance, I hope you dance . . . I hope you dance . . ."

As I watched him dance with his daughter, tears filled my eyes because I knew his mood with me would be only temporary. This was once again about him, not about me. The choice he made to become a husband and father was conflicting with his career as a marine. He thought he would be able to control both, but it was simply impossible.

CHAPTER 51

ANNAPOLIS, MD, SUMMER AND FALL OF 2006

"I am an example-setting father that raises children who positively influence our nation, society, family and friends for generations. Our family name becomes synonymous with integrity, valor, character, commitment, spiritual/mental/ physical toughness, leadership, charisma and justice."
D. A. Zembiec

It was apparent from the first few days of Fallyn's life Doug was destined to be a father. I, on the other hand, wasn't sure about myself as a mother. Initially, my doubts began when I wasn't able to breast-feed due to a low milk supply. It was horrific spending the first six weeks of motherhood with either Fallyn or a breast pump attached to my body. Breast-feeding was supposed to be an "incredible bonding experience," but, to me, it felt like an exhausting task. My body was destroyed from the C-section, and I was also suffering with a mild case of postpartum depression, which drew me even further away from my daughter. Doug definitely, "stepped up to the plate" for the sake of our family.

In the meantime, Doug was working through his demons of having a wife incapable of breast-feeding, as well as being denied sexual intimacy for several weeks. I couldn't help but feel sorry for him about the "sex thing." After all, he was deployed for nearly three months before her birth, leaving a cute "mother-to-be" in her peak months, only to come back to a wife bloated and scarred from a horrifying birthing experience. Not to mention the fact that he missed the birth in the first place. I continuously felt his animosity, but unfortunately, there was nothing to help us except time.

As the weeks after Fallyn's birth turned into months, our life and relationship began to adjust. We learned how to accept the things we couldn't change and move in another direction to benefit our relationship and our daughter. We decided, together, to give up on breast-feeding, which brought a breath of fresh air into our home and Fallyn's little jaundiced body. Every decision we made was together, which was a difficult task for two people who were joining mature lives into one. Doug would always say, "Communication is the hardest thing in a relationship, but is also the key to a strong relationship." In a way, I was emotionally closed, and Doug was able to open a side of me I thought never existed.

Life was moving along in a positive direction as I began to turn back into my "old" self, which benefited both daddy and daughter. I was also getting ready to return to work, and we were able to choose an au pair from Costa Rica who would care for Fallyn during the day. She was also good company to have if Doug was asked to go away for work.

Everything was falling into place in the Zembiec family, and even our "shack on the water" was transformed into a beautiful waterfront home in Annapolis, Maryland. We were able to host several parties in our new home while Doug's dream of having his Naval Academy friends over during Navy football games was finally coming to fruition. We hosted several friends and their families for Navy games with our house becoming known as the "Comfort Inn" in Annapolis. It was a great time as Fallyn and I watched her daddy and his friends jumping and swimming with Vahli in Chase Creek before and after the games.

During homecoming in 2006, when Navy played Rutgers, we hosted several friends, which included some old friends of Don and Jo Ann's, Tom and Karen. Tom and Karen's son went to college at Rutgers, which was one of the main reasons they were coming to Annapolis for the game. Both parties looked forward to an incredible competition. Doug was extremely keyed up about this game because he knew someone who was able to get us into Sups Tent and the press box at the Navy Marine Corps Stadium. My husband was well-known at the Naval Academy with his vivacious personality and his efforts to help out the wrestling team during his free time. The coaches of the wrestling team appreciated Doug's help, and he was, therefore, able to sometimes get special privileges.

Homecoming games for the Mids were always extra special with graduates and their families traveling from all parts of the country and world to attend the games. On this day, the stadium was filled to capacity overlooking a beautiful and clear fall day in Annapolis. When we arrived at the Sups Tent, it was already filled with excited Navy fans who were carefully viewing our friends in the red and white attire; Navy fans were loyal to their team, but also knew how to respect the competition.

As the game rolled along, our faithful Mids were being rolled over by a tough Rutgers team. By halftime, the score was 20 to 0, and the Navy fans were beginning to lose hope about any chance for a comeback. I wasn't going to give up hope until the final seconds of the game, but there was a force on Rutgers by the name of Ray Rice, who was unstoppable. He was running all over our defense in his little 5 foot 8 frame, and I was hoping our coaches would adjust their game plan to stop this guy.

Doug was overly anxious to leave the Sup's Tent because he heard a small rumor that Senator McCain was being housed in the Press Box. He wanted desperately to meet the former prisoner of war and war hero who he completely respected; especially due to the possibility of Senator McCain being the presidential Republican nominee in 2008. Doug was worried about the upcoming election due to all the controversy surrounding President Bush and his choice to invade Iraq. He was concerned regarding the possibility of our country electing a Democratic president with his lingering fear of the new president withdrawing our troops from Iraq before finishing the job. Doug was there and saw all the death and destruction, all the loss of Iraqi and American lives and all the hatred of the terrorists. Therefore, he knew how important it was to establish a democracy in this country to help fight terrorism and to honor all the lives lost in the fight.

When we approached the Press Box, there were several guards monitoring the entryway. Doug was immediately recognized by his friend who placed our group on the elevator leading to the box. We walked into the room which was very quiet due to the soundproof windows facing the field. As I turned to my right, I noticed my husband gallantly walking toward a man with white hair and dressed in a suit. I knew it had to be Senator McCain, but I was, once again, amazed at Doug's confidence as he proceeded to strike up a conversation with the senator. When Doug was finished talking, he turned, looked my way and motioned for me to walk over. I was hesitant at first, but knew I didn't have a choice in the matter. For some reason, I was a little nervous. After all, this man was an icon and a state senator.

Doug sensed my apprehension and walked over to me and said, "Babe, what's wrong?"

I answered, "I don't know, I'm a little nervous. It's Senator McCain!"

He smiled at me and said, "Honey, he's just a man. He's done great things for our nation, but you'll see. He's a humble guy."

Doug grabbed my hand and escorted me over to meet Senator McCain. I reached my hand out to shake his, but he gave me a hug instead. And like Doug said, he was just a humble man. We ended up watching the remainder of the game in the Press Box and stared in disbelief through the glass windows as Rutgers overpowered the Mids in a 34 to 0 victory!

CHAPTER 52

ANNAPOLIS, MD, SPRING OF 2007

*"I am an empowering motivational husband. I energize my wife
to raise a strong family and maintain an exceptional, satisfying
lifelong romance."*
D. A. Zembiec

After a very long two years of adjusting to marriage and parenthood, Doug and I were once again completely connected with each other. Our relationship was growing stronger each day, and I was entirely back to my old self after standing the test of motherhood and marriage. Doug would always say, "That which doesn't kill you can only make you stronger." All of my new challenges were definitely making me and my husband stronger people.

One thing was certain for both of us . . . Our daughter, Fallyn Justice Zembiec, was truly a gift from the heavens above. She was the happiest baby who smiled all the time, ate everything we fed her and slept through night. When we took her out to Sunday brunch, other patrons would be amazed at the large amounts of smoked salmon and avocados she consumed. More important, Fallyn was already showing signs of being "Doug-like" well before her first birthday. I was elated how she resembled her father in many ways, and I joked on several occasions about being just an "alien carrier" for Doug's baby. Doug would just laugh and try to make me feel better by saying she looked and acted like me "a little bit." It didn't matter to me. She was happy, healthy and besides, I loved her daddy and was happy she was like him.

We were living a happy life and things were progressing as we had planned until Doug was once again called to action. He was being sent away for another deployment, but this time, it was going to be Iraq, and this time, I didn't want him to go. For some reason, I felt like Doug was finally content with our life because he was feeling both challenged and comforted, but knew he would never, ever, give up the call of duty. I, therefore, pretended I was happy for him to go. He was relieved knowing I would always support his career, no matter what the cost. So, instead of crying the blues, I focused on all the wonderful things in my life: I was a working mother who was able to successfully balance both career and motherhood. I was also busy planning our daughter's first birthday party that would follow Hawaiian tradition and be a "baby luau."

March 24, 2007, was the date for Fallyn's "Baby Luau" party. Doug was born in Kona, Hawaii, and first birthday parties were traditionally baby luaus. It was customary for Hawaiian families, regardless of ethnicity, to hold a luau to celebrate a child's first birthday because in Polynesian cultures, the first birthday was considered a major milestone. Doug's mom was born and raised in Kona, and even though she moved to the mainland to attend college and marry Doug's dad, she returned to Kona and gave birth to Doug. Therefore, we thought it would be a great idea to celebrate our daughter's Hawaiian culture. Moreover, luaus were great parties and our reputation for having these types of gatherings was almost expected. This party was also special because Doug was leaving for his deployment on March 30th, and this event would be the last family gathering until he returned in June.

Even with all of the party planning, my husband, the vast explorer, was on a mission to visit as many friends as he possibly could before he left for Iraq; especially those who wouldn't be attending the birthday party. We traveled as a family to Chicago to visit Jon and Anya for a long weekend. We visited my family and had them over for several family dinners. We went to visit Navy's assistant wrestling coach and his family. And finally, Doug went solo to North Carolina, disguising his trip as "scheduled diver training," to see Chris and Aurora. His original plan was just a day trip, but after a quick phone call home to get my blessing, he ended up staying for the night. In fact, Doug was in such a great mood when he returned home, I told him he should have more "alone" time with his friends.

After several hours of planning, buying, inviting and cooking, I was ready for my baby's first party. We served teriyaki beef and chicken, Huli Huli chicken, potato salad, fruit salad, long rice and Mai Tais. Our house was decorated with palm tree lights, hula skirt tablecloths, tiki balloons, luau piñatas and Hawaiian lanterns. On our deck, we had electric tiki lights and tiki torches, as well as a huge palm tree cooler large enough to house a case of water and two cases of beer. We also had an area set up in our carport for the kids that housed "Hawaiian-themed games." The "shack on the water" was successfully converted into a Hawaiian paradise fit for a Polynesian queen.

As our guests arrived, we greeted each person by placing a Hawaiian lei around their necks, which was customary in Hawaiian culture. The lei custom was introduced to the Hawaiian islands by early Polynesian voyagers, who took an incredible journey from Tahiti, navigating by the stars in sailing canoes. With these early settlers, the lei tradition in Hawaii was born. Leis were constructed of flowers, leaves, shells, seeds, nuts, feathers, and even bone and teeth of various animals. In Hawaiian tradition, these garlands were worn by ancient Hawaiians to beautify themselves and distinguish themselves from others. However, we weren't very picky about our leis; our guests were given a color choice of whatever we purchased from Party City.

My daughter was the birthday Hawaiian princess, but was oblivious to all the fuss. She played around with her little baby friends while my mother, Jo Ann and the other women "oohed" and "ahhed" at all Fallyn's wondrous milestones. My husband was in charge of keeping the men occupied on the deck with stories, drinks and cigars while I was running around making sure the older kids were entertained with our planned games. When it came time for Fallyn to eat her cake, the entire party gathered in our picturesque dining room and viewed the sun setting on the Severn River with all the pink, yellow and oranges hues while singing happy birthday to our phenomenal Fallyn Justice Zembiec. She was one, and it was time to give her a little brother or sister.

It was our plan and the next step in continuing the Zembiec legacy, to try for another baby when Doug returned home in June. There were several things Doug was planning for his family. His first goal was to take me on a "second" honeymoon that he would actually arrange and implement this time. Doug wanted to make things right after his initial failure. We were going to Idaho for at least ten days of self-discovery, baby making and house hunting. It was going to be nice to just sit back and let him plan our trip, which I knew excited him.

All of my dreams were coming true especially after he promised me he wasn't going anywhere for a long time when he returned from this deployment. We missed him, and finally, I felt like he missed us. And when Doug asked me to get a babysitter for Fallyn so I could take him to the base, I jumped at the chance. He always had someone else take him because he didn't want to "inconvenience" his family. This usually caused a fight, a fight I never won, but this time he wanted me to take him, and I was honored.

On March 30, 2007, after several bites of Fallyn's official "birthday" cake and another round of singing happy birthday to the princess on her actual birthday, we packed the car and headed north on Route 50. During our drive, I sat quietly while listening to Doug talk about our future as he devoured several chocolate peanut butter eggs with his right leg moving back and forth. He popped the chocolate eggs in his mouth as though he was eating popcorn at a movie theater. While he ate, he said, "Babe, I can't wait to get back this time. I'm planning a great trip for us. We'll take Fallyn to New Mexico and let my parents watch her, and then we'll rent a car and drive north to Idaho. We can stay at some of the places where I stayed with my dad. All I have to do is book the rooms. I promise it'll be great." I simply stared at him and smiled. For some reason, I wasn't very talkative and now understood why he would never let me take him to the base. Doug broke my silence by saying, "You know, if something ever happens to me, I would want you to move on with your life. I would want you to be happy again someday and not be alone." Before I could answer he added, "I'm not going to die, though, so don't worry."

At first, I didn't know what to say. In fact, I was angry when I retorted, "Douglas, don't ever say those things again! I know you're not going to die! Why do you have to bring this stuff up now when you're getting ready to get on a plane to the most dangerous place in the world?"

By the look on his face, I knew he was regretful for saying those things, but he was confident when he answered, "Honey, we are at war. Of course I don't think I'm going to die, but I've never told you that before. I never brought it up because I don't think I'm going to die, but you need to know I would be okay with you being with someone else if I do."

I cried when I answered, "Douglas, I don't think I could ever be with another man again if something happened to you. You're the best thing that ever happened to me."

Doug clenched my hand with full force and said, "Babe, I'm not going to die. Besides, Fallyn needs a couple of brothers to make her strong."

After I left him, I drove back to Annapolis feeling completely empty, as if I was on a road to nowhere; traveling on black asphalt streets with bright flashing lights. Doug talked of things that never crossed my mind because I either didn't want to believe them or simply chose not to believe them. Military wives, by no means, ever talked about their husbands dying. Death was taboo, and if you thought about it or spoke about it, there was little chance for your survival. Therefore, when my aimless drive brought me back to 1501 Circle Drive, I chose to erase all memories of our conversation because I wanted to live.

CHAPTER 53

ANNAPOLIS, MD, MAY 10, 2007

"Do and become what you think about most."
D. A. Zembiec

My husband was the most incredible man in the universe. In between fighting for our country, he also found the time to be a great husband, a great father and a great son. As soon as my phone rang, I knew it was him, calling from Iraq. We were separated physically by thousands of miles, but his calls always reinforced my day and gave me reassurance that he was safe.

On most mornings, Doug did call, but this morning our conversation left a special treat when our gregarious young daughter said "Dada" for the first time. I hoped it would keep a smile on his face when he went out to get the bad guys since our phone call ended abruptly when he told me he was getting ready to leave on a mission. However, I wasn't worried. Doug was highly trained and had done this stuff thousands of times before. I felt at ease after I hung up the phone and methodically went about my busy day.

For the first time in five years, going to work was satisfying. My career was taking a new turn after I made the decision to take a specialty position with Amylin Pharmaceuticals. A good friend of mine who was a hiring manager for Amylin recruited me, knowing I would be interested in selling pharmaceuticals in the diabetes industry. We worked together on another pharmaceutical endeavor and she discovered that, unfortunately, both my mom and dad were being treated for Type II diabetes, and my grandmother died due to complications from Type II diabetes.

I was lucky to have a great mother-in-law who was able to keep Fallyn for me when I went through training in San Diego during the month of April. If it wasn't for my huge support system, I would never have been able to take the position. Doug knew how excited I was about working for Amylin. Even though his career always came first, he was supportive of my livelihood. He never questioned my decision to move to another company; he only helped me make it happen by volunteering his mother to stay with our daughter.

I spent two weeks in La Jolla, California, for initial sales training and wished I could visit Doug's old home when he was stationed at Camp Pendleton and lived in Laguna Niguel. Unfortunately, sales training was intense and overwhelming, which didn't allow for any "extra" activities. My husband knew I was busy when I forgot to wish him a happy birthday on April 14, 2007, but I did remember the next day, and when I apologized, he brushed if off by saying, "Babe, you know April 14th isn't really my birthday. I was born the day I became a marine. It's more important for you say happy birthday on November 10th." *Of course I already knew this about my husband. Maybe that was why I forgot to say happy birthday in the first place.* I thought to myself. My husband wasn't just a marine, he was *The* marine.

In pharmaceutical sales, being able to see at least five doctors, face to face, was considered a successful day. The industry was changing and pharmaceutical jobs were becoming more like UPS delivery representatives instead of medical information specialists. I didn't like the changes and knew I would eventually have to find another career, but today, I was able to spread my knowledge about Byetta to several physicians, even without having a scheduled lunch. I chalked it up to "new rep luck," which would last for about six weeks, but then you became like everyone else. Or maybe it wasn't luck after all, but the call I received from my husband that made me feel safe and secure. It didn't matter. My day was going well, and I couldn't help but think about my life and how great it was.

On my way home, as I drove down Ritchie Highway, I became gloriously aware of the world and my calling. I glanced to my left to see the Big Vanilla Fitness Center, the place where I moaned and groaned as I worked with a trainer to lose my baby weight. The sight of the huge "vanilla" building made me sigh because I felt content with my weight, knowing I was back to my prepregnancy size. I glanced to my right and saw Doug's favorite McDonald's and laughed aloud as I thought about his ridiculous eating habits. His menu items were so extreme…always three fish sandwiches, a 6 piece chicken nuggets, a large blue

POWERade and a cookies and cream McFlurry on his visits to the Golden Arches. I would have to look up the calorie content and see if he reached his goal of 4000 calories per day with just lunch! Even though I made him promise to NEVER feed our children junk from McDonald's, I was hiding my envy for his ability to eat that junk and still maintain 7 percent body fat.

As I made a right turn onto Severn Way, I passed over the B&A Trail, a place where we would walk our daughter while struggling to keep Vahli tame, and I noticed many runners and bikers enjoying their individual forms of stress relief. My drive continued on through the Pines on the Severn, down several steep hills and turns, which led to Chase Creek. The sun was just beginning to set on the sparkling water, and I could see the reflection of my dock and gleaming, directly above the creek bank, was my red, beautiful house that seemed to smile at me.

By the time I turned on Circle Drive, I knew I was home, and this was where I was supposed to be right here and right now. At first, I thought Doug returning from Iraq in 2004 was the happiest day of my life, and then I thought my wedding day was the happiest, but both times I was dead wrong. Today was because all my dreams were coming true: my husband and I were completely in love, my daughter was incredible, my house was finally a home and I treasured my new job. Doug and I were turning our goals into reality, and it felt good.

When I carefully backed my car down our steep driveway, I realized the depth of the hill wasn't so bad after all. The beautiful pink puffy flowers hovering around the stairway banister caught my attention as they mingled with the purple and pink azaleas in the midst of green ivy. Everything was different now. I was learning to appreciate the beauty in this house, not because of its outward appearance, but because of the substance it contained inside: a happy family.

I entered my home and was greeted with a smiling baby whose eyes were as bright as the shimmering water I saw only seconds before. She ran to me, and I picked her up, snuggled my face in her tiny little neck and smelled her baby scent. Fallyn was heavenly.

The remainder of my day was spent playing with my little girl until I gently placed her in her crib among the fantasy safari animals surrounding her bedroom. I loved her room. It was hand painted with "girly" safari animals that included a giraffe smelling violets, a lion hiding in tall African grass and a parrot perched on a green leafy branch. All had long, cascading eyelashes that gave them a feminine characteristic. Her wonderful godmother generously donated brightly colored stuffed animals conveniently scattered through the room; these animals accented the walls perfectly. My husband told me to spare no expense when decorating his daughter's first bedroom, and I gladly accepted his gesture.

She usually fell asleep quickly in her African wonderland by the time I crept to the upstairs living area and glanced at her television monitor. The screen was black and white, but I could always make out her long, dark eyelashes scraping the top of her cheekbone when she was resting. However, on this night, May 10, 2007, when I glanced at the screen almost 45 minutes later, I could see the glowing eyes of little Fallyn Justice.

My initial thought was to go downstairs and give her a soothing rub on the back, but she wasn't restless or crying. She was smiling. It seemed as though she was staring at something in her room that was making her happy. I didn't have a sense of fear, only curiosity, so I went about my evening, and when Vahli and I retired for the night, I checked the monitor for a second time and noticed my daughter resting like a cherub on a white puffy cloud.

CHAPTER 54

ANNAPOLIS, MD, SUNDAY, OCTOBER 28, 2007

"Anyone can give up; it's the easiest thing in the world to do. But to hold it together when everyone else would understand if you fell apart, that's true strength."
Unknown

For six lingering months, I ran along a path filled with sorrow, anguish and denial while I prepared my physical body for the 2007 Marine Corps Marathon. I wondered on many days how I got to this point and what was going to happen when I completed this goal. What was I going to do next? The marathon training kept me sane in a world where nothing seemed real. My day for redemption had finally come, and I was going to run this marathon with a fire ignited from within the recesses of my broken heart.

There were several others following in my path, who, like me, were suffering without Doug and used exercise as their way to slay the demon we all knew as grief. Several of Doug's classmates from the Naval Academy Class of '95 decided to participate in the run, but went a step above and beyond the call of duty.

After Doug's death, the Class of '95 was in disbelief when they realized their graduating class had lost six of its members in battle: Major Doug Zembiec, USMC, Major Megan McClung, USMC, LCMR Erik Kristensen, USN, Lt. Rich Pugh, USN, Lt. Bruce Donald, USN and Ltjg Brendan Duffy, USN. In fact, the Class of '95 lost more members than any other class since the Vietnam era. Feeling compelled to raise awareness for their lost comrades, a few members of '95 decided to initiate a charity called "Run To Honor." The Class was able to reach out to several members of '95 and the families of the fallen who participated in the event. Some people signed up to run, while others were scheduled to be cheering bystanders. T-shirts were made honoring the heroes with their names imprinted on the back of the shirts and the Class of '95 emblem was placed on the front along with "Run To Honor" surrounding the crest. The "Run To Honor" group also sponsored a spaghetti dinner on Saturday, October 27, 2007, where Kap and Colonel Ripley were honored speakers. I was asked to be part of all the festivities, but, unfortunately, wasn't able to emotionally handle the situation. It was too soon after Doug's death. I wasn't ready . . . and wasn't sure if I ever would be. I, therefore, had several family members and friends over to my house for our own spaghetti dinner and was able to relax and hopefully get some sleep before my race. My house was filled with the "all-star" cast of friends: Andre, Steph, Liz, Christine, Chris Sanbar, another classmate of Doug's who flew in from California, Stevie, Don, Jo Ann, Ed Solis and Ben Wagner. Bridget, Kap and Melissa went to the dinner, but came over to my place for dessert and our final preparations for the morning to come.

Before Kap left for the evening, he gave me some Ironman words of wisdom: "Pam, you should wake up by 5:30 A.M. and eat something light, like a waffle. Have coffee if you usually drink it. By 8:00 A.M., you will be good to go for a while, but should eat a PowerGel or Gu every 45 minutes. And, of course, drink at every stop."

I reached hard from within to gather a smile on my face and said, "Kap, I remember your advice from the first marathon, but I guess it doesn't work if you decide to poison your body with alcohol 48 hours before race day." For the first time since Doug's death, we both chuckled as we remembered a fun time with his best friend and my soul mate.

On this marathon morning, I was awake when the alarm clock rang at 5:30 A.M. I couldn't sleep; I was too anxious. Bridget already warned me about the "premarathon" jitters which usually occurred the night before the race. She emphasized the importance of good sleep two nights prior to the marathon, and I willingly accepted her advice. I was torn between two worlds: in my first world, I was excited to get this race completed because my life for the past six months was entirely focused on this run, and in my second world, I was terrified at not knowing what I was going to do next to keep me going. One thing was certain; I was trained and ready. Therefore, nothing was going to keep me from my goal. This race was dedicated to my husband, to the father of my daughter, to the son of Don and Jo Ann and to the True American War Hero.

My inner strength had carried me this far, and it gave me the courage to eagerly jump out of my bed into the blackness of my room. I quietly tiptoed to my closet where I had carefully placed my race day clothes the night before. I made up my mind to wear inconspicuous race attire. A red shirt, white bra and blue shorts, the same thing I wore in the Half. I wasn't prepared to wear the Run to Honor shirt that was given to me by Doug's Naval Academy buddies. My friends warned me about the media attention the Run to Honor Team would get throughout the race, and I didn't want any unnecessary disturbances on this day. It was too important. Besides, this race was personal to me; it was for me, for my sanity and for my husband—not for the rest of the world.

I closed the door to my walk-in closet and turned on the light in order to find my way around. After slowly slathering my body with Vaseline and body glide, I dressed into my race clothes and sat peacefully on my closet floor. This closet had become my personal refuge since Doug's death; it contained all my sacred possessions. It was my place to read his love letters, to look through his journals and to smell his clothes. Whenever I needed to think or to make a decision, I went to the closet and asked my husband for his advice by searching his journal entries, always finding an answer. Doug made sure this closet was built for me after we bought the house and I never, ever, thought I would shed so many tears in such a place. In many ways, I felt like this room was my passageway to Doug. It seemed right for me to sit in my special place before the race and gather my thoughts.

Before leaving the closet, I cradled my husband's lumberjack shirt in my arms to breath in his scent. The smell invigorated me while I read from his journal. For some reason, I was drawn to a very simple statement: "I trust you to do the right thing, and I believe in you." The words echoed through my mind, and I felt as though Doug was talking to me through whatever heaven he was in. I realized he had always trusted and believed in me, but what was the right thing? I thought I knew the answer to this question, but now, shattered by my grief, I wasn't so sure. For now, running the Marine Corps Marathon was the right thing and feeling satisfied with this answer, I gathered my race day face and left my sanctuary.

Bridget arrived right on time, and we jumped into her minivan headed to the nation's capital. Transportation for marathon runners usually included parking at a Metro stop, and then traveling the remainder of the way by Metro to the race start. This avoided the overcrowded parking conditions. The Marine Corps Marathon, also known as "The People's Marathon," was well liked and attracted runners from all over the United States. The course was friendly for first-time marathon runners with little hills and exceptional scenery. Anyone who has ever run in a marathon knows the importance of those two factors. Bridget and I were lucky this year due to a friendly gesture from a Marine Corps general who gave me a parking pass for the event. We were able to park close to the event while also being supplied with a shuttle to the race start.

The weather called for beautiful blue skies with low humidity and mild temperatures; perfect race day conditions. However, the dawn before the morning skies was filled with misty clouds and cool breezes, deceiving the weather forecast. My body was shivering from both the chill of the air and my nervousness from within. Each burst of chilly air made my legs turn light purple with goose bumps covering every inch. I thought to myself, *Did I wear the right clothes?* Bridget read my mind when she assured me the cold weather was only temporary.

The group of us made our way to the starting line in between stopping for photographs with several Run to Honor racers. Everyone treated me with admiration and respect, telling me both "thank you" and "sorry for your loss." Several classmates shared stories about Doug and how his example inspired them in their lives. I could tell from their words how much my husband meant to them as well. It seemed the impact of Doug's death spanned many lives, and I started to feel "not so alone" in my grief.

Finally, as we waited patiently in the midst of several thousand competitors, the wave of moving legs began. Initially, it was a shuffle, which turned into a creeping jog, and finally, into a slow run. I maneuvered in and out of slower runners trying to find my way out of the congestion and into free space. My slow run turned into a fast run, and Bridget stopped us as soon as she heard the beeping alarm of her watch. We were running the race according to the "Galloway Method," which allowed for walk breaks at the end of each 10-minute mile. Basically, this method broke the marathon into twenty-six segments, which permitted proper hydration and eating during the walk breaks. I hoped this method would increase my speed and get me to my goal. However, when Bridget told me to stop, it took every ounce of inner strength to do it. The adrenaline pushed through my body, and I wanted to progress further, especially with the noise of the crowds. I was on a higher level of functioning and felt like

I could go as fast as a roadrunner. My partner and mentor yelled again, and I forced my body to stop. Bridget made sure we drank water and kept a quick walking pace for the minute. When the buzzer rang, I was pleasantly surprised because the minute went by so quickly. I sprinted at the sound and moved further along the racecourse.

The miles went on as we passed over the Key Bridge and into Georgetown. All my memories of Doug came flowing into my mind like waves crashing into crevices of rocks on a rugged shoreline. He loved Georgetown and everything it had to offer; from the Barnes & Noble bookstore on the corner of Jefferson and M streets to the belly dancers at Mie N Yu. I remembered the time Ray and Doug dressed up as French maids at the Old Glory Saloon for Halloween when everyone else wasn't. I remembered when we went to Sequoias for dinner right before I found out I was pregnant, and I remembered the night we spent at Modern after the 8th and I parade. I also remembered the time a group of us went to the Kennedy Center while enjoying an evening filled with culture and elegance. The memories were moving through my mind, body and into my legs as I ran.

As we passed the monuments, the first one that caught my eye was the Lincoln Memorial, bringing back memories of the night I tried to sit on Lincoln's lap. This city, our nation's capital, represented the reasons why Doug fought for his country and spending time there was precious for both of us. Running this race took me back through the years I spent with Doug and each year, no matter where we lived, we always made our way back to Washington, D.C. I was able to share my stories with Bridget, and she listened carefully while monitoring our time, water and food. She was my savior and friend.

I noticed several people wearing the Run to Honor shirts, and I chatted as much as I could through the 26-mile emotional roller-coaster ride. There were times I couldn't speak because the memories filled my throat with sorrow as tears slowly rolled down my cheeks. I also noticed one spectator who seemed to be at all the main viewing points along the course. He was carrying the Run to Honor sign and kept yelling, "Go, Pam, go!"

At some point along the route, I realized I hadn't seen my daughter. My family was supposed to bring Fallyn and they were going to cheer for me along the racecourse. I desperately searched for Fallyn along the roadside, and when I couldn't find my daughter in the crowd, it never failed, I would always see the same spectator holding the Run to Honor sign. His words helped keep me going. Bridget did her best to alter my train of thought as I kept my hunting eyes open for Fallyn. My daughter was my inspiration in many ways and would be the one to help carry on her father's legacy.

When we reached Hains Point, I was quickly reminded of the awful calf cramps that almost ended the race during my first marathon, and once again, thoughts of Doug flooded my brain as I recalled his inspiring words that gave me the strength to finish. He was so patient, caring and proud. I only hoped that wherever he was, I was making him proud today. It was amazing how different I felt in comparison to the last time I ran on this road. This time, my body was much stronger and my legs weren't bothering me at all; I was able to keep a steady pace throughout the long, tedious stretch of Hains Point without worrying about beating the bridge.

Once we got to Crystal City, I knew I was almost finished, but I was tired, really tired. I entered into mile 22 feeling run-down and ready to end this thing. My body was beginning to cross into a state that only a marathon runner understood. It was the time when your physical body stopped functioning, and your mental toughness took over. I kept pushing forward through this difficult period, even though my body gave way to stomach cramps, muscle aches and exterior knee pain.

When we passed through Arlington National Cemetery, my aches and pains temporarily subsided when I gave way to feelings of respect and admiration for not only my husband, but for all the heroes who made the ultimate sacrifice for their country. It was because of these brave Americans I was able to make it through this day, and I was fulfilled, knowing my run was in their honor as well as in honor of the one person I loved most in the world.

I ran by the rows of white tombstones, each engraved with words I could barely recognize, as the sound of Trace Adkins's "Arlington" streamed in my mind, reminding me of the day I buried my husband: *And I'm proud to be on this peaceful piece of property. I'm on sacred ground, and I'm in the best of company. I'm thankful for those things thankful for the things I've done. I can rest in peace. I'm one of the chosen ones . . . I made it to Arlington . . ."*

And then I saw her, my beautiful brown-eyed girl looking at me as she smiled and cried out "Mama!" Fallyn instantly reached out her arms for me to hold her, and I grabbed her hands and kissed her chubby little cheeks, then quickly moved ahead. In the distance, I could hear her screaming for me, which brought tears to my eyes. She inspired me to move faster, even though my legs weren't doing much for me any longer. My pace was slowing down, and my mind was getting weak.

Chris and Ed tried to lighten the picture by telling jokes and making fun of me when I took a potty break behind a bush in front of the Pentagon, only to find a Porta Potty hiding one hundred meters around the corner. Chris gave me his shirt to use for toilet paper and was now running bare chested. I tried desperately to keep going, but I could barely move with still 1 mile to go. Tears started pouring out of my eyes, and I lost control of my emotions. The stoicism I maintained over the past six months melted away on the hot, black ground like ice dissolving on a hot summer day. I began to cry out loud as my friends remained by my side, supporting me through those final steps up the quarter-mile climb and over the big red Marine Corps' finish line. I looked over at Bridget and her smiling face. She stopped her watch and said, "Four hours and 48 minutes."

Making it over the finish line without my husband brought me to the realization my life was different now, and there was nothing I could do to change it back to the way it was. As much as I tried to pretend like this horrible thing had never happened, I knew someday I would be forced to face the truth: Doug was gone. The fairy-tale life I had was now something in my past, and I had two options: to stay there in fear or move forward with courage. Something about finishing that race, the one I ran with him only three years beforehand, prepared me for the latter. I was going to move forward with courage, knowing in my heart he would always be by my side; maybe not in body, but always in spirit.

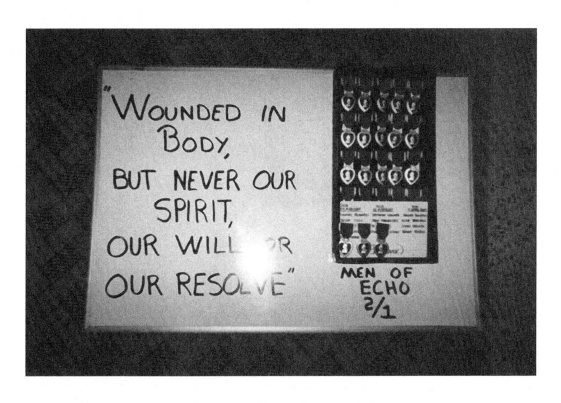

EPILOGUE

Following the Marine Corps Marathon in 2007, I finally allowed myself to feel the loss of my husband. I couldn't be the stoic wife any longer. I was unable to fulfill my duties as a pharmaceutical representative. It was extremely difficult going into physician's offices with a happy smiling face. I decided to leave my company, stay home with Fallyn and work on us. I found my way by traveling back and forth to Virginia Beach and New Mexico so I didn't have to be in my house for an extended period of time. In a sense, I was running away from my pain and Doug's presence. I felt like he was always right next to me when I was in my Annapolis home. Fallyn also had this habit of waving in the air and calling out *daddy* when no one else was in sight. Finally, during the spring of 2008, Fallyn and I moved out of our house and into a small condominium a few miles away. It was a nice way for me to free myself of Doug's presence and try to move forward.

However, the wounds were constantly being reopened by many award ceremonies honoring Doug's valor. I was and am still overjoyed by how the military, the Naval Academy and the NCAA, have all given awards memorializing Doug. There have also been golf tournaments and scholarships named after my husband. He's been written about in books and articles and has his own Wikipedia page. All of these things will keep Doug's memory alive for generations to come.

I fought desperately to try and fix my pain by loving Fallyn, by exercising and by talking to my friends and family. Nothing worked. I just couldn't get out of the clouds. Fortunately, a good friend of mine suggested I join a woman's therapy group. She found this group helpful for her when she was going through a similar situation. I made the decision to join the group and met with them on a weekly basis. The therapist leading the group suggested I see her for individual sessions to compliment the group therapy. *The moment I made the step to accept the fact that I did need help to get through this loss was the moment I began to move forward with my life.* My therapist taught me it was okay to miss Doug everyday. She taught me it was okay to fail because I was grieving and she taught me to take care of me so I could take care of Fallyn. I also took responsibility for my grief by accepting it and knowing that the pain of Doug's death will never go away. I would survive by learning how to live with the pain and by honoring his memory along with the memory of our lives together.

Part of my healing process began by writing a short story about my life and the reasons why I joined the women's group. That short story, written 6 years ago, was the initial stage of this book.

CPSIA information can be obtained
at www.ICGtesting.com
Printed in the USA
BVOW04s0042190617
486865BV00013B/33/P